A Million and One Gods

A Million and One Gods

THE PERSISTENCE OF POLYTHEISM

PAGE duBOIS

Harvard University Press

Cambridge, Massachusetts
London, England
2014

Cataloging-in-Publication Data available from the Library of Congress

ISBN: 978-0-674-72883-7 (alk. paper)

For John

Contents

Introduction   *1*

1   The Prejudice against Polytheism   *16*

2   Greeks, Romans, and Their Many Gods   *50*

3   The Polytheism of Monotheism   *86*

4   The Politics of Polytheism   *129*

Epilogue   *167*

Notes   *175*

Acknowledgments   *193*

Index   *195*

Introduction

Then all the men which knew that their wives had burned incense unto other gods, and all the women that stood by, a great multitude, even all the people that dwelt in the land of Egypt, in Path-ros, answered Jeremiah, saying, As for the word that thou hast spoken unto us in the name of the LORD, we will not hearken unto thee. But we will certainly do whatsoever things goeth forth out of our own mouth, to burn incense unto the queen of heaven, and to pour out drink offerings unto her, as we have done, we, and our fathers, our kings and our princes, in the cities of Judah, and in the streets of Jerusalem; for *then* had we plenty of victuals, and were well, and saw no evil. But since we have left off to burn incense to the queen of heaven, and pour out drink offerings unto her, we have wanted all *things,* and have been consumed by the sword and by the famine. And when we burned incense to the queen of heaven, and poured out drink offerings unto her, did we make her cakes to worship her, and pour out drink offerings unto her, without our men? (*Jeremiah* 44.15–19, King James Version, 1611).

This passage from the (Hebrew) Bible, translated in the seventeenth century by Protestant Christians, with its reference to the "queen of heaven," points to one of the paradoxes of contemporary Western societies. Their history, a history of polytheisms, of the ancient Israelites, ancient Greeks and Romans, has been interpreted as a triumphant progress toward monotheism. Yet, like the Judaean women settled in Egypt, who stubbornly cleaved to their goddess, some people still worship a goddess, and others *many* gods, while a persistent and sometimes unconscious prejudice against polytheism denies legitimacy to religious traditions that surround us. Polytheism survives in many different forms, within so-called monotheism, for example in Catholicism, target of Protestant polemic and violence in the seventeenth century and after, as well as in declared polytheistic traditions. Mine is an argument not in support of pluralism, but for the recognition of both the persistence of polytheism, and a disdain and condescension toward it, conscious or not, that persist as well. I consider not just what some people call religious "pluralism," that is, a U.S. or a U.K. that contains many different varieties of religion, from Pentecostal Christianity to Mormonism to Islam to Hinduism, but also the unsettled boundaries between some of these traditions, relatively monotheist, and those traditions that are polytheist, that is, that recognize *many* gods.[1] My point here is not to defend polytheism, but to show how difficult it is to discuss it responsibly when it is treated as a curiosity or primitive residue, in the "routine," the unexamined assumption that monotheism is a superior development out of polytheism. The rigidity of this claim may speak to the monotheisms' defensiveness concerning their own legacies, and even practices, of polytheism.

Polytheism provides a rich and various vocabulary for naming forces, powers, beings. My fascination with, even delight in, a sublime array of multiple divinities, the million and one gods, comes from a childhood populated by gods, plural. And from years of teaching courses on the ancient Greeks, taking the greatest pleasure in the complexity of ancient polytheism, only to encounter again and again the response that such beliefs are merely a benighted stage on the way to monotheist enlightenment.

Yet from the beginning, at the first words of the seminal, fundamental text of the monotheisms, the Hebrew Bible, sacred not only to Jews, but also to Christians and Muslims, in the book of *Genesis,* we find polytheism. After the narrative of the creation, thought to be a late, priestly addition to the text, and after the second creation of human beings, one male, the female derived from the body of the male, and after the forbidden consumption of fruit from the tree of the knowledge of good and evil, in a beautiful scene we find the god walking in the garden in the cool of the evening, and calling out to his creatures, "Where are you?" Adam and Eve cower in fear, and the god interrogates Adam and learns of the trespass. And he complains: "See, the man has become like one of *us*, knowing good and evil; and now, he might reach out his hand and take also from the tree of life, and eat, and live forever" (*Genesis* 3.22–23; emphasis added).[2] Fearing that these beings are coming to resemble "us," that is, *the gods, plural,* he drives them from the garden.

The scene resembles the origin myth of the Maya people of Mesoamerica, recorded in the *Popul Vuh* and recounting a series of creations. Their gods first made animals, then human beings of mud, who were unsatisfactory because their flesh crumbled and dissolved in water. The gods created effigies of wood, but these too failed to satisfy and were destroyed. Finally four human beings were fashioned out of white and yellow maize:

> Perfectly they saw, perfectly they knew everything under the sky, whenever they looked. The moment they turned around and looked around in the sky, on the earth, everything was seen without any obstruction . . . As they looked, their knowledge became intense. Their sight passed through trees, through rocks, through lakes, through seas, through mountains, through plains (*Popul Vuh*, 147).[3]

The perfection of these beings disturbs the gods; they see too much, know too much. The gods fear that the human beings will "become as great as gods . . . Their deeds would become equal to ours, just because their knowledge reaches so far." The gods "take them apart just a little" (*Popul Vuh*, 148), reducing the maize people to lesser creatures:

> And when they changed the nature of their works, their designs, it was enough that the eyes be marred by the Heart of Sky. They were blinded as the face of a mirror is breathed upon. Their vision flickered. And now it was only from close up that they could see what was there with any clarity.
>
> And such was the loss of the means of understanding, along with the means of knowing everything, by the four humans (*Popul Vuh*, 148).

Neither the Hebrews' nor the Mayans' gods wish to share the universe with human beings, their creatures, their creations, who threaten to equal the gods themselves, or to challenge their power. So, after a time, they reduce their creatures, or expel them from a garden in which they might learn not just the difference between good and evil, but also the secret of life, the key to divine immortality. Although an outsider might balk at the notion that human beings must humbly accept their inferiority to the gods, the parallelism between these two narratives ultimately breaks down. While the Mayans recognize the existence of many gods, the monotheisms, descended from the Hebrew Bible, officially do not. The dominant religions of "the West" misrecognize their relationship to polytheism and posit an "original" monotheism that distinguishes them as morally and ethical superior to other peoples of this earth.

In this book, I rely on the definition of "religion" proposed by Hans Penner: "Religion is 'a verbal and nonverbal structure of interaction with superhuman being(s).'"[4] These superhuman beings are the many gods. There are of course other definitions of "religion"; anthropologists recognize a vast array of practices, as well as the difficulty of adjusting the vocabulary of the West, the North, to that vast array: "We have a word for religion. This is a convenient label that we use to put together all the ideas, actions, rules, and objects that have to do with the existence and properties of superhuman agents such as God. Not everyone has this explicit concept . . ."[5] Richard King, in *Orientalism and Religion: Postcolonial Theory, India and "the Mystic East,"* recalls the formulation of the concept "religion" in the work of the Roman jurist and politician Cicero, who traced the etymology of the word to the Latin verb *relegere,* "to re-trace or re-read"; that is, religion is repetition, respect for the fathers, tradition (Cicero, *De Natura Deorum* II.72). "As such it represented the teachings of one's ancestors and was essentially not open to question."[6] Such an understanding of religion required the continuance of received rituals, honoring the gods. King contrasts this view of religion with that of the early Christians:

> In the third century CE we find the Christian writer Lactantius explicitly rejecting Cicero's etymology, arguing instead that *religio* derives from *re-ligare,* meaning to bind together or link. Thus, for Lactantius, *religio* "is a worship of the true; superstition of the false . . . They are superstitious who worship many and false gods; but we who supplicate the one true God are religious."[7]

Christian religion, in this conception, is about a bond between the one true god and a community or a single human being; any person who does not share this bond is a "pagan," a country bumpkin, and eventually a "heathen" (derived from a root denoting forest, uncultivated land, as in heath, and then the person who is similarly uncultivated, savage). So-called pagans, or heathens, recognize many gods.

The seemingly firm and unassailable ground of patriarchal monotheism rests in fact on some unstable ground, etymologically. The word "deity" was formed by Augustine, as *deitas,* on the model of *divinitas* in Latin, from *deus,* "god" (*De Civ. Dei* 7.1). The *Oxford English Dictionary* defines deity as: "the estate or rank of a god; godhood; the personality of a god; the divine quality, character, or nature of God; Godhood, divinity; the divine nature and attributes, the Godhead. A divinity, a divine being, a god; one of the gods worshipped by a people or tribe; an object of worship; a thing or person deified. With capital supreme being as creator of the universe; *the Deity,* the Supreme Being, God."[8]

The word is first cited in the work of Geoffrey Chaucer, in 1374, with reference to Jove, one of the Romans' many gods, as Troilus's "deity" (*Troylus* 3.968); Chaucer uses the word again in *The Franklin's Tale:* "Though Neptunus haue deitee in the See . . ." (*OED* 319); Capgrave's fifteenth-century *Life of St. Katherine* mentions deity in relation to Apollo (4.764); in 1594, Christopher Marlowe and Thomas Nashe put the word in the mouth of the goddess Iuno, Jove's divine mate: "Here lyes my hate, _Æneas_ cursed brat, The boy wherein false destinie delights, The heire of furie, the fauorite of the face, That vgly impe that shall outweare my wrath, And wrong my deitie with high disgrace" (*Dido* 3.2). Another passage is cited in the *OED,* from Hannah More in 1786, in her letter to Lord Gambier: "Polite ears are disgusted to hear their Maker called 'the Lord' in common talk, while serious ones think the fashionable appellation of 'the Deity' sounds extremely Pagan" (1.10.157). The English term "deity," then, was early on associated with the gods of polytheism, of ancient Greece and Rome, and later with "deists," enlightenment types who seemed to the pious "extremely Pagan."

The English word "god" also has an interesting history. It is derived from Teutonic roots, but in Gothic and Old Norse the word follows the neuter declension, that is, no masculine or feminine gender attends the word, the author of the *OED* article on "god" remarking that "the adoption of the masculine concord being presumably due to the Christian use of the word. The neuter sb. [substantive] in its original heathen use, would answer rather to L. [Latin] *numen* than to L. *deus*." So "deity" refers often to the gods of polytheism, and the root of the word "god," once neuter and referring to the *gods* of the Old Teutonic world, must be remade and rendered masculine in English. Further observations on the use of the word "god" in the *OED* include "a superhuman person (regarded as masculine: see Goddess), who is worshipped as having power over nature and the fortunes of mankind; a deity. (Chiefly of heathen divinities)." Further: "Even when applied to the objects of polytheistic worship, the word has often derived from Christian associations." "When the word is applied to heathen deities disparagingly, it is now written with a small initial; when the point of view of the worshipper is to any extent adopted, a capital may be used." Another meaning: "An image or other artificial or natural object (as a pillar, a tree, a brute animal) which is worshipped, either as the symbol of an unseen divinity . . . ; an idol." The second definition is in "the specific Christian and monotheistic sense. The One object of supreme adoration: the Creator and Ruler of the Universe."

For another definition of god, I turn to another dictionary: *The American Heritage Dictionary of the English Language* defines "god" as "a being of supernatural powers or attributes, believed in and worshiped by a people; especially a male deity thought to control some part of nature or reality or to personify some force or activity."[9] The word, according to this dictionary's appendix on etymology, comes from a Germanic root, going back to an Indo-European form meaning "to call, invoke." The god, then, is the one called or invoked. This definition further distinguishes "god" from "goddess," defined simply as "a female deity." "Deity" is "a god or goddess," in a rather circular definition; the reader is referred to the Latin *deus,* "god," and then to another Indo-European root meaning "to shine," and then by extension to the sky, or the heavens. These definitions are marked by their context in American and British English and by the legacy of monotheism; worship in these definitions entails "love," or veneration of a deity, while in polytheism deities are often believed in but not loved, or worshipped—given offerings or even sacrifices—not because of "love," but because of fear or the desire for favor. Ares—sometimes called the "god of war" of the ancient Greeks, of whom more will be said later—a god of destruction, was for Zeus "the most hated of the gods" (*Iliad* 5.890), yet he was one of the pantheon of the many gods.

I prefer a definition of deity that emphasizes supernatural powers, that stresses neither masculine nor feminine gender, and that does not entail "love," but rather includes a belief in supernatural beings that can accompany affects of fear or hatred. Not all of the "gods," the deities of the earth's peoples, are beloved, but they are believed in, respected, and treated with care, as is the Satan who troubles the monotheism, itself sometimes trinitarian, of orthodox Christianity. In the *Handbook of Cultural Psychology*, the contributor Scott Atran, in "Religion's Social and Cognitive Landscape," remarks that:

> All religions follow the same structural contours. They invoke supernatural agents to deal with emotionally eruptive existential anxieties, such as loneliness, calamity, and death. They have malevolent and predatory deities, as well as more benevolent and protective ones (Atran, 445).[10]

That is, in his view, polytheism is the norm.

Even in the context of an increasing secularization, we still find polytheism in contemporary societies. The U.S. and the U.K. count many polytheists among their inhabitants. As advocates of the pluralism landscape point out, people practice the ancient discipline of yoga everywhere, conscious or not of its roots in the Vedic tradition. In the most ancient sites of England and Puritan New England, there are worshippers not only of Jahweh and Allah, but also of the many gods of Hinduism, as well as polytheists of another bent, those who have chosen new forms of old religions, including the worship of the gods of the ancient Greeks. Every major city in the U.S. and the U.K. contains many immigrants, from many parts of the globe, who often bring with them their religions, sometimes polytheisms, sometimes monotheisms radically modified by fusion between their indigenous traditions and missionary Christianity. Even small towns are increasingly marked by these changes, by a leavening of the homogeneity of worship and belief that once characterized the heartlands of America and Britain. Workers arrive from South Asia, Hindus or Muslims, or from Central America, with their mixtures of Maya traditions and Christianity, or new syntheses of Santeria, for example, and from Africa, and the old ways must change, lest they risk annihilation. In Los Angeles, for example, devotion to Our Lady of Guadalupe, a Mexican apparition of the virgin Mary, has led to new forms of representation that sit sometimes uneasily with a more conventional Irish Catholicism in sites like the cathedral of a now disgraced archbishop.

Pluralism is, in general, an acceptance, even welcoming of diversity, whether in political ideas or in religious communities, a model for a diverse, multicultural postmodern society. But, like "multiculturalism," "pluralism" can connote a bland tolerance of difference, allowing for a "marketplace" of ideas, masking prejudice and the structural privileging of one idea or one community over others. Like neoliberal applications of the concept of liberty, in which affirmative action is dismissed in the name of a fictive equality, disregarding historic inequities, pluralism can fail to acknowledge prejudice. My emphasis here is not on the many manifestations of different religions in pluralism, but rather on the endurance of polytheism in all these traditions, on a structure that privileges monotheism, and especially on defensive and perhaps reactive implicit prejudice against polytheism.

Polytheism is not primitive, an early stage of human development, to be transcended as people progress toward a more sophisticated understanding of divinity, nor do religions necessarily oscillate between polytheism and monotheism. Rather, I contend that polytheism is always present, officially or unofficially, and that the attempt to deny its presence produces intolerant assumptions among monotheists and even atheists, who claim a moral superiority to polytheists. Pluralism, in the context of the *separation* of "church" and state, does not take account of different cultural and religious traditions, especially those in which that separation seems artificial and unlivable. The way forward is not clear, but simply to assert the necessity for a "secular" state in these terms produces a daunting contradiction. The separation of church and state in secular North America does in fact assume a "church," and an emptying out of the public sphere. In other contexts, for example in India, secularism has evolved in a multireligious country in which Hindus are a majority, but by no means the only religious community, and in which the state ideally, as a secular democracy, does not favor any religion but recognizes the presence of all. This is not the separation of "church" and state, but an acknowledgement of the multireligious (*not* multi-"confessional"—again, a loaded and culturally specific term) nature of the state.

The question of how to resolve the contradiction between pluralism and polytheisms needs to be posed. Arguments for cohabitation imply a greater openness, not an evacuation of public life, not just tolerance, or toleration, but something more, an attention to the life-worlds of others. It is possible that—like "Jewish democracy," the notion that a democracy can restrict its citizenship to people of one ethnicity or religion—the concept of a *pluralist separation of church and state*" is an oxymoron. For those whose cultural reality entails an immanence of many gods, such a separation is inconceivable, and its imposition an affront to any authentic conception of pluralism.

Recent work on the secularization of modern industrial societies has pointed to the ways in which religious structures persist in the U.S. and U.K., especially Protestant Christian constructs such as the separation of church and state, or the private and public sphere. Saba Mahmood makes this point in *Is Critique Secular?*:

> As much of recent scholarship suggests, contrary to the ideological self-understanding of secularism (as the doctrinal separation of religion and state), secularism has historically entailed the regulation and reformation of religious beliefs, doctrines, and practices to yield a particular normative conception of religion (that is largely Protestant Christian in its contours). Historically speaking, the secular state has not simply cordoned off religion from its regulatory ambitions but sought to remake it through the agency of the law (Mahmood, 87).[11]

The very definition of "religion" privileges Christianity in the U.S. and the U.K., and in Europe as well. In discussing rulings of the European Convention for the Protection of Human Rights, Mahmood emphasizes that its legal reasoning "tends to privilege the cultural and religious beliefs of the majority population" (Mahmood, 86). Peter Danchin notes that "there appears to be a bias in the jurisprudence of the Court . . . toward protecting traditional and established religions and a corresponding insensitivity toward the rights of minority, nontraditional, or unpopular religious groups. . . . Those religions established within a state, either because they are an official religion or have a large number of adherents, are more likely to have their core doctrines recognized as manifestations of religious belief."[12]

Giorgio Agamben has argued that the "division of powers," even the tripartite division of the state into judicial, executive, and legislative branches, echoes the crypto-polytheist structure of the Trinity in Catholic doctrine.[13] As noted in the *New York Times* in 2013, "Even the European Union's flag—a circle of 12 yellow stars on a blue background—has a coded Christian message. Arsène Heitz, a French Catholic who designed the flag in

1955, drew inspiration from Christian iconography of the Virgin Mary wearing a crown with 12 stars. The same 12 stars appear on all euro coins."[14] In the U.S., legal tender bears the legend "In God We Trust." Although these institutions may claim a commitment to secularism, in fact Christianity, either Catholic or Protestant, dominates the public sphere. And in most of the religious contexts surveyed here, including both the Hebraic and Hellenistic sources of Western civilization, now dominated by the Abrahamic monotheisms of Judaism and Christianity, polytheism has endured and disrupts the tidy convictions of worship of a single, patriarchal divinity.

Even though Western secular states want to relegate religion to the outside of the state, in the name of (a Christian) secularism, there may be nonetheless an inevitability to the persistence of polytheism, an undercurrent that cannot be suppressed, a popular culture that holds to its many gods, a recurrent resurfacing of polytheism within monotheism, or an exhaustion of monotheism that dialectically produces polytheism. In contemporary cultures, worship of the masculine, patriarchal, frequently punitive single god of the Hebrew Bible seems difficult for many, especially those conscious of women's rights, to sustain, and polytheism may correspond to deeply felt and perhaps unconscious needs. As psychic life is increasingly seen not to correspond to the Freudian model of a paternal superego, consonant with the patriarchal nuclear family, acknowledgement of the complexity of contemporary psyches becomes more common. A recognition of the many psychic forces at play in consciousness may make polytheism more compatible with life in the twenty-first century. But for some people, difference, internal and external, produces an anxiety that the world is becoming less familiar, less homogeneous, less predictable, more chaotic. Thus the renewed, defensive call to abhor polytheism. In their work on idolatry, Moshe Halbertal and Avishai Margalit discuss the philosophical issues associated with its monotheistic, or biblical condemnation, from the perspective of those who reject paganism. But they acknowledge that: "polytheism . . . by its very nature includes an abundance of gods and modes of ritual worship, and so it has room for different viewpoints and beliefs and therefore is pluralistic. This pluralism is not just the product of compromise but is in fact an ontological pluralism that constitutes a deeper basis for tolerance."[15]

In the world today there are many traditionally polytheist communities, with their own cultural continuities and the formation of subjectivity within these traditions. It seems imperative not to continue to link ethics and morality with monotheism, as some monotheists do. Various cultural traditions, "religious" or not, inform individuals' consciousness, forms of identity, sense of self; these are not necessarily "polytheist" or "monotheist," but may nonetheless differ and have their effects even on persons who do not "believe." Saba Mahmood, for example, describes forms of Muslim subjecthood in a dialogue concerning the violence and protest that erupted when a Danish newspaper published cartoons ridiculing the Prophet Mohammed. In *Is Critique Secular?* she describes subjectivities different and perhaps even unintelligible to those outside this religious tradition. She describes some believers' relationship to the prophet not as worship, but as forms of emulation or identification, the devout trying to live his or her life, corporeal and psychic, in ways that follow the teachings of the prophet not just in the messages conveyed by the *Qur'an,* but also in the later Islamic traditions of anecdotes and stories. While Mahmood insists on not generalizing these conceptions of self to all Muslims, such inclinations help to produce identification with the prophet, with the result that ridicule, mockery, or profanation of him in images causes psychic distress to the believer. We need to be attentive to such versions of psychic formation, to acculturation within traditions, to unconscious, preconscious, collective forms of subjectivation that continue to operate even in those who do not believe. This is something Judith Butler courageously grapples with in her recent book *Parting Ways,* in the name of "cohabitation" with others from other traditions:

> We doubtless make a mistake by reducing the question of religion to a problem of whether an established subject holds to certain "beliefs," when religion often functions as a set of practices and, indeed, as a matrix of subject formation. Perhaps I could not be who I am without a certain formation in religion that in no way implies a specific set of religious beliefs regarding God (the metaphysical reduction) or modes of belief that are distinct from reason (the epistemological reduction). Certain values are embedded in practices and cannot be easily "extracted" from them and made into explicit "beliefs" formulated in propositions. They are lived as part of embodied practices formed and sustained within certain matrices of value (Butler, 22).

Thus her argument for "cohabitation," going back to work of Hannah Arendt, which she ultimately derives from the Jewish experiences of exile and diaspora. Butler emphasizes the point that we do not choose: "To cohabit the earth is prior to any possible community or nation or neighborhood. We might sometimes choose where to live, and who to live by or with, but we cannot choose with whom to cohabit the earth" (Butler, 125).

Cohabitation in this sense is not possible in a context of condescension such as often exists among monotheists. Western scholars as well as unofficial believers can treat monotheism as inevitable, as the flowering of Western civilization and enlightenment, and as ethically superior to polytheism, in a triumphalist and progressist narrative that goes back beyond Hegel. When we naturalize monotheism, or see it as the *telos,* goal or end of religious development, perhaps a stage on the way to atheism, we accept the homologies that have governed Western modernity. God is the father, the father is as a god in the nuclear patriarchal family, and as the superego he governs the psyches of modern possessive individuals. Although in the U.S. we may no longer accept the notion of a "sovereign," while Britons are still subjects to a sovereign, the neatness of homologous psychic, familial, and religious structures can seem to justify them as necessary, true, and inevitable, as "human nature."

As a classicist—someone who studies ancient Greece and who believes the polytheism of ancient Greek society to be inseparable, ineradicably bound up with its legacies of democracy, drama, both tragedy and comedy, and philosophy—I want to insist on the beginnings of Western civilization in polytheism, Hebraic as well as Greek; to argue against a premature monotheism that misreads and misinterprets ancient culture; but also to recognize the persistence of polytheism in the present, in cultures traditionally polytheist and in the others as well.

My argument in this book is:

- Prejudice against polytheism still exists, although it is rarely now labeled as paganism or heathenism.
- Such prejudice is often complicit with racism, which labels some people of color as polytheists, and therefore as primitive, superstitious, and underdeveloped.
- In fact, polytheism is an integral part of the history of the West, of two of its currents, flowing from "Jerusalem" and "Athens."

- Polytheism persists not only in traditionally polytheistic societies and their diasporas, but also in the Abrahamic monotheisms.
- Polytheism may be more consonant with contemporary life, its mixed populations, and its recognition of psychic complexity and interdependence, than a rigorous Protestant monotheism.
- Pluralism and the separation of "church" and state may be incompatible, a pluralist separation of church and state may be an oxymoron, and we need to think more about these questions, to privilege not just one tradition, openly or cryptically, but perhaps to strive to be neutral, as a state, and to "cohabitate."
- Beyond tolerating polytheisms, the U.S. and the U.K. may have something to learn from them.

The chapters of this book are as follows: The first, "The Prejudice against Polytheism," selects some examples of the historic prejudice against polytheism in the modern West, in scholarly circles as well as in popular culture. The second, "Greeks, Romans, and Their Many Gods," shows how the classical cultures of Greece and Rome, at the beginnings of Western civilization, were polytheistic, and how the origins of democracy, to cite just one example, are deeply imbedded in polytheist practices and beliefs. The third, "The Polytheism of Monotheism," shows the difficulties the so-called monotheisms encounter in the efforts to rid their theologies and practices of the vestiges of the many gods of their ancestors. "The Politics of Polytheism," the fourth chapter, discusses some of the ways in which people resistant to the hegemony of the Abrahamic monotheisms have challenged assimilation and annihilation of their traditions. The epilogue provides a brief glimpse of the landscape of the present in the U.S. and the U.K. and argues for recognition of the persistence of polytheism, even in atheist or secular institutions of the modern nation-state, in the monotheism of the dominant groups, and in other communities now part of a global, transnational life-world.

One of the dangers of writing a book like this one is that one can never be master of all the scholarship required. Scholars tend to specialize in a field, to know the languages necessary for working in that field, and spend decades refining and narrowing their focus so that they often become experts in a tiny area of human knowledge. This has great advantages, in that new information can produce breakthroughs in a highly defined and often restricted set of facts and ideas, and these breakthroughs can ripple outward and affect the work of other scholars in nearby fields. But the disadvantage is that it is in such cases difficult to generalize, to see how all fits together, how a tiny bit of information has its place in a big picture. Sometimes scholars are reluctant to take risks, to chance commenting on that big picture, because they fear criticism for stepping out of their field of expertise, relying on the work of other experts, and finding themselves unable to verify absolutely the claims that they are making about the larger whole.

I am a classicist and comparatist who works on the culture of ancient Greece, and who finds the polytheism of the Greeks profoundly fascinating. Here I write about not only the many gods of those Greeks, but also about the phenomenon of polytheism, the many religions of many gods, trying to understand how people through the history of human societies have had many deities, and continue to do so, even when the official religions of their cultures require a strict monotheism, an obedience to, and gratitude to, a single god, usually a male god, a patriarch.

It would be madness to claim to know all the scholarly work, and the languages, ancient and modern, of all these religious traditions, from the language of the sacred texts of Zoroastrianism, the religion of ancient Persia, to the languages spoken by modern Native Americans, first people. In making my arguments, I have relied on my own knowledge about the many gods of the ancient Greeks, on my attachment to them, indeed in part because of their polytheism, and on experts in the many, varied fields of religious studies who have focused on polytheism and monotheism in the societies about which they are expert, and on scholars in philosophy, political theory, and cultural studies interested in the question of religion. Among these are Peter Brown, Judith Butler, Wendy Brown, Gayatri Chakravorty Spivak, Saba Mahmood, Talal Asad, Giorgio Agamben, Jan Assmann, Dipesh Chakrabarty, Peter van Nuffelen and Stephen Mitchell, Robert Parker, Mark S. Smith, Henk Versnel, Jörg Rüpke, Bruce Lincoln, Clifford Ando, Marcel Detienne, Phiroze Vasunia, Wendy Doniger, Simon Gikandi, J. Lorand Matory, Ashis Nandy, and many others. Although I rely often on the work of scholars of religion, this book is not primarily directed toward them, but rather toward readers less specialized in the field of religious studies, interested in the questions of the politics of culture that my arguments engage. This is an essay, a sometimes polemical attempt to think through the implications of the survivals of polytheism in the present.

The religion(s) of ancient Greece serve me often as paradigms for thinking about polytheism, for considering the richness of ethics, philosophy, and democracy generated in the polytheistic contexts of ancient Greek cities. But if I had let myself be confined only to my field of expertise, I would have missed the vast variety of religious experience, belief, and practice in human societies, and the insights that come from setting one's own field of expertise within a wider array of human possibilities. The ancient Greeks look different to me now, as does my appreciation of human invention and ingenuity, loyalty to traditions and powers of improvisation and innovation. The gods are, for many of us, still here, still everywhere.

CHAPTER ONE

The Prejudice against Polytheism

"THE MOST IMPORTANT COMPLIMENT that monotheism has ever paid itself
is that it is the religion of justice. According to the widely held conviction
of the monotheistic religions, morality and law first came into the world
with belief in a single god."[1] Jan Assmann's words accuse the monotheisms
of an enduring view that ethics and the moral life go hand and hand with
the assertion of the existence of one true god, and with the rejection of
the many. Such ethnocentric arrogance has deep roots. If we recognize the
many and various traditions in our heterogeneous societies, both in the
U.S. and in the U.K., and in the globalizing world that we all inhabit, more
and more in virtual or physical proximity with one another, then the call
for homogeneity, for purity, or fundamentals, or orthodoxy, of any kind,
including the monotheist traditions of Judaism, Christianity, and Islam,
seems not just potentially xenophobic or racist, but also impossible to fulfill.
No country on earth, at present, is populated by people of just one form of
worship or belief, devoted to just one god, and we need to acknowledge this,
the persistence of polytheism, the enduring presence of many gods.

Yet a prejudice against polytheism also persists in the West, in the U.S., the U.K., and in Europe. If these nations today are troubled by competing monotheisms in their various manifestations, ideologies of exclusivity and possession, and by the violence that sometimes accompanies them, it may be difficult to acknowledge the prejudice, conscious or unconscious, that guides many monotheists, practicing or not, concerning worshippers of many gods. Unconscious assumptions about the inevitability and value of an evolution from animism to polytheism to monotheism to secularism can in fact veil the ways in which polytheism survives in contemporary hegemonically monotheist cultures, marked by beliefs in the power of Satan or saints. Polytheism threatens, from its first mention in English, as something that must be rooted out from its dangerous presence inside England, Europe, the West, and even from within the self, in the form of the temptations of idolatry. These frequently appear as gendered; primitive peoples are seen as effeminate, weak, or devoted improperly to female divinities. Finding the primitive in other lands allows for its denunciation and its projection outwards. The peoples who indulge in polytheism are distanced in time and in space: the ancient Israelites, the Greeks and Romans, the peoples encountered on voyages of "discovery," conquest, and colonization. But the menace of idolatry and polytheism lurks, still present at home.

THE WORD POLYTHEIST

Some readers may have difficulty thinking their way into polytheism, and this is a historical as well as a contemporary problem. The word *polytheos,* "belonging to many gods," first occurs in ancient Greek. It was used by the refugee Danaids—daughters of Danaus, Greeks by descent, Egyptian by appearance—as early as Aeschylus's tragedy *The Suppliant Women* of about 466–459 BCE (Before the Common Era), to refer to the site of the asylum they seek. These maidens are fleeing their cousins, somehow more fully Egyptian, who want to marry them without their consent. The women call on the Olympian gods, the gods of the heavens, as well as the "ancient gods below, possessing the tomb," that is, the Greeks' chthonic, earthly gods, and "Zeus Savior, keeper of pious men" (lines 21 and following). Their father, in the city, Argos, where they have found a temporary refuge, urges them to call on some of the many gods of the Greeks: Zeus, Apollo, Poseidon, Hermes. And he commands them:

> All gods here at a common altar worship.
> Settle on the sacred ground like doves
> Clustering together, fearing the winged hawks,
> Who hatefully pollute their very blood (Aeschylus, *The Suppliant Maidens*,
>   lines 222–225).[2]

The word *polytheos* itself occurs at line 424 of this tragedy, where the chorus of maidens cries: "See me not seized, from the seat of the many gods," in a verse that emphasizes the multiplicity of the religious practices of the ancient Argives, and all the gods present, who protect these maidens. The predatory Egyptian suitors, threatening their own kind, their cousins, appear to be another kind of polytheist, those who worship "the deities by the Nile" (line 922). The voices liken the pursuing suitors to crocodiles, to two-footed serpents, to spiders, to foot-biting adders.

The Greeks from early on read the Egyptians as consummate polytheists, with their animal-headed, hybrid, human-animal gods, and they will appear again in this book, as we see them set against the monotheists of the Hebrew Bible in the great distinction of the ancient Near East that condemns those who worship many, and therefore necessarily false gods. Aeschylus's tragedy stages a conflict of gods, as the herald of the Egyptians asserts defiantly that he does not fear the gods of Greece, who neither reared him nor brought him to old age. The fifth-century BCE Greek historian Herodotus provided an account of a more harmonious encounter between the gods of the Greeks and those of Egypt. His work on other cultures suggests the possibility of the "translation of names," that different peoples simply call the same gods by different names, but that the many gods themselves are constant and present in those societies that the Greeks themselves encountered in their exploration and colonization of the shores of the ancient Mediterranean.

The Greeks here in Aeschylus's tragedy seem to take pride in emphasizing the anthropomorphism of *their* gods, their human appearances civilized when compared to the animal gods of the barbarians. They remain polytheists for many centuries, even as the Olympian and chthonic gods of Greece begin to share devotees with philosophers, who express doubts about the gods. The pre-Socratic Greek thinker Xenophanes, for example, conveyed skepticism about divinity when he said:

> But if cattle, <horses> or lions had hands
> and were able to draw their hands and perform works like men,
> horses like horses and cattle like cattle
> would draw the forms of gods, and make their bodies
> just like the body <each of them> had.
> . . .
> Ethiopians say that their gods are snub-nosed and black,
> Thracians blue-eyed and red-haired.[3]

Yet popular devotion continued, unmoved by such doubt, in ancient Greece; the mystery cult of the goddesses Persephone and Demeter, for example, persisted for many centuries to come.

A report on the death of the god Pan came relatively early in antiquity, in a text of the Greek author Plutarch, who recounts in *De defectu oraculorum,* "The Obsolescence of Oracles," that during the rule of the Roman emperor Tiberius in the first century CE, the Egyptian pilot Thamus, traveling to Italy, passed by the island of Paxi, and heard a voice call out his name from the land, and when he answered, the voice said: "When you come opposite to Palodes, announce that Great Pan is dead."[4] Those who heard the news cried out in grief, but worship of the god was still apparent to the famous traveler Pausanias a century after Plutarch wrote; he saw shrines, altars, and worshipers of the goatish god. And even after these gods retreated in the face of conversions to Christianity, Judaism, and Islam, they survived in diverse forms—in the zodiac, in astrology, in myth and fictions. Helen Morales, in *Classical Mythology: A Very Short Introduction,* describes how the myth of the rape of the Tyrian girl Europa by Zeus, who seduced her on to his back in the form of a charming little bull, figures in the propaganda urging the cohesion and solidarity of the European community around a common currency, the "euro."[5]

POLYTHEISM IN ENGLISH

The word "polytheist" seems to enter into the English language in the early seventeenth century, as a term of anti-papist condemnation directed at Jesuit missionaries in Asia. These are denounced by a travel writer and man of the newly Protestant church, Samuel Purchas, for building on conversion to Christianity "(the most dangerous to new Converts) an exchanged Polytheisme in worshipping of Saints, Images, and the Host"[6] The Puritan objection to Catholicism derived in part from a perception that Catholicism had corrupted the legacy of monotheism inherited from the ancient Israelites, dispersing and diffusing spiritual energy into a vastly corrupt system of saints, icons, and, as Purchas puts it, "the Host," the communion wafer worshiped like a god, which therefore assumes the very likeness of the graven images forbidden to the ancient Israelites to differentiate them from their idolatrous neighbors—worshipers of golden calves, figurines of voluptuous women, and other such pagan targets of prayer and offerings. The protesting Protestants sought to restore their Christianity to an unadorned, pure adherence to the oldest laws, even though they interpreted and still do interpret many of them rather loosely, such as the commandment to kill a disobedient son at the gates of the city. Where the ancient Greek tragedian distinguished one set of gods from another, the proper Greek gods from the Nilotic, within the spectrum of possible polytheisms, Purchas has moved beyond such discrimination to a critique of the lapse back into polytheism by the Catholics. The problem for Purchas is that the Catholics, bent on converting these peoples, give them an easy way out, a means to continue in their old polytheist traditions, by claiming that their gods resemble those of the Catholics, that their wildly assorted gods and fetishes are equivalent to those honored by worshipers of the one god of Abrahamic monotheism.

It is important to note that it is only from the perspective of a conscious, self-conscious, prescribed, willed monotheism that we can even talk about polytheism. As Jordan Paper, author of *The Deities Are Many: A Polytheistic Theology*, stresses, in the course of an argument that "polytheism is the human cultural norm":

> It is the identification by monotheists that defines polytheism. Polytheists would have no more reason to call themselves such than they would to call themselves "air breathers" or "bipedal."[7]

Polytheism is a term invented by monotheists, to describe others, whom they refer to variously as "pagans," "heathens," "gentiles," "infidels," and "idolators," terms that often carry a heavy weight of condescension or disapproval. People who as a matter of fact worship many gods do not consider themselves "polytheists"; they worship their many gods, and only after encountering the censure of monotheists acknowledge or reject this very foreign concept. As Moshe Halbertal and Avishai Margalit point out: "from the point of view of practitioners, anthropologists, or historians of different pagan religions, the very general category of paganism—a category that includes an enormous variety of religious phenomena—seems empty. . . . The only perspective from which the category of paganism makes any sense is the nonpagan perspective . . ."[8]

The Catholic missionary impulse, which touched the whole of the South Asian subcontinent, and which resembled the Islamic drive to conversion, attempted to rescue the Hindus from a benighted polytheism. If Purchas found that the indigenous polytheism was simply displaced by a disguised form of the same, by means of the Catholic worship of the saints and the fetishization of the host, a mere material object in his view, the Protestants were nonetheless also committed to saving the Hindus from their barbarism. Michel Danino, in a controversial and much-disputed argument against the theory of a historical "Aryan invasion" of India, cites nineteenth-century British missionaries, who, though not using Catholicism as a prop to lure people from traditional polytheism, were nonetheless bent on its eradication. The civil servant Thomas Macaulay, in the notorious 1835 "Minute on Indian Education," posited that Hinduism relied on "a literature admitted to be of small intrinsic value" and that "inculcates the most serious errors on the most important subjects" . . ."hardly reconcilable with reason, with morality, . . . fruitful of monstrous superstitions."[9] Macaulay implies the compatibility of his own religion with reason, with an argument familiar to Christian apologetics that denies any mystical or irrational component to belief in its god(s). Reason is here coextensive with monotheism. And it was understood to be necessary to impose Christianity of a firmly monotheistic type on the natives in order to justify the rational, reason-inculcating institutions of British colonialism. These views have a long history, a long life.[10]

Reflection on the legacy of polytheism, viewed negatively from its earliest usage in English, is a political question because of implicit violence, the forms of conquest that often followed or accompanied the arrival of missionaries throughout the world, because of fundamentalist ideologies, both "polytheist" and monotheist, that divide people who are neighbors, and who kill one another in the name of their own god(s). The *Oxford English Dictionary* defines polytheism as "Belief in, or worship of, many gods (or more than one God.)" In the Christian context of the early use of this term in English, the term polytheist refers to "pagans," or even "heathens." There is a significant distinction made here between belief and worship, as if the two were separable; one can believe without worshiping, or worship without believing. The latter could refer to a circumstance like that of Pascal's famous wager, in which he argued that one could perform the rites of a pious person, and that such a stance might make sense since, if the god and afterlife did exist, one would gain by performing acts of piety, and if they did not, then the effort was pointless but worth the wager. The dictionary entry also alludes to the possibility that a polytheist might believe in or worship many gods, but also, as an alternative hypothesis, that he or she might simply worship more than one, that the smallest addition to one—say, one other god—would make for a polytheist. Is there a religion with two gods, and does not monotheism often posit a god of evil in addition to the patriarchal one, a god or devil in which one believes, but does not worship?

The author of the dictionary entry capitalizes the word God, as if to suggest that the monotheism of Christianity, or of the makers of English dictionaries, requires that the name of the one god of this tradition be God, rather than "god." If there is only one, his name is God, and he receives a capital letter. I often find in translations assigned to my students, where an ancient Greek author has sung, spoken, or written, necessarily without capitalization, since papyrus and manuscripts for many centuries did not mark this distinction, "'the god' did X," that the translator, especially in earlier translations perhaps more marked by an assumed universal monotheism, Christian or Jewish, renders this being as "God." And I point out to them that this distorts the Greek, since often the author is simply referring to whichever god is most present in the text at the time, Apollo, or Zeus, or even just "a god," one who appears in the work without having a specific name: Plato, for example, has Socrates say in his *Apology,* his defense speech before the Athenian jurors who condemned him to death, that "a god," or "the god" commanded him in oracles and dreams (33c), that a prophetic voice prevented him from performing certain actions in the past (40a). Are we to understand that this god is Apollo, a divinity especially dear to Socrates? I don't think we are to understand that Socrates was a monotheist, who worshipped "God."[11]

PREJUDICE AGAINST POLYTHEISTS

In his influential study *How Societies Remember,* Paul Connerton discusses the effects of religious belief, and like many scholars, assumes "religion" to be a matter of Abrahamic monotheism:

> Nowhere is [the] explicit claim to be commemorating an earlier set of founding events in the form of a rite more abundantly expressed than in the great world religions; this claim appears there again and again.[12]

It turns out that "the great world religions" include only Judaism, Christianity, and Islam. So foundation, and memory, and monotheism qualify a religion for greatness and world import, and religions that do not look back to a foundation, such as Hinduism, are neither great nor "world-class." Yet, the *Christian Encyclopedia*'s numbers, approximate but acceptable, suggest that just half the world's population is Christian or Muslim; Hindus and Buddhists together make up a fifth, with Judaism, Sikhism, Jainism, Baha'i, and all other remaining religious comprising less than one percent of the world's religious worshippers.[13]

I come to the question of prejudice against polytheism in part through teaching. In a freshman lecture course I teach on ancient civilizations, including the ancient Near East, Greece, India, and China, students for the most part assume that monotheism is the inevitable, rational, and perfected end of the development of civilization out of barbarism. When I point out that many millions of people on earth at this moment are practicing polytheists, they acknowledge that they consider such persons to be underdeveloped and barbaric. And that is that. The few polytheists in the class are invariably offended by such attitudes, of course. But for the great majority, the *telos,* the final cause of the history of ancient civilizations, implies progress in the movement from the worship of many gods to the worship of one. Try as I might to convince them that the world of the ancient Israelites was polytheistic, they resist. More on this later, when I discuss the polytheistic nature of the Hebrew Bible, but for now, it seems important merely to note that although there are those who want to restore the U.S. and the U.K. to a fundamentally monotheist past, in fact the more we delve into the past, and the further into the past we go, the more we find a constant and often explicit texture of polytheist beliefs and worship, one that gives the lie to a claim that an original, fundamental monotheism, or purity, was ever possible.

Another possible translation or application of the word "polytheist," although it is not cited in the *Oxford English Dictionary,* would be to describe a nation, or a world, whose inhabitants believe in and worship more than one god, or worship two gods, or some variation on this: such a situation is in fact what obtains at present, and one of the goals of this present book is to suggest that the call for return, restoration, purity, and monotheist fundamentalism vainly attempts to master and override a polytheistic reality.

This alternative application of the adjective "polytheist," beyond pluralism, one that pertains not just to an individual human being, but rather to some political entity like a nation, seems to me a logical extension of its meaning. And if we allow for this wider use of the term, a definition that includes collectives as well as persons, then the epithet "polytheist" would apply very well not only to countries where individuals believe in and worship many, or two, or several gods, but also to those countries in Europe and the Americas where the dominant but not exclusive religions have traditionally been monotheist and derived from the Hebrew Bible and the patriarch Abraham. Even these religions, genealogically related to one another, often raise doubts concerning whether the same god is believed in and worshiped by all.

For example, in the early Christian era, when the religion of Jesus was just beginning to take its definitive shape, his followers participated in an intense debate, stimulated by the theologian Marcion of Sinope, who lived in the first and second centuries CE. Now considered to be a heretic, he wanted the new religion to be truly new, to acknowledge that its god, and its other god, the son of that god, were discontinuous with traditional Judaism. He argued that the scriptures of the new religion should not include the Hebrew Bible, with its supreme divinity known by the name Jahweh (or by several other names, significantly, to be discussed later). His argument was that this divinity, however named by its believers and worshipers, was not identical with the one believed in and called upon by Jesus, and therefore that the followers of this later but not necessarily subsequent religious line should base its practices not on the old religion of the Jews and Judaism, but rather should limit itself to those texts that celebrated the god of Jesus. He saw the god of the Hebrew Bible as an Israelite tribal deity utterly unlike the god who sent Jesus to earth, a physical presence who, as *Genesis* recounts, walked in the garden of Eden enjoying a cool evening breeze. Elsewhere, however, this divinity appears vengeful and cruel, and Marcion hoped to establish a canon for Christianity that discriminated between the scriptures revered by the Jews and those associated with the life and teachings of Jesus. Others argued more successfully that since Jesus was a Jew, as were his earliest followers, continuity with the old law should be maintained, although Marcion's efforts, and his large body of followers, stimulated the efforts by what was becoming a more orthodox Christianity to draw a line between legitimate scripture and *apocrypha*, delegitimized writings deemed unacceptable to the fluctuating theological consensus. But the question of whether the god of the one and the god of the other are the same can certainly be asked, as the later Christians do not follow the laws set down for religious Israelites, however much the Protestants, another tendency that broke away from a dominant tradition, might urge a selective return to the commands of the Hebrew Bible. Christians, to cite one of many examples, do not restrict their diets according to the ancient rules and do not follow the Sabbath restrictions: do not request, for example, that the city authorities adjust the traffic lights in their neighborhood so that they need not labor, that is, push the button indicating a desire for the light to change so they can cross the street, on their Sabbath.

In a textbook adopted for the world history series of courses I teach in, the editors set forth what they call "the revolutions" that shaped human history, including among these, along with Greek philosophy, "ethical monotheism." They confirm a representation of the course of history as progress from the superstition and primitiveness of polytheism, proto- or pre-ethical, to the enlightened world of "ethical" monotheism, that is, to a religion where a single god pronounces ethical commandments. The suggestion lingers that there is no ethics where there is no such single god, no such list of rules for life. But in fact, as I will argue here, there is no evidence that those who live or lived under many gods were any less ethical than those who became monotheists. The ancient Greeks, for example, although they did not receive or record a set of commandments or recognize a single god of covenant, reward, and punishment, elaborated laws and philosophy in other domains of life and considered with great intensity how human beings might conduct themselves properly with regard to one another. Similarly, the ethics of ancient China, a polytheistic culture, emphasized not divine commandments but the harmonious conduct of human beings in relation to one another, especially in the Confucian tradition, and to the natural world, among Taoists.

Yet the prejudice against polytheism and polytheists, the exclusive definition of Western civilization as monotheist, manifests itself in many cultural situations. In the eighteenth century, the politician William Pitt the Elder, arguing against the "Roman" Catholics, said: "The errors of Rome are rank idolatry, a subversion of all civil as well as religious liberty, and the utter disgrace of reason and of human nature."[14] In *Our Church: A Personal History of the Church of England,* the English philosopher Roger Scruton takes for granted the monotheism of his church and country, in an implicit slap at "others" who have arrived recently from elsewhere. Scruton appears irritated by that fact that some people do not share his understanding of the continuing centrality of the Protestant Church of England to national identity: "It seems to me that our country is greatly misunderstood by the many influential people who fail to see that our national church remains part of its identity, and the key to its past." Of course, the established monotheism and monarchy of the Church of England are contested aspects of Britain's present state and, indeed, a "key to its past," in the sense that the Reformation and centuries of missionary work linked to colonialism have produced estrangements and enmities that continue to have their impact on Britain's international and domestic politics.[15]

Mark C. Taylor, a noted expert on religion, casts light on Scruton's view in *After God:*

> Throughout the nineteenth century, there were only four acknowledged categories of religion: Christianity, Judaism, Mohammedism (any one of which might be regarded as true), and the rest, that is, paganism, heathenism, idolatry and polytheism (all of which were declared false) (Taylor, 6).[16]

Taylor acknowledges the idea of world religions, developed in the 1920s, which included other living traditions, including Hinduism. Yet his views seem to reflect an immanent presupposition, taking monotheism for granted. For example:

> To function religiously, symbolic networks must address theological, anthropological, and cosmological issues. These three dimensions of experience are

articulated in the interrelated figures of God, self, and world or their functional equivalents. Theology, anthropology, and cosmology mutually condition each other: the way in which God is imagined determines the way in which the self and the world are conceived and vice versa. In theistic traditions, for example, God is believed to be a quasi-personal being who creates and governs the world. As we will see in detail below, traditionally there have been two alternatives within the parameters of this vision: either God's will follows God's reason, in which case the world is ultimately comprehensible, or God's will is antecedent to reason, in which case the world is radically contingent and irreducibly mysterious (Taylor, 22).

Taylor argues for understanding religion as a "complex adaptive network," involving co-implication. His is meant to be a general theory of "theistic" religion, but it reveals the degree to which the paradigm is monotheism. "God's will," "God's reason" assume one mind, a monism of divine prescience. There is no room for a conflict of wills, a conflict of reasons, a pantheon of divinities.[17] And he argues for an ethics that is "after God." "If," as Taylor writes in an embrace of co-implication, complexity, cooperation, volatility, and uncertainty, "the divine is neither an underlying One, which dissolves differences, nor a transcendent Other, which divides more than unites, but is incarnate in the eternal restlessness of becoming, then life in this world is infinitely valuable. The figure of this infinite life is water—" (Taylor, 377). Why not multiplicity of "the divine," *many* restless gods?

In an article in *Critical Terms for Religious Studies,* Francis Schussler Fiorenza and Gordon D. Kaufman grapple with the word God.[18] (There is no article on "gods.") "We begin our reflections here with 'God' as a proper name since throughout the literary period of English [this has] been the predominant usage, and what had been 'the original heathen sense' of the word came to be 'apprehended as a transferred use of this'; 'a *god*', in this view, is a supposed being put in the place of *God,* or an imperfect conception of *God.*" They cite the *OED:* "In the 'specific Christian and monotheistic sense' of this word, it was often used 'in contexts where the One True God is contrasted with the false gods of heathenism'" (Fiorenza and Kaufman, 137). Their article goes on to examine this conception of God, the one God of monotheism. They admit feminist critiques of gendering of this God, to the extent of citing Rosemary Ruether on God/ess, yet there is the one, god the God; Gaia the earth sits awkwardly in such a cosmos.[19]

HISTORY OF RELIGION

In his article "Religion, Religions, Religious," Jonathan Z. Smith shows how the category "religion" was expanded and understood anew in the sixteenth century, after the European encounter with New World peoples.[20] He points out that "'Religion' is not a native category. It is not a first person term of self-characterization. It is a category imposed from the outside on some aspect of native culture. It is the other, in these instances colonialists, who are solely responsible for the content of the term" (Smith, 269). It is, he argues, not a theological but an anthropological term.

> The most common form of classifying religions, found both in native categories and in scholarly literature, is dualistic and can be reduced, regardless of what differentium is employed, to "theirs" and "ours." By the time of the fourth-century Christian Latin apologists, a strong dual vocabulary was well in place and could be deployed interchangeably regardless of the individual histories of the terms: "our religion"/"their religion," with the latter often expressed through generic terms such as "heathenism," "paganism," or "idolatry"; "true religion"/"false religion"; "spiritual" (or "internal") religion/"material (or "external") religion; "monotheism" (although this term, itself, is a relatively late construction)/"polytheism"; "religion"/"superstition"; "religion"/"magic" (Smith, 276).

Smith points out that this dualistic vocabulary was available to label heresies, in the polemics of Protestants against Catholics, and for "the evaluation of the newly encountered religions beginning in the sixteenth century" (Smith, 276). The so-called Abrahamic religions were then one set, posed against "an undifferentiated other" (Smith, 276). In the gradual differentiation of the "others," the prejudices persist. Smith traces the development in the nineteenth-century study of religion of distinctions between "natural religions" and "ethical religions," or "race religions" and "founded religions" (Smith, 278), "world religions" of which Christianity is, to quote Cornelius Petrus Thiele, "incommensurably high above both its rivals [Islam and Buddhism]" (Smith, 279).

As Smith wryly notes: "It is impossible to escape the suspicion that a world religion is simply a religion like ours . . ." (Smith, 280). And, at least in the public sphere in the U.S. and the U.K., such descriptions remain hegemonic, controlling the dominant discourse and defining the problem in terms of ethics and the opposition between monotheism and atheism, rather than incorporating more inclusive definitions of the divine, which in itself, as an abstract noun, formed from an adjective, like the Greek philosophical terms "the good," suggests a monolithic substance rather than a multiplicity.

As Guy Stroumsa shows in his exhaustive study of the beginnings of the field of religious studies, scholarship on these questions begins with the encounter with others, in the new worlds of earliest colonialism. In *A New Science: The Discovery of Religion in the Age of Reason,* he writes:

> From the beginning of the Spanish conquest, the religious identity of New World peoples presented a capital problem. When referring to the practices and beliefs of the conquered empires, those established by the Aztecs in Mexico or by the Incas in Peru, the Spaniards remained unable to speak of natural religion. The only available way was therefore to compare them with already-known practices and beliefs in an effort to think about the new religions with the help of existing concepts meant to describe the religious multiplicity of the world (Stroumsa, 15).[21]

The conquerors, driven to examine the rituals of the peoples they encountered, "compared these rituals with those of idolatrous religions, of course, such as those of the Greeks, Romans, or Carthaginians" (Stroumsa, 15). They also saw resemblances to the rites of the Hebrew Bible, and even to some Christian rituals. As the interest of scholars moved toward the east, "East Asian religions remained classified as belonging to the 'fourth form' of religion, the other three being Judaism, Christianity, and Islam" (Stroumsa, 28). There is judgment concerning idolaters, but also fascination. "Such works as Vossius's *De Theologia Gentili* were officially intended to expose idolatry wherever it hid by searching for its roots. Yet it is hard to avoid the impression that these works also reflect a hidden attraction to the richness of polytheistic mythologies and cults. Moreover, they certainly encouraged an avowed sympathy for such ancient beliefs in the gods" (Stroumsa, 33). And such attitudes, sometimes held by missionary priests, allowed for an expansion of the traditional opposition between true and false religion. "It is in great measure thanks to American 'idolatry' that modern students of religion learned to free themselves of theological blinkers and, in the practice of scholarship, put the idea of truth inside brackets" (Stroumsa, 24).[22] Stroumsa further notes: "Thanks to [Sir William] Jones's intellectual prowess, European scholars were finally able to start deciphering the great literature of India and to study its religious traditions. In striking contradistinction with Confucianism, however, Brahmanism was only conceived as paganism, and as such its religious tradition was despised. Thus, in 1616, the Jesuit Fernandes Transcoso describes the beliefs of the Brahmans as 'absurdities, infamies, lies'" (Stroumsa, 158). Stroumsa traces with meticulous care the development of the field of religious studies, stimulated by the discoveries of early colonialism.

Yet in popular culture and the public sphere, prejudice against polytheism endures. Garry Wills, in *Why Priests?*, critical of the entrenched hierarchies of the Catholic church while affirming his Catholicism, extends an olive branch to fellow Christians, including Protestants. And, he adds:

> That does not mean we can forget our foreparents, the Jews. They, after all, gave us the one God they taught us to worship . . . Nor do I count out monotheistic believers of other sorts. Though they do not accept our Creed, they are also children of the same one God (there are not two), who cares about them in ways we may not comprehend. [23]

Wills's tolerance and compassion barely extend to Muslims, part of the Abrahamic genealogy, and not at all to polytheists of any kind; does his God "care" for them?

THE DEFENSE OF MONOTHEISM

Christian "apologetics," the practice of defending Christianity against other forms of worship, began in the early church, at first bent on protecting the Christians against persecutions by the Romans, and eventually directed against the beliefs of pagans, or heathens, who were seen to worship false, nonexistent gods whom the Christians could not acknowledge. Tertullian wrote an *Apologeticum,* that is, a "defense" (rather than an apology in the English sense of the word). Justin Martyr expressed his defense of Christianity in terms of the injustice of persecution of Christians by the Roman imperial state and linked his arguments in favor of a single god with philosophical notions of *logos,* the "reason" that governs the cosmos. *Logos,* the "word," "reason," had emerged in the work of such pre-Socratic thinkers as Heraclitus, again in the works of the Stoics; in the arguments of the philosophers, the cosmos itself, the universe, the "order," was in antiquity gradually more and more seen to be a single great reasoning mind that controls all things. In associating the one god, God, with this word, this reason, the evangelist John forged a bond between a philosophical monism and monotheism: "In the beginning was the word," in Greek, *logos.* Justin Martyr sees Jesus as the earthly manifestation of this *logos,* this philosophical "reason."

Later apologetics focused on the rivalry among the Abrahamic religions; Christian apologists argued for the greater excellence of their creed, in relation to the other monotheisms. At the time of the European discoveries, voyages into the rest of the world—the shock of encounter with thriving and flourishing polytheisms in the Americas, in Asia, and in Africa—brought new life to the defense of Christianity as the colonizers augmented their claims to ethical and social and religious preeminence with a conviction of ethnic superiority. Even faced with the highly evolved civilization of China, they found ways to argue for Christianity's preeminence, as the Jesuits saw in Chinese deference to Tian, "heaven," in practice nothing like the single divinity of Christianity, an analogous figure to the god of their monotheistic doctrines. And, as in the case of Samuel Purchas, in the works of the Protestants, the split between Catholics and Protestants in Europe led to analogies made between "pagans"—the polytheists seen as primitive peoples—and idolatrous Catholics. These polemics replaced "apologetics," the defense of Christianity against paganism, and were themselves overtaken eventually by the challenges of the Enlightenment, some of whose leading lights dismissed organized, official religion as irrational and a vestige of more primitive times.

Yet many enlightenment figures saw religious belief and practices as compatible with reason. Although John Locke was in favor of religious toleration, he wrote a text entitled *The Reasonableness of Christianity,* published in 1695, and accepted the validity of divine revelation, of the miracles, indeed of all the Biblical text. "Reason" did not for him exclude the intervention of supernatural powers into the human world. Locke was also an important figure in the evolution of Western culture toward an emphasis on the individual, at the center of liberal ideology. As C. P. Macpherson described Locke's political thinking:

The individual with which he starts has already been created in the image of market man. Individuals are by nature equally free from the jurisdiction of others. The human essence is freedom from any relations other than those a man enters with a view to his own interest. The individual's freedom is rightly limited only by the requirements of others' freedom. The individual is proprietor of his own person, for which he owes nothing to society. He is free to alienate his capacity to labour, but not his whole person. Society is a series of relations between proprietors. Political society is a contractual device for the protection of proprietors and the orderly regulation of their relations.[24]

Such views are compatible with ideas on religion focused on a single deity, and on the use of reason to support the worship of such a god. The relationship between the individual and his god, a god of reason, is a matter of independence, not imbeddedness in an interdependent, polytheist environment.

Immanuel Kant, although critical of German pietism and of the performance of fetishized religious acts, nonetheless in his treatise *Religion within the Limits of Reason Alone* (1793) argued that human beings have innate moral intuitions, must act in relation to their moral duty, and that the Summum Bonum, the highest good of human existence, includes virtue and happiness; the one God is the guarantor of the link between them and of a future life after death for those who live virtuously, in which they will find perfect happiness. Basing his arguments "on reason alone," Kant's analogy between human reason and the reason of the cosmos seems to require a single mind, a divine mind, a God, even though this argument proceeds by analogy, not by logic or reason.

In the work of the French Catholic viscount René de Chateaubriand, we find another version of the defense of Christianity. Shocked by the writers of the French enlightenment—anti-establishment figures like Voltaire—and by the violence of the French Revolution, Chateaubriand wrote his *Génie du christianisme ou les beautés de la religion chrétienne*, published in 1802. He there commits himself to demonstrating that the Christian religion is excellent not because it comes from God, but that it comes from God because it is excellent (Chateaubriand, 48).[25]

It was . . . necessary to prove that the Christian religion, of all the religions that ever existed, is the most humane, the most favorable to liberty and to the arts and sciences; that the modern world is indebted to it for every improvement, from agriculture to the abstract sciences . . . It was necessary to prove that nothing is more divine than its morality—nothing more lovely and more sublime than its tenets, its doctrine, and its worship; that it encourages genius, corrects the taste, develops the virtuous passions, imparts energy to the ideas, presents noble images to the writer, and perfect models to the artist . . . (Chateaubriand , 49).

One of the strongest arguments put forth by Chateaubriand is that Christianity is consistent with "reason," although he offers few detailed proofs in this regard. He mocks the creation narratives of other societies, while assuming that his own, that of the Hebrew Bible, corresponds to reason, with its transcendent god who says: "Let there be light." Unreasonably,

in the East Indies an elephant supports the globe; in Peru, the sun made all things; in Canada, the great hare is the father of the world; in Greenland, man sprang from a shell-fish (Chateaubriand, 109).

He provides no arguments concerning why his story is more virtuous, more true, more reasonable. Chateaubriand surveys earlier philosophical thinkers and finds them wanting, arguing that there can be no morality without the promise of heaven or hell after death, a system of rewards and punishments: "men no sooner divest themselves of the idea of a God than they rush into every species of crime, in spite of laws and executioners" (Chateaubriand, 190). Atheists are such criminals. "The rewards which Christianity promises to virtue, and the punishments with which it threatens guilt, produce at the first glance a conviction of the truth" (Chateaubriand, 203).

Christians generously commit themselves to spreading their message: "Idolatrous nations knew nothing of that divine enthusiasm which animates the apostle of the gospel" (Chateaubriand, 557). This accusation of apathy serves as a reproach to the ancient philosophers who never left the pleasures of Athens, while Christian missionaries have courageously gone forth to save the souls of those who "still languished in the darkness of idolatry. They were filled with compassion on beholding this degradation of man . . ." (Chateaubriand, 557). Chateaubriand surveys, with extensive praise, the missions to the Levant, America, India, and China. In discussing the missions of the Antilles, he raises the awkward question of slavery, but deftly handles it by claiming that while the Protestants, an inferior variety of Christians, deferred baptism of their slaves until the moment of death, to secure their labor until the end, the Catholics on the other hand "finally succeeded in abolishing [slavery] from Europe" (Chateaubriand, 587 n. 1). In an interesting confluence of interests, the American translator calls the reader's attention to the French author's references to the 1801 slave revolution in Haiti, which Chateaubriand denounces: "A vain, boasting philanthropy has ruined everything. Even the sentiment of pity has been extinguished; for who would now dare to espouse the cause of the blacks after the crimes which they have committed?" (Chateaubriand, 588). The American translator notes: "The author had before his eyes the massacres of St. Domingo, which had but recently occurred. His remarks on the ultra philanthropy of his time will be easily applied in our own day and country" (Chateaubriand, 588, n. 1, translator's note). The translator writes in 1856, just before the American civil war. Chateaubriand claims the abolition of slavery, nonetheless, for Christianity, even though slavery persisted in Europe for almost two thousand years after the time of Jesus.[26]

Chateaubriand attributes all the excellences of modern Europe to the effects of Christianity. In relation to ancient Rome, he claims: "The passions under polytheism would soon have overturned a government which is preserved only by the accuracy of its counterpoises" (Chateaubriand, 662). Only Christianity espouses a doctrine of moral equality, producing in society "an internal tranquility, a continuous exercise of the most peaceful virtues . . . The meanest of Christians, if a virtuous man, is more moral than was the most eminent of the philosophers of antiquity" (Chateaubriand, 663). In a somewhat delirious and enthusiastic summation of his arguments, Chateaubriand claims that "in literature, characters appear more interesting and the passions more energetic under the Christian dispensation than they were under polytheism. The latter exhibited no dramatic feature, no struggles between natural desire and virtue" (Chateaubriand, 665). So much for Homer, Greek tragedy, Vergil's *Aeneid,* and all the rest.

HEGEL ON THE RELIGIONS

In his lectures on religion, delivered over a period of years from 1821 to 1831, the great and influential German philosopher Georg Wilhelm Friedrich Hegel considered the polytheisms he knew, under the rubric of "determinate," "particular," or "ethnic" religions, lacking the necessary and further evolution to the consummate, "conceptual" form of religion that he finds in his version of Protestant Christianity. In a survey of the world's religions, so-called determinate religions include the worshippers of inferior, or "nature" gods, counting "inferior, natural, and unfree human beings" as their correlates, and ranking beneath, or before, the highest form, "the consummate religion" (Hegel, 203).[27] "So far as the historical development is concerned, nature religion is the religion of 'the East.' The second form of religion, namely that in which the spiritual elevates itself above the natural, is in one aspect the religion of sublimity (that of the Jews) and in the other aspect the religion of beauty (that of the Greeks)" (Hegel, 208). After these stages comes Roman religion, the religion of "external purposiveness or expediency" (Hegel, 209), a necessary prelude to the triumph of Protestant Christianity.

Hostile to the Romantic interest in India, or its idealization, as he sees it, Hegel classes polytheist Hinduism as an early phase in the evolution toward perfection, making an effort, nonetheless, to convey its nature to his listening students. As he expresses it: "It is difficult to get the sense of an alien religion from within. To put oneself in the place of a dog requires the sensibilities of a dog" (Hegel, 224). (In the anonymous transcript of these lectures, an elephant takes the place of the dog.) After attempting to describe Chinese religions, then Buddhism or Lamaism, he arrives at the Indians, and comments that one aspect of Hinduism is "the distinction into many powers, and these many powers [depicted] as a plurality of deities—an unbridled polytheism that has not yet progressed to the beauty of figure. These are not yet the beautiful deities of Greek religion . . ." (Hegel, 271). Hegel also notes with regret that the Indians "personify" phenomena and powers, sometimes as animals: "They do not have hospitals for sick people, but they do for sick cattle" (Hegel, 282). And he continues with his invidious comparisons of Hindu to Greek divinities; in ancient Greece "the beautiful imagination of human beings animates everything, ensouls everything, represents everything as inspirited" (Hegel, 289). With the Hindus, in contrast, "it is a wild and unruly mode . . . [Their] liberality has its ground in an impoverished image of themselves and, to be precise, in the fact that their humanity does not yet have in it the content of freedom, of the eternal, of actual being truly in and for itself, and they do not yet know that their own content or specification is nobler than the content of a spring or a tree"

(Hegel, 289). "There is a concrete expansion of this unspeakable and end-lessly variable superstition, these tremendous fetters and limitations" (Hegel, 290). Human life is valueless, like a sip of water. (The 1831 lecture adds: "Particular activity is held of little account; only stupefaction is valued, and all we are then left with is the organic life of the animal. When no freedom, no morality, no ethical life is present, then power is known only as internal, obscure power, such as pertains both the animals and to those people in the most complete torpor" [Hegel, 290, n. 251].) This theme of an absence of ethics had been developed earlier in the 1827 lectures:

> Just as the superstition arising from this lack of freedom is unbounded, so it follows that there is no ethics to be found, no determinate form of rational freedom, no right, no duty. The Hindu people are utterly sunk in the depths of an unethical life (Hegel, 291).

No understanding of *dharma, karma,* or a politically generated ethics here.

PREJUDICE IN CONTEMPORARY POPULAR CULTURE

Such pernicious argumentation as Hegel's might seem irrelevant today, but unfortunately such ignorance and condemnation thrive in the present. From the online site Yahoo Answers!, to the question "why is monotheism seen as superior to polytheism?" a response by Juvegirl, reproduced verbatim:

> In a polytheism, the gods had various traits, few of them good, ethical or altruistic. It is only after Abraham that we find a religion, tied to one God, that encourages ethical behaviour in its adherents.
>
> One might argue that we have failed to act ethically, but that's another discussion.
>
> If you look at roman, greek or hindu gods, some of them might have good points, but by and large, they have serious human failings, and to a greater degree than humans. Moreover, worshipping these gods was a requirement but not a path to salvation. No one prayed to Hera for salvation. You made your sacrifices, you observed the feasts, and that was that. It was unimport-ant how you lived your life.
>
> We take such ideas as "Don't steal" and "Don't kill" for granted today but it wasn't always the case. So, in that sense, we could say that by imposing a

moral and ethical standard on those who accept it, monotheism has been a force for the good. Again, I'm not saying monotheism was as successful as we might have liked in this regard, but it made some headway.

That's the best I've got, based on the context you asked and the restrictions imposed.[28]

From religiousforums.com, from John Martin, "sophomore member," this answer to the question: "Is Monotheism Superior to Polytheism?," posted May 27, 2013, again cited word for word:

Human beings grow in their relationship with God. The first stage is nature worship or Totemism. Second stage is polytheism in which many gods are worshiped. Third stage is henotheism in which t.here is an acceptance of many gods but one god is considered superior to the other gods. The next sate is Dualistic monotheism which affirms the existence of only one supreme God, other gods are seen more like angles, inferior to him. Creation is seen as a creature of God.This stage brings the problem of evil, omnipotence, omniscience and omnipresence. The next stage can be described qualified non-dualistic monotheism, which affirms the existence of one God and creation is seen as the manifestation of God(It is not pantheism, everything is God). But creation is not identical with God. There will be subtle essential difference between God and creation. This goes beyond good and evil. The next stage can be described as the non-dualistic monotheism, which affirms that there is only one God and everything comes from that one God and returns to that one God, like a piece of ice that comes from the water and returns to water. This experience goes beyond the problem of evil, beyond the problems created by the impotence, omnipresence and omniscience. Creation is essentially one with God but functionally different life water and ice. Water and ice are essentially one but functionally different. This is also an evolution of human being. A human being who was at the mercy of God in the initial stages realizes being one with God. Jesus Christ said:'the Father and I are one'. This is the experience of non-dualistic monotheism. Each stage makes human beings powerful. Hence we can say, polytheism is higher than nature worship. Henotheism is higher than polytheism. Dualistic monotheism is higher than polytheism. Qualified non-dualistic monotheism is higher than Dualistic monotheism and Non-dualistic monotheism is higher than Qualified non-dualistic monotheism, because it helps human beings to realize that they are one with God or God alone is.[29]

The writers express views essentially consistent with those of Hegel. And they are part of the soup of popular culture, and of much popular religious discourse, today. The evidence for physical evolution, for the evolution of human beings from apes, unknown to Hegel, has come to provide a model for the cultural evolution he described. Some purist Christians, including some of my students, reject the evidence concerning biological evolution, as well as any evolution in the domain of religion: The God made the world, dictated the Bible to Moses, and then idolators fell away from the truth. But for others in contemporary culture, the confluence of these two, physical and cultural evolution, provides a prop for those who believe that their monotheist Christianity is superior to all "earlier" forms of religion.

The trajectory of progress from nature to consummate religion, and the argument for the inevitable superiority of this last form of belief, marks the unwitting, or perhaps deliberate claims of Christianity's ethical ascendancy over its primitive antecedents. Hegel's description of the development of religion moves from East to West, from China to Tibet to India to Persia to Egypt to Greece to Israel to Rome. Theirs are the "determinate" religions, those of the first few "nature religions," the lowest form, but each representing a higher development than the one before. The Greeks and the Israelites have not "nature" religions, but spiritual beliefs, "being-for-self," and these two, the Greek the religion of beauty, the Israelite the religion of sublimity, are synthesized in the Roman religion of purposiveness, the purpose being dominion over the empire, guaranteed by Jupiter Capitolinus and by the emperor himself. The climax comes with Christianity, the consummate religion, the religion of the concept. All that precedes is prelude, underdevelopment, necessary but insufficient stages in the progress towards the Protestant Christianity of the nineteenth century. And these stages of development are paradoxically located elsewhere simultaneously both geographically and temporally: the Hindus are *still* primitive in 1827, while the ancient Greeks inhabit an earlier time.

The discovery of evolution in the biological sciences has only served to strengthen the narrative of progress in popular ideas of religion. The analogy with development from apes to humans has been superimposed on cultural practices, and just as *homo sapiens sapiens* is the final and perfected product of evolution, Protestant Christianity appears to its adherents as the perfect end of cultural development.

INDIVIDUALISM AND ETHICS

To one looking at these developments from outside, from the perspective of ancient Greek and Roman polytheism, or ancient Vedic or contemporary Hinduism, all the arguments appear remarkably tautological, circular, ethnocentric, and no more anchored in reason and logic than any other religious point of view. And one might observe also that, within the Western tradition, such views gradually center more and more on the individual, from the time of ancient Greece and Thucydides's speech, attributed to Pericles, in which Athens celebrates itself as the protector of private life:

> It is true that our government is called a democracy, because its administration is in the hands, not of the few, but of the man; yet while as regards the law all men are on an equality for the settlement of their private disputes, as regards the value set on them it is as each man is in any way distinguished that he is preferred to public honours . . . And not only in our public life are we liberal, but also as regards our freedom from suspicion of one another in the pursuits of every-day life; for we do not feel resentment at our neighbor if he does as he likes, nor yet do we put on sour looks which, though harmless, are painful to behold . . . [w]e thus avoid giving offence in our private intercourse . . . (2.37.1–2).[30]
>
> [O]ur city as a whole is the school of Hellas, and . . . each individual amongst us could in his own person, with the utmost grace and versatility, prove himself self-sufficient in the most varied forms of activity (2.41.1).

Such an understanding of private life, of the self-sufficient individual, distinguishes the Western political, philosophical, and religious traditions. Richard Nisbett remarks:

> The Greeks, more than any other ancient peoples, and in fact more than most people on the planet today, had a remarkable sense of personal *agency*—the sense that they were in charge of their own lives and free to act as they chose . . . A strong sense of individual identity accompanied the Greek sense of personal agency.[31]

These traditions do not die.

The influential work of C. P. Macpherson on "possessive individualism," cited earlier, aiming at the heart of Anglo-Saxon liberalism, stressed the significance of subsequent development of such ideas of selfhood in the political theory of the West.[32] The individual reasoning consciousness of Descartes's "Cogito ergo sum," "I think therefore I am," leads eventually, and not without challenge, to the individualism of contemporary advertising: "You're worth it," "Be all that you can be!" In such an environment, a religious tradition that imagines a special relationship with a divinity who himself is an individual, a reasoning mind, thus seems more and more plausible, natural, even inevitable. In a circular pattern of reasoning, that god is imagined to secure the morality of a society made up of individuals just like him. This however, rather than a proof, rather than "human nature," is a specific mutation, peculiar to the Western tradition.

As Pascal Boyer observes, from the perspective of an anthropologist:

> In no human society is it considered all right, morally defensible to kill your siblings in order to have exclusive access to your parents' attention and resources. In no society is it all right to see other members of the group in great danger without offering some help. Yet the societies in question may have vastly different religious concepts. So there is some suspicion that perhaps the link between religion and morality is what psychologists and anthropologists call a rationalization, an ad hoc explanation of moral imperatives that we would have regardless of religion (Boyer, 24).[33]

Pascal Boyer also cites Richard Dawkins, who said that the one very simple procedure through which people obtain their religion is "heredity" (cited without source in Boyer, 317). Boyer sums it up: "people generally adhere to the specific religious commitments of their community and ignore other variants as largely irrelevant" (Boyer, 317). This does not mean that religions, or societies, that do not lodge guarantees of morality in a system of rewards and punishments after death, governed by a single divinity, are unethical or immoral. It is only through the Western discovery of difference that monotheism became the norm, polytheism the other. If the many polytheisms seem primitive to monotheists, these latter attribute a chaotic, underdeveloped ethics to polytheists, and such attribution may be a consequence of an unwarranted projection from their location within an untheorized, unrealized horizon of monotheism, the separation of church and state, and the smug conviction of superiority and inevitability that has grown out of Christian hegemony, especially in predominantly Protestant countries.

THE GENIUS OF POLYTHEISM

Appreciations of the richness of the polytheisms of the world are rare in the context of monotheistic triumphalism, in which the inevitable emergence of monotheism establishes justice, the rule of law, and a personal relationship to a deity. In fact, as Jan Assmann shows, ethics, morality, justice all exist in polytheistic cultures; it is the peculiarity of monotheism to locate the question of justice exclusively in the domain of religion.[34] The French anthropologist Marc Augé, in his *Génie du paganisme,* his title a reply to Chateaubriand's *Génie du christianisme,* does, exceptionally, celebrate "paganism," "heathenism," all that is not monotheism. Augé accuses the European left of denouncing ethnocide, but of failing to take seriously the pagan gods of Africa, America, and Oceania (Augé, 97).[35] In Augé's view, to take them seriously would be to acknowledge that they constitute a materialist ordering of the world, and to recognize their kinship with the Greek gods. Accepting the transcendent nature of monotheism, and attributing immanence to the pagans, he claims: "The paganisms carry no presentiment of Christianity; no paganism extols the love of God or that of one's neighbor" (Augé, 97–98). He stresses that the Greek gods, no more than African gods, stand out for their morality; they have a generally invisible familiarity with human beings: they can help, succor, counsel, but also, if they become hostile, can make sick or unhappy. He distinguishes between paganism and Christianity according to (at least) three criteria: the persecuting consciousness of evil *(la conscience persécutive du mal),* the sense of force, and the immanence of the divine world in the human. "Paganism admits that man can commit errors but has no conception of sin" (Augé, 100).

African religions are the touchstone for Augé, even given their erosion in situations of colonialism and postcolonialism, but he continually quadrangulates among African religions, Confucianism, ancient Greek polytheism, and Christianity. And he points to "the convergence between monotheism and centralized power and . . . the extraordinary destiny of Christianity and to a lesser extent, of Islam in this regard" (Augé, 108).

> The most pertinent opposition that can be drawn in the religious domain would set on one side the religions of the unique and personal God, on the other the polytheisms. The history of the world, whether we like it or not,

is in great part the history of their encounter. If the pagan polytheisms have always lost, . . . it is, among other reasons, because of their exceptional capacity for tolerance . . . *(vertu de tolérance)* (Augé, 109).

Augé is critical of pious considerations of the equality of religions, which often come from hypocrisy and "approximation," and mask too often "the effects of domination and alienation which characterize the relations between unequal political powers" (Augé, 109–110).

In his introduction, Augé argues *for* "paganism":

> [Paganism] is never dualist and opposes neither the spirit to the body nor faith to knowledge. It does not constitute morality as a principle external to the relations of force and meaning that the chance events, the hazards of individual and social life represent. It postulates a continuity between biological order and social order, which on the one hand relativizes the opposition between individual life and the collectivity in which it is inscribed, and on the other hand tends to make every problem, individual or social, a problem of reading: it postulates that all events produce signs, and all signs meaning. . . . Therefore it greets novelty with interest and a spirit of tolerance; always ready to add to its list of gods, it conceives of addition, alternance, but not synthesis (Augé, 19–20).

And polytheism has no missionary practice, no sense that others should be improved, if necessary by force, through conversion to one's own, superior, way of life (Augé, 20).

Jordan Paper, in *The Deities Are Many: A Polytheistic Theology,* writes as a convert to polytheism and provides an essential meditation on these questions. As he argues, "polytheism is a monotheistic construct. Polytheists have no reason to have a term for themselves, since polytheism is the human cultural norm" (Paper, 104). But one problem with his claim to produce "a polytheistic theology" per se is that there can be no unitary polytheist theology, no list of polytheist values, since there are multiple, various, and radically different polytheisms, lumped together only from the perspective of monotheism, which defines them, or it—polytheism—as its other. Paper's "theology," deeply informed by Chinese and Native North American ideas, is his own.

Michael York's *Pagan Theology: Paganism as a World Religion* seeks to provide the ground for both a definition of a world-wide paganism, and a definition fluid enough to allow for many different forms; paganism is an affirmation of interactive and polymorphic sacred relationship by the individual or community with the tangible, sentient, and nonempirical (York, 162).[36]

As the author acknowledges, this is far from a credo, and so open that almost any religion, any relationship to the supernatural, would fit into this category. In fact, as he shows, there are many paganisms, many polytheisms, and those fashioned by contemporary thinkers, influenced by new age spirituality, can only be seen as one aspect of an extremely heterogeneous spectrum. He distinguishes Christianity from paganism by noting that while the Christian god is transcendent, the gods of paganism, and even pagan monism, are immanent, that is, residing not beyond the physical world, but in it. Yet the claim for paganism as "world religion" seems possible only from the perspective of a scholar of religious studies, not an "emic" category, not an "immanent" category, since believers in one form of paganism, still a term of disapprobation, I would think, would not recognize believers in another form as participating in the same, single "world" religion.

And there are dangers inherent in some new forms of paganism, deriving from Nazi ideology, for example, forms that perpetuate racist and anti-Semitic ideologies, at times in the guise of music such as "black metal." Moshe Halbertal and Avishai Margalit, in their valuable treatise *Idolatry,* trace the history of paganism and its associations with idol worship (Halbertal and Margalit, 9–36). They demonstrate that in the Hebrew Bible the root metaphor for the understanding of idolatry is the marital relation; the metaphor is anthropomorphic, adultery exemplifying a flawed personal relationship that is then extended to the relationship between worshipper and divinity. "The sin of idolatry is whoredom" (Halbertal and Margalit, 13). In subsequent developments of the concept, especially in the context of Judaism, idolatry comes to signify rebellion against God as sovereign, improperly anthropomorphizing the deity, using pictorial representations to depict him, worshipping an intermediary, worshipping the wrong object wrongly. Eventually the meaning of idolatry extends to the worship of something else besides God—money, for example. Finally, in an inversion in the hands of Nietzsche and neopagans, paganism is celebrated: "Nietzsche articulates the opposition between the nonpagan God and the pagan gods as one between the uninstinctual, transcendent, emasculated, life-denying God and the heroic, instinctual, life-affirming gods" (Halbertal and Margalit,

250). These ideas, misread, some would argue, lead eventually to the horrors of Nazism, and its descendants, violent Aryanist neopagans. Perhaps some of the current prejudice against polytheism, and polytheists, derives from anxiety, the misrecognizing of all polytheists as espousing these ideologies of hatred and genocide.

CULTURAL PSYCHOLOGY

The model of the psyche adduced by Freud, with a paternalistic superego, an ego struggling with reality, and the demands of an unruly unconscious, corresponds well to a certain model of the nuclear family, with patriarchal father at its head, a child in development, and a possibly feminine and chaotic underpinning. If such a version of psychic and familial life long governed Western modernity, it also provides support for another "monotheist" religion with a father god, a son, and a holy spirit, with the added presence, in some versions of Christianity, of a holy mother, not a god herself, but worthy of veneration. As the psychoanalytic model of the psyche and the self, the subject, changes, under the influence of Lacanians and object-relations theorists and in other tendencies of contemporary thinking about psychic life, perhaps the religious triad of traditional orthodox Christian monotheism will be eroded as well. The family is changing, expanding, adapting to same-sex partners and parents, and it may be that the redundancy of a religion and a nuclear family—as Deleuze and Guattari call it, "mommy-daddy me"—provides a new moment of openness to nonmonotheist ideas in religious life as well.[37]

The field of cultural psychology has been exploring different varieties of selfhood in varied cultural settings and has produced evidence that might be relevant to questions of monotheism, individualism, and separate selves in relation to other traditions that have a more diffuse or diverse sense of divinities. With the model of a single god, watching and judging—or "what would Jesus do?" or "will this action lead to heaven or hell?," Jesus on one's shoulder, Jesus as one's *personal* savior—one result, overdetermined of course by other social, economic, and political factors, is not necessarily a superior ethics, a superior morality, but rather a worldview centered on the self. The fiction writer Gish Jen has referred to the difference between East and West as a distinction between an "interdependent" and an "independent" self.

She remarks on "just how individualistic Western art and narrative are" (Jen, 58).[38] As a second-generation Chinese-American, Jen argues for both: "We need both the interdependent and the independent self. But how interdependent of me to see them as two poles of human experience that cannot be disengaged" (Jen, 158–159).

I would suggest that among the many factors influencing the difference between interdependent and independent psychological types, often categorized as "East Asian" vs. "European" or "European American" (including everyone except people of Asian ancestry— that is, African and Latino and indigenous Americans as well), is rather a distinction between people encultured in a monotheist situation and those who are not. As Richard E. Nisbett has remarked:

> Eastern religions are characterized by tolerance and interpenetration of religious ideas. One can be a Confucian, a Buddhist, *and* a Christian in Korea, in Japan (and in China prior to the revolution). Religious wars in the East have been relatively rare, whereas they have been endemic in the West for hundreds of years. Monotheism often carries with it the insistence that everyone accede to the same notion of God.[39]

Nisbett himself subscribes to the distinction between interdependent and independent psychological development and cites the psychological experiments that back up these claims.

Although it is dangerous, always, to reify these differences and to suggest somehow that they represent essential aspects of culture, it may be that such distinctions, produced by many factors, historical, social, economic, and cultural, also correspond to the elaboration of religious ideas in different societies, and that the hegemonically Protestant U.S. and U.K. prize individualism to the exclusion of other ways of coexisting with other human beings that might be more consistent with polytheism. If the Western European style of Protestant individualism can reach an extremity of selfishness, an indifferent neoliberalism interpreted positively as "liberty," the alternative can be negatively viewed as faceless conformity rather than "harmony." Each can learn from the other; the rigid pseudo-separation of religion and the public sphere in the Western Protestant model might change to accommodate other perspectives, including those of polytheists, and rigid independence open to a new interdependence.

This is not a matter of tolerance, or toleration, but rather of a more fully realized cohabitation.

POLYTHEISM BECOMING MONOTHEISM?

In *A Place at the Multicultural Table: The Development of an American Hinduism,* Prema A. Kurien considers questions of assimilation, transformation, and dialogue with the "homeland," South Asia, in her discussion of Hinduism and polytheism in the U.S.[40] She records the debates, conflicts, and heated interventions of Hindus and people of South Asian traditions in the context of a hegemonic Christian monotheism. Some American Hindus have challenged what they see as misrepresentations of Hinduism in America:

> Many American Hindu spokespersons object to the characterization of their religion as "polytheistic" and "idol worshipping." They point out that although the Hindu pantheon consists of an array of deities, many Hindus believe that all of these deities are different forms manifested by one Supreme Being. They argue that most Hindus have a primary deity that they worship, and some traditions (such as Vaishnavism) only acknowledge the existence of that primary deity. For all of these reasons, they have claimed that Hinduism is in reality a monotheistic religion. Others maintain that neither Western conception ("monotheism" or "polytheism") is suitable to describe Hindu notions of the divine. Similarly, most American Hindu leaders find the English term "idol" offensive, since it has the negative connotation that the worshiper considers the graven image to be divine (Kurien, 187).

Kurien points out that the "umbrella Indian organizations are dominated by upper-class, upper-caste males, and these characteristics go a long way in shaping the content of the ethnicity they represent. . . . Faced with the pressures of racism and assimilation, Hindu Americans strive to perfect a model-minority image of themselves and their culture" (Kurien, 187). The model minority disavows idol worship, the caste system, the oppression of women, and even polytheism. There have been vigorous critiques, even denunciations, of American religious studies scholars, and accusations of a Eurocentric bias in the representations of Hindus and Hinduism, which peaked in the attendance of dissident Hindus at the annual meeting of the American Academy of Religion in 2000.

After September 11, 2001, after ignorant and misguided and violent assaults on Hindus and Sikhs who were thought to be Muslims, "Hindus began to take pride in polytheism, arguing that monotheism led to triumphalism, proselytization, and violence against other faith communities" (Kurien, 197–198).[41] Yet in California, some Hindu spokepersons have objected furiously to the presentation of Hinduism in textbooks destined for sixth-grade social studies and demanded changes:

> Material referring to the plurality of deities, beliefs, and forms of worship in Hinduism was redacted and the texts were revised to portray Hinduism as a monotheistic religion based on Vedic texts. Second, the caste system was dissociated from Hinduism, its hereditary nature was not mentioned, and passages describing its oppressive nature were modified. Third, references to patriarchy or the unequal treatment of women were erased. Finally, the Aryan invasion/migration argument was dismissed as having been "disproved" by contemporary evidence (Kurien, 204).

These changes were accepted by the curriculum commission, whose actions in turn excited reactions from such noted scholars as Michael Witzel, professor of Sanskrit and Indian studies at Harvard University, who objected to the changes as lacking scholarly validity and based on religious and political criteria. Kurien attributes aspects of these debates to what J. L. Matory might call "dialogue," ongoing exchanges between a homeland and a diasporic community, with advocates of the Hindutva agenda of the BJP, the Bharatiya Janata Party, the Indian People's Party in India, endorsing some of these positions.

Kurien summarizes:

> Pressures to assimilate to Western culture in both the colonial and the immigrant contexts led Hindu leaders to construct an organized, monotheistic, textually and historically based Hinduism . . . that emulates the Abrahamic religions they criticize. However, we have seen that when Hindu leaders want to distinguish themselves from these religions, they celebrate the polytheism and the fluid, pluralistic, nonhistorically bound nature of the religion (Kurien, 242).

The encounter with monotheism, especially hegemonic Christianity and Islam, continues to produce these complex representations of Hinduism.

It is only through the Western discovery of difference that monotheism became the norm, polytheism its other. Monotheism is seen as a signal human achievement religiously, philosophically, and ethically. Yet alternate religious and philosophical strains need not indulge in the "degradation" of polytheism, and the other strengths of polytheisms and their different modes of ethical, political, and religious engagement need to be engaged and appreciated. The work of Félix Guattari and Gilles Deleuze, who in *A Thousand Plateaus* discuss the opposition between arboreal and rhizomatic structure, between rigid symmetries and nomadic trajectories, might serve to characterize the virtues of polytheism without reifying or setting them in hierarchical opposition to monotheism.[42] These religious forms differ; they do not represent a Hegelian progress from origin to perfection. Protestant forms of austerity, for example, from the point of view of polytheists, may appear rigid, controlling, colorless, repressive, and repressed. In a Western world that often judges beauty in terms of what is imagined to be "the classical," as in the (misunderstood) pure white marmoreal pedimental architecture and sculpture of ancient Greece, other forms of representation can seem disturbing, ugly, or irrational, in an unwitting prejudice against the multiplicity of polytheisms. Polytheist practices, read by some as excessive, overly corporeal, disordered, even "messy," may accompany an assumption that polytheists are morally defective, that such forms of life are inherently and willfully chaotic, and such assumptions interfere with scholarly work as well as with the exercise of democracies.

DEBATES ON RELIGION IN THE PUBLIC SPHERE

The fear of, rejection of, or dismissal or disregard of polytheism continues, even in the most enlightened of contexts. In *The Power of Religion in the Public Sphere,* a collective volume with essays by Charles Taylor, Jürgen Habermas, Judith Butler, and Cornel West, there is little mention of any religion other than Christianity, Judaism, and Islam.[43] The hallowed public sphere, per se, taken for granted as a necessity of modernity in the West, is yet acknowledged by some participants in these debates to be religiously encoded due to the traditions of Protestant separation between church and state. Judith Butler addresses this issue: "If the public sphere is a Protestant accomplishment, as several scholars have argued, then public life presupposes and reaffirms one dominant religious tradition *as* the secular."

> Some religions are not only already "inside" the public sphere, but they help to establish a set of criteria that delimit the public from the private. This happens when some religions are relegated to the "outside"—either as "the private" or as the threat to the public as such—while others function to support and delimit the public sphere itself. If we could not have the distinction between public and private were it not for the Protestant injunction to privatize religion, the religion—or one dominant religious tradition—underwrites the very framework within which we are operating (Butler, 71).[44]

Nonetheless, in this volume there is barely a mention of traditions outside the Abrahamic. Native Americans are gestured at, in the context of genocide of indigenous peoples (Butler, 97); Gandhi is mentioned, briefly (Butler, 116). Butler remarks, in the dialogic portion of the book:

> I do worry that some of the conceptual frameworks we have for linking secularization with modernization actually assume certain kinds of religions as the relevant ones. Which religion got secularized? Which set of religions is left behind, which now, as Thomas Friedman would say about Islam, represent the premodern? (Butler, 104).

Although Islam is frequently demonized in the West, represented polemically and ideologically as primitive and underdeveloped, polytheism has virtually no place in this conversation about religion in the U.S. public sphere. In fact, Cornel West acknowledges both abhorrence about it, and its persistence: "Christians like myself say you must forever be vigilant in critiques of idolatry. Why? Because idolatry is shot through all of us" (Butler, 105). "Idolatry" is an old, familiar word, pejoratively associated still with paganism, heathenism, superstition, magic, and polytheism.

CHAPTER TWO

Greeks, Romans, and Their Many Gods

THE OATH OF the Athenian ephebes, pronounced at the threshold of manhood, at the moment of induction into the citizen military of the ancient Greek city, reveals the extent to which membership in this elite body, the citizenry that was the city, flourished under the watch of the democratic Athenians' many gods:

> I will not bring dishonour on my sacred arms nor will I abandon my comrade wherever I shall be stationed. I will defend the rights of gods and men and will not leave my country smaller, when I die, but greater and better, so far as I am able by myself and with the help of all. I will respect the rulers of the time duly and the existing ordinances duly and all others which may be established in the future. And if anyone seeks to destroy the ordinances I will oppose him so far as I am able by myself and with the help of all. I will honour the cults of my fathers. Witnesses to this shall be the gods Agraulus, Hestia, Enyo, Enyalius, Ares, Athena the Warrior, Zeus, Thallo, Auxo, Hegemone, Heracles, and the boundaries of my native land, wheat, barley, vines, olive-trees, fig-trees . . . [1]

If we still consider the two streams of antiquity coming from "Jerusalem" and "Athens" to be the sources of Western civilization, Western as such, then the polytheism of the ancient Greeks (and Romans) must be taken into account, not just as a rejected past, a heathenism or paganism overcome by the encounter with "Jerusalem," but also as a living legacy, a presence in the everyday life of the twenty-first century. The worship of the gods of the ancient Greeks and Romans is not dead. When beginning to write this book, I came across a phenomenon previously unknown to me, a wide and varied practice today of so-called pagan polytheism in a form called Hellenismos. Sarah Kate Istra Winter, the priestess also known as Oinokhoe, "Wine-Pourer" in ancient Greek, in a 2008 book thanks, among others: her "former temple, Kin of the Old Gods, with which I had many of my formative ritual experiences, and my first ecstatic rites" (Winter, 5).[2] She writes that 57% of the Hellenic polytheist community surveyed follows the ancient Athenian festival calendar, that the classicist Walter Burkert is their favorite secondary source on Hellenic religion, that Hellenismos competes with Druidry, Santeria, "Reclaiming Witchcraft," and something intriguingly called "Sumerian Reconstruction" (Winter, 137–144). This is just one of the places in which the worship of the ancient gods persists in contemporary culture.

A seminal text in the history of ideas, Jean Seznec's *The Survival of the Pagan Gods,* catalogued the ways in which the gods of the ancient Greeks and Romans resisted their disappearance after the triumph of Christianity and survived in the forms of Renaissance astrology, in the zodiac, in mythological allegories, and in art and poetry: "astrology continued to keep alive the veneration for the gods for which it had served as shelter since classical times."[3] Not just in the works of Shakespeare, but elsewhere, these gods live on, as Atlas still shrugs, and people acknowledge the power of Gemini, the twins, the constellation Castor and Pollux, brothers of Helen of Troy and like her born from an egg hatched by Leda, raped by Zeus, who appeared to her in the form of a swan. In this contact with the god in the guise of a bird, William Butler Yeats, in "Leda and the Swan," saw the devastating consequences of a mixture of kinds for humankind, and the heedlessness of the divinity to his human victim and her people:

A shudder in the loins engenders there
The broken wall, the burning roof and tower

And Agamemnon dead.

                    Being so caught up,
So mastered by the brute blood of the air,
Did she put on his knowledge with his power
Before the indifferent beak could let her drop?[4]

These gods reappear again and again, in popular culture, in young adult fictions like the Percy Jackson series by Rick Riordan, in films, and in many video games that present a vast, jumbled array of divinities from ancient Greece and Rome, as well as Norse and Egyptian gods. Psychoanalysts debate the significance of the Oedipus complex, which Freud proposed, with confirmation in the Greek tragedy of Sophocles. The figure of Sophocles's Antigone has inspired scholars from Hegel to Lacan to Judith Butler to Bonnie Honig.[5] We still use the ancient stories of the Greeks and are informed, formed by the beginnings of Western civilization in one of the classical Mediterranean cultures. Simon Goldhill remarks:

> Describing the "not us" is a fundamental strategy for defining the "us." Wearing nothing but a penis-gourd is "exotic," "foreign" and instantly recognizable as a cultural sign that does not belong to us—except as a self-defining other world.
>
> The trouble is that ancient Greece cannot be just "the other." It's one of those privileged sources from which modern Western culture derives its own values.[6]

He makes these comments in a chapter tellingly entitled "Doing What Comes Naturally?" in a section of his book called "Who Do You Think You Are?" Like many peoples, we tend to see our own social arrangements as natural, inevitable, consistent with "human nature," and some of what we find natural—ideas concerning the psyche, the individual, the democratic citizen—comes to us from the polytheistic ancient Greeks.

In a novel called *Gods Behaving Badly,* Marie Phillips presents a story of the ancient Greek gods literally surviving, squatting in a wreck of a house in contemporary London.[7] Their habits have not changed; the novel begins with a talking tree, victim of the god Apollo's treatment of an unwilling lover. There is incest, drunkenness, much riotously bad behavior, as the gods try to come to terms with their waning power. Their believers have fallen away, and their potency has diminished. The great goddess Aphrodite, for example, has found employment as a phone-sex worker. The novel climaxes with a trip to the underground underworld, and a Tinkerbell-like moment in which only the belief of believers can preserve the life, even immortality, of these charming and amoral creatures. The great pleasure of the text comes from the incongruous juxtaposition of once-immortal ancient beings with contemporary urban life.

But what was the polytheism of the ancient Greeks and Romans, in which the characters of what we now call "myth," characters like the Zeus-swan, were gods—gods and goddesses to be worshipped? Some of the debates within religious studies at present are at the periphery of my concerns here—such issues as the possibility that the conversion from ancient polytheism to revolutionary monotheism, that is to Judaism and then to Christianity, produced religious violence, the question of whether the ancient Greeks and Romans "believed" in our sense in their gods, or whether Greek polytheism was a *kosmos,* an order, or rather a *chaos,* an untidy mess.[8] I'm concerned more centrally, throughout this book, with how the persistence of the polytheism of the Greeks and Romans, and many others, still plays a role in forming the West's concepts of subjectivity, philosophy, and democracy. In this chapter I survey briefly the complicated field of ancient Greek worship of the gods, and then focus on one god, Dionysos, and on one worshipper, Sappho, to give the flavor of what polytheism meant in the ancient Greek world. I conclude with a brief survey of ancient Roman religion, and a discussion of how our own perspective, usually grounded in centuries of monotheist culture, makes it difficult for us to appreciate ancient polytheism, one of the valuable legacies we receive from Greek and Roman antiquity.

THE POLYTHEISM OF ANCIENT GREECE

One might argue that the polytheism of the ancient Greeks and Romans, although accessible to the audience of young adult novels and games, is obscured in the accounts that trace the heritage of "Western civilization" back to Athens. The official account proudly acknowledges the "invention" of democracy by the Greeks. This element of the legacy of the past of Western civilization, in an imaginary genealogy, can be imposed by armies as a poisoned gift to conquered peoples, even as the Greeks' and Romans' polytheism is relegated to the realm of "mythology," material for children's picture books. Yet the ancient Greeks, like most of the peoples of ancient societies all over the world, were polytheists, believers in many gods. They lived in the myriad city-states called *poleis,* scattered over the Greek mainland, the islands of the Aegean Sea, North Africa, the western coast of Asia, the shores of the Black Sea, Sicily, and the coasts of what are now Italy and France. We know most about the ancient *polis* Athens, which survived through the so-called Dark Ages after the collapse of Bronze Age Mycenaean and Minoan civilization and was a crucial early contributor to the history of the West, along with Mesopotamian and Israelite culture. The Athenians saw themselves as inventors of democracy, philosophy, and Western drama, both tragedy and comedy, and at the height of their civilization built magnificent public buildings, including the Parthenon, a sacred building on their acropolis dedicated to the goddess Athena, and wrote such seminal texts as *Oedipus Rex* by Sophocles, the dialogues of Plato, the history of the Peloponnesian War by Thucydides. Their polytheism was not barbaric, not "heathen," not primitive, but the beliefs and practices of highly sophisticated, civilized, often learned and cultured persons.

Students are taught that the Greek gods made up a neat pantheon ("all the gods") consisting of twelve divinities with clearly delineated powers. Although the twelve may wobble from one version of the pantheon to another, this orderly procession, with Zeus the father of the gods at the top of the list, governing the rest from Mount Olympus, seems to be the predominant idea of ancient polytheism. But according to Robert Parker, author of the recent *Polytheism and Society at Athens,* "Greek polytheism is indescribable . . . Gods overflowed like clothes from an over-filled drawer which no one felt obliged to tidy" (Parker, 387).[9] Responding to scholarly attempts to order the Greek pantheon, Parker sets such efforts at understanding Greek polytheism against what he regards as the chaotic illogic in actual religious practices; referring to some of the evidence we have on these matters, he laments: "It is difficult to read a sacrificial calendar or a few pages of Pausanias without bewilderment" (Parker, 445). Although he has done much to illuminate the details of Athenian polytheist worship, Parker remains skeptical about tidying up the drawer.

PAUL AND THE ATHENIAN GODS

The apostle Paul, when he arrived on his missionary travels in Athens to try to convert the Athenians and their philosophers to Christianity, before his encounter with the worshippers of Artemis at Ephesus, said to his audience: "Athenians, I see how extremely religious you are in every way" (*Acts* 17.22). The Greek word he uses here, translated as "extremely religious," is *deisidaimonesterous,* that is, literally: "more-fearful-of-the-'daimons'." "The *daimons*" is one way in which the ancient Greeks referred to their many gods and goddesses. It was also the name of the men of the golden age, a past time of perfection, men who seemed to form a link between the gods and human beings, and it refers as well, eventually, to evil spirits, demons, or devils. On Paul's lips the word may seem complimentary, in that he is attempting to win the attention and favor of his Athenian audience, who are skeptical, some saying: "He seems to be a proclaimer of foreign divinities" (*Acts* 17.18). This was one of the charges that brought about Socrates's execution, that he was introducing new gods to the Athenians, and Paul's being brought to the Areopagus, a place where trials were held, may suggest that he had been accused of a similar crime. Paul could also here be insinuating that the Athenians are "idolators," since the text of *Acts* describes him as "deeply distressed to see that the city was full of idols" (*Acts* 17.16). In his address to the Athenians, after his ambiguous remark about their fear of *daimons,* he notes their shrine erected "To an unknown god," and makes much of the fact that *his* god is near to all, and hinting that with this shrine they may have already acknowledged the only true god, *his* one god.

ATHENIAN POLYTHEISM

Many of the Athenians were indeed "fearful," or respectful, or reverential, in all respects, with regard to their very many *daimones,* or gods, although some philosophers may have in the course of time become more skeptical or even indifferent towards the gods. Yet popular religion continued to revere the many divinities of the pantheon. Exemplary of the polymorphous untidiness of actual worship are the divinities invoked in time of war. Ancient Greek war is today most often associated with the god Ares, who was, according to Homer, the most hated by Zeus of all the gods (*Iliad* 5.890); yet Ares had temples on the island of Crete and on the mainland in the Peloponnesus. Cretan cities seem to have offered sacrifices to Ares and his lover Aphrodite, wife of the smith god Hephaistos. Oaths sworn to the lovers by young military recruits may be connected to the homosexual bond among young warriors. As noted earlier, gods, the supernatural beings, need not be loved to be revered, believed in, worshiped, and feared. Ares, hated, was nonetheless an important divinity to the ancient Greeks.

Yet to experiment with or *play* with the other gods implicated in war, as the classical scholar Marcel Detienne has urged, is to come to terms, in Athens alone, with Athena, Enyo, Enyalios, Ares and Athena Areia (invoked by the ephebes, the military recruits, in their oath), Athena Nike, and the Hyakinthides Parthenoi (Detienne, 137–138).[10] These latter were Attic heroines, who "had saved the city by themselves serving, on a variously identified occasion, as the pre-battle offerings demanded by the gods as price of victory" (Parker, 399). The sacrificed heroines came themselves to receive pre-battle sacrifices. Also implicated in war were Zeus, especially as Zeus Tropaios ("Of the Turn"), and Artemis Agrotera, who received a pre-battle *sphagion,* a "slaughter-sacrifice." The wild Arcadian goatish god Pan also figured in the field of battle, and the sacred space of Apollo Lykeios, associated with wolves, was "the main training ground for the cavalry and hoplites of Athens" (Parker, 402). To say that Ares is *the* god of war, as potted histories of ancient Greek religion have it, is to tidy up this picture mercilessly.

A TANGLED NETWORK OF GODS

As Parker notes, "each god is one among many" (Parker, 6). And, as is already clear from the list of the gods associated with war, the names of the principal gods bore added "epithets," verbal qualifiers that connected them with particular aspects of their being, and /or with particular localities in which they were worshipped. Artemis, the virgin goddess of wild animals, of the hunt, of the Asian city Ephesus, associated with the Zoroastrian goddess Anahita there, and with the virgin Mary, was in one of her aspects called *agrotera,* "wild," "the huntress," with respect to the battlefield. This divinity, a goddess linked to childbirth and to female rites of passage, worshipped by virgin girls dressed as little bears, was also honored with a procession that supposedly fulfilled a vow made before the great battle of Marathon, when the Athenians along with other Greeks (but not the Spartans, delayed by observance of a lunar eclipse) defeated the Persian emperor's army and saved mainland Greece from conquest and incorporation in his huge empire. The Athenians had vowed to sacrifice as many goats as enemies killed, and when they ran out of goats, pledged five hundred a year at Artemis Agrotera's festival. Artemis Mounichia was associated with the bright moonlight that aided the Greeks in the battle of Salamis, another victory over the Persians, while Artemis Phosphoros, "light-bearer," had given light in darkness to the defenders of democracy during the civil war at the end of the fifth century BCE. She marked the borders that separate civilization from savagery, and her help was summoned in time of war. As Parker puts it:

> She intervenes in situations of a special type, not ordinary battles but those that form part of a "war of total destruction," one that threatens the annihilation of an independent state. Such an annihilation would mean the destruction of temples, agora, a laying waste of civilized forms: Artemis is patrolling the borders . . . (Parker, 401).

The additions to divine names, then, are many, and mark specific forms of worship—in groves, shrines, temples, processions—connected with past events, with particular places sacred to the gods, to aspects of their many powers, which are not limited to such simple features as "virginity," for example. Zeus, father of the gods, in Athens alone was known as Agoraios, Alexeterios, Boulaios, Eleutherios, Epakrios, Epiteleios Philios, Euboules, Herkeios, Hypatos, Hypsistos, Kenaios, Ktesios, Meilichios, Moiragetes, Morios, Naios, Olympios, Pankrates, Patroos, Philios, Phratrios, Polieus, Soter, Teleios, and Tropaios. And each of these additions to the name of Zeus had specific reference—to his role in politics; to other gods of the pantheon; to places in Athens and its surrounding territory, Attica; to the household; to Mount Olympus; to the turn in battle, and so on.

The worship of the gods of the ancient Greeks and the Romans formed a huge self-contradictory universe, where the divinities can seem both playful and brutal; it is very different from the universe of monotheism, defined at least officially as a cosmos of judgment, where a single god knows, watches, and judges all. And it is almost impossible to separate out religion, as a category, from the rest of life in the ancient world. Although we may strive to mark off religion as an independent part of social existence, as within the "private sphere," in antiquity what we think of as religion, a relationship to the supernatural, was completely intertwined with what we might see as the separate realms of politics, literature, music, architecture, drama, entertainment, and everyday life. Implicitly, Greek and Roman religion provides a critique of that understanding of reality—a ludic—that is, playful—temporal, densely populated landscape of radical otherness. Such are the joys of polytheism. Rather than a paternal divinity of reward and punishment, or even one of crucifixion, resurrection, and forgiveness, the ancient Greeks experienced divinity everywhere, immanently, embodied anthropomorphically at times, sometimes generous, sometimes dangerous, and not to be confused with ethical "commandments." Although poets, statesmen, and philosophers reflected on ethical and moral questions, these were not adjudicated by remote divinities.

The god Dionysos gave human beings wine as a gift; he is in the wine, in the drinker when he drinks it. A famous Greek vase, made for wine-drinking, shows Dionysos at sea; the wine, when it filled the vase, represented the wine-dark sea, and Dionysos appeared as one tipped the vase to drink it, the god's gift to suffering humankind. The goddess Aphrodite put desire into human beings, a desire for coupling with another person, and one insults her when rejecting her gift. Coming to terms with this understanding of the world allows us to denaturalize, demystify our own, compare it to another way of mapping almost everything—divinity, desire, gender, politics—or to acknowledge an unrecognized debt to these ways of experiencing existence.

In the polytheistic societies of ancient Greece and Rome, people worshiped many gods and goddesses, in many different cults, with various rituals and with many forms of sacrifice. As noted above, there were gods of the cities, of villages, of particular spots—mountain tops, springs, caves, temples. Ancient polytheism was not the sum of many individual religions. These gods were worshipped at the same place and at the same time by the same community and the same individual—the *totality* of the gods constituted the divine world. The Greek pantheon was not a closed, harmonious system, but was rather unstable, full of gaps, without a sacred, canonical scripture, without prophets, with no set time and place of origin. For some scholars, rather than a chaotic and unmappable landscape, the gods represent a complex system that embodies all the various and significant different forces, powers, forms of energy for human beings. For example, Aphrodite can represent both the joyful consummation of sexuality, and the accompanying pains of yearning and desire. In any case, this is a world in which everything is *full* of *gods,* not an absent, patriarchal, transcendent, judgmental god, but a world of divine energies and forces, not coherent, not directed from a center, but perhaps more reflective of the complexity of human experience than the positing of an eternal father, or a transcendent single divinity of forgiveness, reward and punishment.

SAPPHO

Whether the landscape of divinity in ancient Greece is an untidy drawer or a complex system of forces, describing it here would be impossible. Greek polytheism embraces a vast array of ritual practices, sacrifices, festivals, and processions, as well as an immense multiplicity of gods. Although our knowledge of these is constantly being enriched by scholarship and archaeological findings, most of our information comes from elite texts preserved somewhat haphazardly over millennia. We know less about the everyday practices of worshippers. Any discussion of this rich and complex word relies to a lesser or greater degree inevitably on these elite texts, including the great and enduring poetry and prose of lyric singers, tragedians and comic writers, historians and philosophers.

Before discussing just one god among the many, Dionysos, I look at just one worshipper among many, the sixth-century BCE Greek poet from the island of Lesbos, Sappho, whose magnificent poetry survives in fragments, often quoted by other ancient authors, or found on shreds of ancient papyrus in the garbage dumps of ancient Egypt. Sappho is appropriate as a single example, since her life is so often misread in terms of her devotion to a single divinity. In this poem—a prayer, a hymn, perhaps—Sappho calls the goddess Aphrodite from her father Zeus's home in the heavens and entreats her to help her devotee, here explicitly named Sappho:

> Upon your intricately wrought throne, deathless Aphrodite,
> child of Zeus weaving lures, I beg you
> don't break my heart with longing nor with grief,
>   oh queen,
> but come here. If once at another time
> you heard my cry from afar,

and you responded, and came leaving your father's house—
    golden—

chariot yoked. Beautiful they brought you,
quick sparrows over the black earth,
densely whirring wings from heaven
     through mid-sky.

All at once they arrived, and you, blessed goddess,
a smile on your deathless face,
asked what I was feeling again and why
     was I calling again,

and what for myself I most want to happen
in my frenzied heart? "Whom again do I persuade
to take you back into her love? Who,
     Sappho, is doing you wrong?

"If she runs off, soon she'll be chasing.
If she refuses to accept gifts, she'll give them.
If she doesn't love, soon she will love,
     even unwillingly."

Come now again, free me from painful
care. Whatsoever my heart desires to happen,
make it happen. You yourself
     fight on my side.[11]

Is this a religious hymn, a prayer, a playful parody of a hymn?

Feminist classical scholars have tended to frame Sappho as a love poet, rather than the composer of ritual hymns, and as a worshipper of Aphrodite to the exclusion of other gods. In part because of the intensity of this poem, the atmosphere of intimate supplication, and the way in which the worship of Aphrodite corresponds to our own ideas, aesthetic and religious, constructed through the legacy of Sappho's verse, we may read her poetry through the lens of this particular devotion as a "henotheism," that is, devotion to one particular, favorite god among the many of a polytheistic pantheon. The introduction to Paul Roche's translation *Love Songs of Sappho,* republished in 1998, begins: "The ancient Greek poet Sappho writes of Aphrodite the goddess of sexuality, of soft beds, roses, groves sacred to the goddess . . ."[12] I am the author of this statement. Like other twentieth-century literary and feminist classical scholars, I read Sappho as a lover and a poet and as a single-minded devotee of Aphrodite.

But if Sappho has often been associated exclusively with Aphrodite, other gods populate her songs, other gods *besides, beside* Aphrodite. Sappho was a polytheist, like the other inhabitants of the archaic Greek world, and not just a worshipper of the goddess of sexual desire. Some of the many gods who inhabit Sappho's poems do seem to belong to the world of Aphrodite, the world of sexuality. Eros, god of desire, for example, shook her heart, as does a wind falling upon mountain oaks (fragment 47); that Eros descended from heaven, dressed in a purple cloak (fragment 54); fragment 130, from Hephaistion's *Handbook on Meter,* quotes Sappho: "Eros, the limb-loosener, again stirs me / like a sweet bitter irresistible creeping beast." Other divinities mentioned include those associated with Sappho's vocation as a singer. She often names the Muses, sometimes accompanied by the Graces, but this too might be seen as related to a devotion to Aphrodite.

But what of other divinities addressed by Sappho, more sharply distinguished from Aphrodite? The most significant of these were the gods of a triple shrine on the island of Lesbos, invoked in a song that demonstrates most fully the polytheistic reference of Sappho's work. This is fragment 17, which summons not Aphrodite, but the goddess *Hera:*

> Near me, as I pray you that you may appear
> Lady Hera : : your elegant figure
> to whom the sons of Atreus prayed.
>   Those glorious kings
>
> having won many prizes,
> first around Ilium, then on the high sea,
> but then setting out for this place
>   were not able to complete the voyage
>
> until they appealed to you and to Zeus of the supplicants
> and to Thyone's son who excites desire.

Now be gracious, and help me also
   in accord with the ancient ways.

Sacred and beautiful :
: maidens
gather round
      : :

: :

       to be :
:   to arrive at the shrine

How are we to understand this reference to Hera, associated most often with weddings and marriage rather than with seduction? Wife and sister of Zeus, Hera was not deified as a mother: her son the monster Typhaon was born without a father, that is, "parthenogenically," as was Hephaistos, the smith and artisan god, whom his mother threw out of Olympos when she saw his crippled body. Hera was known in myths for persecuting the hero and god Herakles, for her violent rage against the god Dionysos and against Proitos's daughters, punished for resistance to Dionysos; at her instigation Herakles killed his wife and children in Thebes in a fit of madness. Sappho addresses Hera in a hymn that is a reminder of the enormous risks taken by voyagers at sea in antiquity; travelers and their friends and families often accompanied embarkations with vows and sacrifice, libation and prayer to the gods, and garlands thrown into the sea. The Homeric visit of Menelaos to Lesbos concerned the insecurity and dangers of crossing from Troy, in Asia, back to Greece. Sappho's fragment 17 is just one moment where we see another Sappho, not the single-minded, erotically fixed, ecstatic worshipper of Aphrodite, as she asks for help from Hera for safe passage by sea for some friend or companion or lover.

The whole city of Mytilene, Sappho's city, was said to celebrate a festival in honor of the god Apollo in the fifth century BCE. The direct address to Hera rather than to Apollo in Sappho's fragment 17, a prayer to beg her to manifest herself to the singer of the song, strikingly widens and opens the sense of Sappho as addresser of divinity, one focused perhaps on female divinity. Although Sappho's songs do not include a hymn to Eos, the Dawn, possibly worshipped in Sparta, she does allude to the story of the goddess of dawn and that goddess's kidnapping of the beautiful mortal Tithonos, in fragment 58. And Alkaios, Sappho's contemporary, confirms the polytheism practiced on Lesbos in his fragment 129:

> The Lesbians established this great conspicuous precinct to be held in common, and put in it altars of the blessed immortals, and they entitled Zeus God of Suppliants and you, the Aeolian, Glorious Goddess, Mother of all, and this third they named Kemelios, Dionysus, eater of raw flesh.[13]

The Italian scholar Giovanni Tarditi argued that these altars represent not the Sapphic triad, but a very ancient Aegean religious form consisting of two masculine divinities subordinated to a goddess at the center, related to pre-Hellenic and proto-Hellenic triads. This goddess bears the name "Eolia" here; she is the protectress not only of the Lesbians, but of all the surrounding Aeolians, Greeks of the Eastern Mediterranean, and her cult was thought by Tarditi to be very ancient.[14]

Alkaios names Zeus first, and asks the three gods of the shrine to hear his prayer, to rescue him and his friends from hardship and exile, and to allow an avenger to pursue his enemy, Pittakos, ruler of Mytilene. Elsewhere Alkaios nostalgically recalls the Lesbian precinct of Hera and its famous beauty contest, and he sings of a glorious cache of archaic weaponry. Alkaios's polytheist practice illuminates Sappho's. She may be declining to acknowledge Apollo, subordinating Zeus to Hera, refusing the militarist connotations of many of Alkaios's songs, as in other of her poems she turns from the Homeric legacy celebrating warriors and war, in fragment 16 choosing the girl Anaktoria over cavalrymen, infantry, and ships at sea. Here she demonstrates a particular desire, for her girl, over an abstract definition of "the most beautiful" that will lead eventually to the abstractions of a philosophical monism.[15] Her selection of female deities also seems significant, centering on Aphrodite and Hera while subordinating Zeus and Apollo. In any case, we see Sappho the polytheist, worshipper of many gods, whether male or female, among them Aphrodite, goddess of sexual desire, and Dionysos, the god of ecstatic possession, and the joys of wine. In the works of Sappho, known best as a worshipper of the goddess Aphrodite and celebrated in antiquity for her erotic poetry praising and longing for women, we see not an exclusive focus on this one goddess, but a rich array of divinities, including Hera, the dawn goddess

Eos, and other divinities associated with love, desire, poetry, marriage, and even Dionysos himself.

DIONYSOS

Dionysos is just one of the many gods of the classical city. In his worship, we find a vast range of cultic celebration, including phallic processions, sacred marriages between mortal women and the god, and the magnificent dramatic festivals of the city of Athens, which included tragedy and comedy and brought together the whole of the city in honor of the god. If I focus here on this one god, Dionysos, it is not only because he becomes so important in the development of Christianity in the postclassical world, but also because he is a compelling exemplar in the network of relations that made up Greek polytheism.[16] His worship was never localized, and to catch him in a net may be impossible, but I can try to give a sense of the richness of worship of this, just one of the many gods. Dionysos is called *lusios,* the "liberator," eater of raw flesh, god of liquid things—wine, sap, semen. He is the god of orgiastic aspects of Greek religious life, possession and ecstasy. The *Homeric Hymn* to the god calls him "boisterous Dionysos of the ivy-wreathed head."[17] When compared to the god Apollo, patron of the Delphic oracle, god of prophecy and philosophy, and a complex divinity in his own right, Dionysos has been described as embodying a different kind of masculinity, erasing the boundary between male and female, and a different class affiliation, appearing as the people's god, in opposition to the aristocratic Apollo.[18]

Long thought to be a foreign god, imported from Asia perhaps, the name of Dionysos actually appears in very early records showing that he was worshiped in Greece itself in the Mycenaean age, on tablets written in Linear B, the most ancient form of Greek, from about 1250 BCE. Dionysos had no fixed site of worship; he was mobile, wandering, and was honored everywhere. The narrative, the myth, recounts that he was twice-born, with an exceptional beginning that marks him as extraordinary even among the gods, even though he was not always included in the pantheon of the twelve Olympians. His mother Semele was one of the daughters of Kadmos; he had come from Phoenicia, on the western coast of Asia, to find his sister Europa, abducted by Zeus, and instead founded the Greek city of Thebes.

The libidinous god Zeus was then enamored of Semele; his wife Hera was, as always, jealous of the mortal object of her brother/husband's affections, and she is said to have appeared as an old woman to Semele and encouraged her to test her lover, to ask him to appear in all his splendor as a divinity, as if she were his immortal consort, as he would appear to Hera herself. Semele maneuvered Zeus into promising her any favor she wanted; she asked him to appear as he did to the goddess. He came in a blast of glory and thunderbolts, and Semele was consumed by lightning. Her unborn child was taken up by Zeus and sewn into his own thigh. Thus the god Dionysos was twice born, once of a mortal woman, once of the god, and so through this second birth, through a strange moment of masculine pregnancy, with his father wounded and opened up, Dionysos achieved immortality. After his double birth, the god Dionysos was given to the nymphs of Nysa to raise, and they became his followers. In one version of his life, he was said to be vulnerable to death, to have been dismembered by the Titans, the generation of gods who preceded the Olympians, and then reborn.

In many of the "myths" or stories told of the god's life, the theme is the overcoming of resistance. Seen as a newcomer, bringing his gift of wine, he enters communities in which some residents resist worshiping him; eventually he overpowers them, often destroying them in the process. He represents the violent force of liberation, and like Aphrodite, who embodies the sometimes violent force of sexual desire, he can be cruel and ruthless. In works of art, and perhaps in ritual as well, Dionysos is associated with a force seeking freedom, the energy to break bonds, often bringing with him an anti-order; he is the other always present, ready to emerge, the irrational and the sacred erupting into the everyday, scrambling orderly hierarchical political and masculine values of the city. He was imagined arriving in Greece from India, the East, with his followers, escorted in a triumphal chariot as he comes. Vase painters often depict him accompanied by this entourage; his devotees make up a *thiasos,* an unbounded community of those filled with his presence; worshipers include women, slaves, and citizens together, and in myth and art he travels leading satyrs, wild spirits of the woods, quasi-human, with some bestial part, always with erect penises, their virility not about fertility and reproduction, but about lust, arousal for its own sake. The satyrs are shown in works of art with horses' tails or goats' horns, ears, or legs. Highly libidinous, they are fond of dancing, and are seen at times with *silenoi,* older satyrs, often drunken; these bestial characters behave aggressively, sexually, toward women in the company. Dionysos also moves accompanied by nymphs or maenads—"women driven mad"—who wore fawn skins, carried sacred wands, and performed miracles, making fountains of milk or wine spring up from the earth. Inhumanly strong in moments of Dionysiac possession, they tear up bulls and human beings with their bare hands and engage in the eating of raw flesh, undoing the order of sacrifice, the principal rite of ancient Greek worship. Subversive of neat categories of difference, these possessed women are invulnerable to weapons, suckle animals, and constitute a feminine presence at the heart of Dionysos worship. The women running wild in the mountains, whether real or imaginary, differ from proper matrons, citizen-class worshippers of the goddess of grain, Demeter; they represent the Other inside, ready to erupt and undo the order of the city. Alexander the Great was represented as a new Dionysos, a conqueror who went eastward and then returned, bringing with him new ways and new companions.

Euripides's *Bacchae* presented the story of Pentheus, king of Thebes after Kadmos, in a tragedy named for the "bacchantes," the maddened worshippers of Bacchus, another name for Dionysos. Pentheus refused to worship Dionysos, even to recognize his divinity, and comes on stage revealing that he is appalled by a newcomer to the city adorned with Dionysos's long curly hair, bearing his effeminate "Asiatic" look. The young Pentheus holds rigidly to virility, clarity, rationality, transparency, and order, in the face of this stranger who has arrived in Thebes, claiming to be an emissary of the god. Dionysos, or the stranger, sends the women from the city up on to the mountain top to honor him, and Pentheus tries to stop them, imprisoning the stranger. But the prison bursts open, and the god appears, in a terrible and haunting scene convincing Pentheus to dress in women's clothing and go himself up to the mountain to see the women worshiping. The god, as he seduces and pulls the young king into madness, shows the power of the force he summons; his maenads, the maddened, possessed women who commit violence in his name, sing hymns in praise of the god:

He is sweet upon the mountains. He drops to the earth from the running packs.
He wears the holy fawn-skin. He hunts the wild goat and kills it.
He delights in the raw flesh.

He runs to the mountains of Phrygia, to the mountains of Lydia he runs!
He is Bromius who leads us! Evohe!

With milk the earth flows! It flows with wine!
It runs with the nectar of bees! (lines 135–142)[19]

These words of praise, in the ecstatic song of Dionysos's female followers—
male performers dressed as women—give many names to the god who, like
others named earlier, has many aspects, many places.

Pentheus, dressed as a woman, spies on the peaceful maenads, the "bacchantes," from high up in a tree. But he is spotted, pulled down, torn to
pieces, perhaps devoured raw by his own mother, in a scene described by a
messenger who witnessed the horrors of the bacchantes driven into a frenzy
by this trespass into their women's rites. Pentheus's mother Agave descends
from the mountain and appears back in the city with his head as a trophy,
believing she has killed a lion cub, and in a horrific, grotesque, and painful
scene, emerges from her Dionysos-induced madness to recognize that the
head she carries is that of her own son.

This tragedy recognizes the impossibility, the potential insanity of
attempting to maintain absolute reason with no room for irrational, unex-
pected wildness and femininity. Dionysos appears here as the wildness at
the heart of civilization—nature, fertility, the incomprehensible—and there
are other such stories of his ability to undo the orderly hierarchical city. In
Argos, the daughters of Proitos would not recognize the divinity of Dionysos, went mad, and destroyed their own children. The daughters of Min-
yas refused to come out and worship Dionysos, staying home like proper
citizen women to perform their household duties, to weave. But phantoms
of wild beasts filled their room, their weaving began to turn into vines, and
they too went mad. King Ikarios received Dionysos gladly, and the god gave
him the gift of wine. Ikarios in turn presented the gift to his people; experiencing the effects of intoxication, they thought they had been poisoned and
killed their king, while the daughters of the city hung themselves.

Another such story is told in a *Homeric Hymn* to the god: Dionysos
appears and pirates steal him, thinking he would make an excellent slave,
but they cannot hold him: "first throughout the swift black ship sweet and
fragrant wine / formed a gurgling stream and a divine smell / arose as all
the crew watched in mute wonder."[20] This is the same pattern of restraint,

resistance, the attempt to control the god, and here too he bursts free, becoming a lion, then a bear.

> And next on the topmost sail a vine spread about
> all over, and many grapes were hanging down
> in clusters. Then round the mast dark ivy twined,
> luxuriant with flowers and lovely growing berries [21]

Dionysos slips away from the control of these pirates, whom he turns into dolphins, as easily as he escapes the prison of Thebes.

Dionysos has a few erotic adventures, including a love affair with Ariadne, daughter of Minos, ruler of the island of Crete. The hero Theseus came from Athens to be sacrificed to the Minotaur, and Ariadne, falling in love with him, gave him a ball of thread so he could enter the labyrinth, kill the Minotaur, and find his way out again. Theseus sailed away with Ariadne as far as Naxos, where he abandoned her; she was found by Dionysos, who married her. And scenes of the two in art become emblematic of marriage. Yet Dionysos, a male god, often has an ambiguous sexual identity, very different from Apollo's. He is shown with long curly hair, crossing the boundary between masculine and feminine, the liberator from rigid gender categories. Ancient Athens was a society in which male and female persons were usually separated, women of the citizen class segregated inside their homes. But Dionysos encourages Pentheus to dress in women's clothes and leads women astray, encouraging them to leave home and run wild.

Dionysos is the god of wine and of intoxicated ecstasy, of drunkenness, a welcome change in consciousness, especially for the poorer classes of the city; drunkenness was seen as a possession by something divine, like madness, possession by the god. In the celebrations of Dionysos, a mass phenomenon, the worshiper becomes the divinity, both called Bacchus; there is a blurring of personality, *enthousiasmos* as it called in Greek, the god "inside," an ecstasy very different from the order and discretion of the oracular, prophetic god Apollo.

The Greeks celebrated many Dionysos festivals, most connected with wine, featuring phallic processions and the opening of the new wine. In one festival, the wife of the "king," a priest, was given to Dionysos in a ritual sex act, a so-called sacred marriage. As god of wine, he was honored as a delight to mortals and a giver of joy, stilling cares and bringing sleep and

oblivion from everyday pains and suffering. Thus his worship also sometimes entailed an association between drunkenness and death; dismember-
ment is invoked in some of the rituals and myths about the god.

Perhaps because of his association with possession, with the crossing
of gender boundaries, and the power of actors to assume both male and
female personas, Dionysos was also god of the theater in the ancient Greek
world. Both tragedy and comedy were not just modes of entertainment
in Greece, but were political-religious institutions, which some scholars
believe were crucial to the development of Athenian democracy, "rule by
the people." The city held dramatic festivals in Dionysos's honor, and in
tragic contests the stories of the past, "mythology," were embodied on
the stage in the theatrical resurrection of aristocratic heroes and gods. An
actor himself might be possessed by Dionysos, wearing a mask, sometimes
dressing in women's clothes, inhabited by otherness, becoming an other
on the city's stage.[22]

The democratic city arranged for these productions, supported by the
wealthy in a form of taxation, and eventually paid citizens to attend several
days of theatrical performances at the end of which prizes were awarded;
the priests and priestesses of the city sat in reserved spots at center stage.
The tragedies and comedies were performed in honor of the god. In addition to tragedies like the *Bacchae,* the only such play we have in which
a plot directly concerned Dionysos, there were comedies in which actors
wore padded buttocks and large, drooping, padded phalluses, recalling
the ritual phallic processions performed in honor of Dionysos, the people's
god. While Euripides's *Bacchae* presents the danger, power, and cruelty of
this god, Aristophanes's comedy *Frogs* exhibits Dionysos as a character who
verges frequently on the ridiculous. When descending to the underworld to
bring back one of the great, dead tragedians to the city in trouble, traveling
with his slave Xanthias, the comic character Dionysos betrays an impressive
cowardice when faced with Hades's doorkeeper:

> *Dionysus:* My butt runneth over; let us pray.
> *Xanthias:* Stand up right now, you clown, before somebody sees you!
> *Dionysus:* But I feel faint. Please, give me a wet sponge for my heart.
> *Xanthias:* Here, take this and apply it. Where is it? Ye golden gods, is that
>   where you keep your heart?
> *Dionysus:* Yes, it got scared and sneaked down to my colon.[23]

The marvelous translation by Jeffrey Henderson restores the scatological, obscene nature of this scene and the indignities to which the god is subjected. After this bodily disgrace, the god forces his slave to exchange costumes with him, and spends some of the comedy pretending to be not only a mortal, but a slave, and thus subject to torture. Although to modern viewers these scenes, with an actor playing a god made cowardly and ridiculous, can seem baffling, Dionysos is here a familiar character, one subject to mockery and excess, perhaps just because he is a god especially associated with democracy and the *demos,* the people of the city. It is difficult to imagine the lofty Apollo treated with such irreverence in a comedy.

The dramatic festivals of Athens were performed in honor of Dionysos, and there were other such celebrations of this favorite, popular god. The Athenians marked the opening of the new year's wine with the Anthesteria, which included slaves dining with their masters, the arrival of Dionysos in the city on a wheeled, sacred black ship, and the sacred marriage of the "king"-priest's wife with the god. The first two days of this festival of three days were dedicated to Dionysos, the last to Hermes Chthonios, Hermes of the earth, of the underworld. At the Dionysia, the choruses were said to gratify the other gods, and especially the twelve gods with their dances (Xenophon, *Hipparchus* 3.2). And colonists who had long ago left the city of Athens were required to send a phallus to be carried in a sacred procession; on a vase, we see a phallus on a long wooden pole, given an eye, carried by men with erect penises. The phallus is ridden by a huge figure who himself has a tiny rider on top.

As noted earlier, each god of the Greeks was one among many, and their significance derives from their sometimes contradictory positioning within a polytheism, a spectrum of many gods. Dionysos is not Apollo, cool god of prophecy, music, foundation of cities, civilization, disease and healing, murder and its purification; he is not Demeter, goddess of the grain and the dry food that sustains humankind; he is not Hermes, guide of dead souls into the underworld; not Pan, the truly wild goat god of Arcadia; not Athena, goddess of weaving, guardian of the city of Athens. Dionysos is the god of female delirium and male sexual frenzy, often stimulated by wine, and thus different from Aphrodite, goddess of desire between two lovers. Worship of Dionysos, who remains cool and aloof from the ecstasy and lust of his followers, takes place within the wider context of the complex and wide-reaching array, changing over time, that the Greeks saw as the supernatural dimension of the cosmos, whose gods intervened rarely in the world of human beings, but which nonetheless imbued every aspect of everyday life with divinity.

The god Dionysos, worshipped as Bacchus by the Romans, comes into Christian iconography. Themes of suffering and liberation, as well as the connection between wine and blood, the eating of raw flesh, imaginatively link the two divinities, and early Christian images showed Jesus as Dionysos, Dionysiac worshipers participating like the pagan bacchantes in the communion, the eating of the god's body and drinking his blood. Early Christian art is rich with Dionysiac associations, whether in boisterous representations of agape feasting, in the miracle of water-into-wine at Cana, in vine and wine motifs alluding to the Eucharist, and most markedly in the use of Dionysiac facial traits for representations of the Messiah, the Christ.[24] These images of Jesus, the one god among three, present an example of the survival and persistence of ancient polytheism into Christianity.

NEW GODS

The world of Greek gods seems to us, as Parker, Burkert, and Versnel note, untidy, messy, and full of variety. Although the Athenians indicted Socrates for introducing new gods, on the other hand they appear to have felt little need to exclude any god who arrives from elsewhere, sometimes with the many slaves who became part of the city's religious life, as in the case of a goddess like Bendis, who came from Thrace, to the far north. She resembled Artemis, depicted as a huntress carrying two spears. Bendis arrived in Athens first in 430 BCE, in the midst of the classical period; the Athenians installed a treasury, that is, a building for precious objects, in honor of Bendis and another goddess from far away, Adrasteia from Phrygia in Asia Minor, administered by officials called the "Treasurers of the Other Gods." Then later, in 413 BCE, Bendis was assigned a priestess, and a great festival to honor her began to be celebrated in the port of Athens, the Piraeus. Plato begins the great dialogue *The Republic* with this account of Bendis worship:

> I went down yesterday to the Piraeus, the son of Ariston, to pay my devotions to the goddess, and also because I wished to see how they would conduct the festival, since this was its inauguration.

> I thought the procession of the citizens very fine, but it was no better than the show made by the marching of the Thracian contingent (*Republic,* 327a).[25]

As the narrator is leaving, he is persuaded to wait, since there is to be a torchlight race on horseback in honor of the goddess, and a night festival as well. It is in the course of the subsequent conversation at the house of a *metic,* a resident non-Athenian, that we hear Sophocles's famous remark about his love life:

> I remember hearing Sophocles the poet greeted by a fellow who asked, How about your service of Aphrodite, Sophocles—is your natural force still unabated? And he replied, Hush, man, most gladly have I escaped this thing you talk of, as if I had run away from a raging and savage beast of a master (*Republic,* 329b–c).

Service, devotion, to this goddess is pleasure and pain; without the benefit of modern medical intervention, the old man must accept the tranquility and release from this particular form of worship of one of the many gods. And as time goes on, as the philosophical tradition begun by Plato matures, with many philosophical schools emerging in the period between the classical ages of Greece and Rome, elite thinkers begin to base their lives on other principles than devotion to the gods, on the motive of the avoidance of the very sort of intensity and suffering, caused by the goddess Aphrodite, that Sophocles had rejoiced in escaping.

ROME

We are familiar with a Rome presented in movies and on television, a Rome in which the pagan Romans are played by British actors with upper-class accents, and where the heroic characters are the poor Christians, the slaves, and the gladiators. Usually, even though they are persecuted, tortured, or crucified, these social inferiors triumph, literally or symbolically, over the cruel, heartless, pagan Roman imperial machine. This is just one of the ways in which a position within dominant monotheism makes for a particular understanding of ancient Roman culture and religion, an understanding that overlooks the complexity and interest of Rome itself, which during its empire was an extraordinary mixture of tradition, borrowed beliefs, and immigrant transformation of tradition.

The poet Ovid reports in his *Amores* on a procession watched as he attempts to seduce the woman seated beside him, an intention that colors his ironic view of the great gods:

> But now the procession comes—quiet everyone,
>> it's time to applaud—and with golden pomp they come.
> Victory leads the passing parade with wings unfurled—
>> let this women yield, goddess, make my love invincible!
> Clap loud for Neptune, you who love to sail the waves!
>> Not for me a life at sea, I choose dry land instead.
> Roar loud for Mars, all you soldiers! I can't stand weapons.
>> Give peace a chance, love is all I need or want.
> Augury depends on Phoebus, the hunter prays to Phoebe,
>> the skilled hands of artisans applaud Minerva.
> Farm people rise to greet Ceres and good-natured Bacchus,
>> the boxer cheers for Pollux, the horse-soldier for Castor.
> But we, oh lovely Venus, we give praise to you, and applaud
>> the boy whose potent bow shoots love.
> Smile, dear goddess, on my sweet endeavor, and
>> make my new heartthrob finally yield.
> The goddess nodded to give a favoring sign . . . (*Amores*, 3.2.43–58).[26]

These are the "great" gods, familiar from the Greek pantheon; Venus, as an indigenous Italic *numen,* or spirit, may have been associated with herb-gardens, and her name suggested "charm, or beauty." The association of Venus with the Greek goddess Aphrodite might have come through worship of the Greek divinity in Sicily. Venus figures as a great generating force of dynamism and fertile energy in Lucretius's *De Rerum Natura.* In Virgil's *Aeneid* she is the immortal patron and helper of the hero Aeneas; he, her son, child of Aphrodite by the Trojan Anchises, is eventually seen as the founder of Rome and as the ancestor of the family of Julius Caesar and his adopted son, Augustus, the first *princeps,* the first "first citizen," first among equals, the *de facto* first emperor, monarch of the Roman empire.

The classical period of ancient Greece, and of ancient Athens in particular, was brief; the history of Rome is long and involves the integration of many different peoples into a huge and long-lasting empire. The Romans themselves expressed interest in the history of their religion, or rather religions, and sometimes tried to separate out a pure, native origin from various other strains that came to be part of Roman worship. The Roman writer Varro, in the second century BCE, wrote a huge treatise on the city's various priesthoods, augurs or diviners, sacred spaces, festivals and the religious calendar, rituals, and gods. From the beginnings, the tiny village on one of seven hills incorporated complex fusions of Latin and Italic traditions, those of the neighboring Etruscans, to their north, and later influences from the Greeks who had colonized parts of southern Italy and Sicily. As the renowned expert on Roman religion Jörg Rüpke writes:

> Despite the standardized name-equivalents given in a mythological handbook such as *Gods and Heroes of Classical Antiquity,* where Ares and Mars, Zeus and Jupiter, Aphrodite and Venus appear as straight-forward synonyms, Roman polytheism was very different from Greek. The internal structure of the pantheon, for example, was far less clearly marked; the various deities were placed on a more or less equal footing, not in a clear hierarchy (Rüpke, 16).[27]

And Rüpke notes that, from its beginnings, Roman religion was characterized by the addition of new gods to the pantheon: "The Roman stories about the gods emphasize new divinities that were introduced at various times rather than the details of the behavior of the old ones towards each other" (Rüpke, 16).

The gods worshipped by the Romans included the great gods, but also local spirits, gods with limited, specific types of responsibility, gods of particular localities, and also humans who had become divine—ancestors, heroic individuals who ascended to the heavens, *daimons* like those of the Greeks, and eventually, in the imperial period, the emperors themselves. Priests oversaw public cults associated with the city of Rome, with elaborate celebrations of ritual. Julius Caesar was worshipped as a divinity before his assassination and his becoming a god became official in 42 BCE. Foreign gods arrived in Rome, brought by their worshippers, new to the empire, including slaves. The Senate in 293 BCE admitted worship of the Greek god Asklepios, god of healing, called in Latin Aesculapius, and in 205 BCE the Mater Magna, the Great Mother of the gods from Asia Minor, was brought, a black stone, to Rome, and given a prominent site in public space.

Not all of the gods considered to be from afar were welcomed by all Romans. The god Bacchus, associated with the Greek Dionysos, was worshipped passionately in orgiastic celebrations called Bacchanalia, and disapproval of his rites grew in the second century BCE. The Roman historian Livy recounts that "To *religio* were added the pleasures of wine and banquets, by which the minds of many were corrupted" (Livy 39.8.3). Finally, in 186 BCE the Senate decided to suppress the private cult of the god. The senators condemned the nighttime rituals, which involved wine and women. Clifford Ando, in *The Matter of the Gods,* cites the Senate's decree forbidding such excesses:

> Let no one want to perform [Bacchic] rites in secret, let no one want to perform [Bacchic] rites in public or private or outside the City . . . (Ando, 12).[28]

The vigorous suppression of these cultic rites responded to dangers associated with improper mingling and foreignness. And later, in the time of the emperors, Juvenal, in his *Satires,* condemned the arrival of foreign ways and foreign cults in Rome: "I cannot stand a Greekified Rome. Yet how few of our dregs are Achaeans? The Syrian Orontes has for a long time now been polluting the Tiber, bringing with it its language and customs, its slanting strings along with pipers, its native tom-toms too, and the girls who are told to offer themselves for sale at the Circus" (*Satires,* 3.61–65).[29] If the evocation of a noble, austere, purely Latin past was based on a fantasy of a paradise lost, there was no lack of resistance to what was seen as dangerous contamination and corruption of the old ways by foreign influences, especially those from the further Greek and eastern reaches of what had become an immense imperial territory.

As the Romans assimilated many gods into their religious practices, and as their territory further expanded, the contamination of what were seen as very ancient local traditions by these new gods continued to worry conservative thinkers, who looked back to what they imagined as a simpler, purer past. In the imperial period, as Rüpke notes:

> The administrative and military elite operated over the whole empire, the emperors came from Spain, Africa, Syria, Illyricum. Slaves (in decreasing numbers), merchants, "economic refugees" and "intellectuals" all came to Rome, to the centre. To that centre came also Egyptian cults (Isis and

Sarapis), Syrian cultures (Jupiter Dolichenus, Jupiter Heliopolitanus, Sol Elagabalus . . .), an allegedly Persian cult (Mithras), Palestinian cultures (Jews, Christians); and Rome was anyway the residence of the *deus praesens,* the ever-present god, that is, the ruling Princeps himself (Rüpke, 238).

The great complexity, over many centuries, of Roman polytheism, can't really be described in this context. The point is that this long-lived culture, source of so many Western ideas concerning literary genres, philosophical traditions, republicanism, law, imperial order, and peace achieved through ruthless militarism, was a culture *full of gods,* from a great variety of localities and peoples, with little sense that the spectrum of divinities needed to be edited down or vetted for purity.[30] The founders of the American state modeled their republic on that of the Romans, maintaining its practice of slavery, but ignoring its polytheism.

APULEIUS

A brilliant novel of the second century CE by the Roman African and Platonist Apuleius, from the same part of North Africa as the later Augustine, gives some of the flavor of the great diversity and difference of the many gods of the Roman imperial period. Apuleius was forced to stand trial in Africa after time spent in Athens, Egypt, and Rome, accused in a provincial town of magical practices. He describes a world full of many cults in his *Metamorphoses,* usually called "The Golden Ass." The hero of this novel, one Lucius, traveling in Greece, on his way encounters images of the goddess Diana, mentions Venus and Cupid, Bacchus, a Chaldean astrologer, the gods of Memphis in Egypt, Hercules, and others of the many gods. Experimenting with magic on his travels to Thessaly, a notorious site of witches, Lucius is transformed into a donkey, complete with hooves, tail, and long and hairy ears, his only consolation "the enormous increase in the size of a certain organ of mine" (*Golden Ass,* 71).[31]

The ass lives through many adventures, and like Lucius, encounters belief in many gods and religious institutions, including Mars, the Salian College at Rome, a priestly group, Juno, Ceres, more Cupid, Vulcan, Pluto and Proserpina, Jupiter, Apollo, Fortuna, and eunuch priests of the Great Goddess of Syria, among others. The ass, after many torments, falls into the hands of a baker and his wife, who use him to work their mill. The wife was, the narrator reports, "the wickedest woman I met in all my travels" (*Golden Ass*, 203). Among her many faults:

> She was malicious, cruel, spiteful, lecherous, drunken, selfish, obstinate, as mean in her petty thefts as she was wasteful in her grand orgies, and an enemy of all that was honest and clean. She also professed perfect scorn for the Immortals and rejected all true religion in favour of a fantastic and blasphemous cult of an "Only God." In his honour she practiced various absurd ceremonies which gave her the excuse of getting drunk in the day and playing the whore at all hours (*Golden Ass*, 203–204).

Such is the narrator's scorn for the monotheist.

After further adventures, and the humiliating threat of being forced to commit public bestiality, as a beast, at a performance of the judgment of Paris, the ass flees, and the Moon-goddess appears to him. He bathes himself in the sea, purifying himself, prays to this supreme goddess, whether she be called queen of heaven, Ceres, Venus, Artemis, or Proserpina, and the goddess reveals herself to him in a dream. She tells him of her many names:

> Some know me as Juno, some as Bellona of the Battles, others as Hecate, others again as Rhamnusia, but both races of Aethiopians, whose lands the morning sun first shines upon, and the Egyptians who excel in ancient learning and worship me with ceremonies proper to my godhead, call me by my true name, Queen Isis (*Golden Ass*, 265).

The goddess has taken pity on the man transformed into an ass, an animal she despises, and tells him that if he attends a procession held in her honor and plucks with his ass's muzzle the roses carried by the High Priest of her cult, he will be transformed back into a man.

The next day's procession dazzles with its excess; there are worshippers dressed as soldiers, men in women's dress, gladiators, philosophers, a bear dressed as a woman, and an ape disguised as Jupiter's cupbearer Ganymede. The musicians of the synthetic Egyptian-Greek god Serapis, manufactured by the Ptolemaic rulers of post-Alexandrian Egypt, lead a crowd of initiates to the cult of the goddess, and following them comes the jackal-headed Anubis, Egyptian god of the dead. Finally appears the High Priest, carrying a garland of roses, which the ass Lucius eats. His human shape returns. Finally, he is initiated into the cult of this ancient Egyptian goddess, who has come to represent all female divinities. He reports:

> I approached the very gates of death and set one foot on Proserpine's threshold, yet was permitted to return, rapt through all the elements. At midnight I saw the sun shining as if it were noon; I entered the presence of the gods of the under-world and the gods of the upper-world, stood near and worshipped them (*Golden Ass,* 280).

Even though Lucius devotes himself with particular intensity to the goddess Isis, he remains a polytheist and honors all the gods, including Osiris, brother-husband of Isis, who manifests himself to Lucius in a dream and seems to guarantee his good fortune as a barrister.

This marvelous tale, full of characters and adventure, displays the range and complexity of the religious life of imperial Rome. In addition to the old colleges of priests of the ancient capital, the many gods of the Latin, Italic, and Etruscan peoples who became part of the Roman state, and the adopted Greek gods, we find a vast array of others who have become part of the Roman pantheon over time. These gods, including such divinities as Isis, Osiris, and Serapis, change their nature as their worshippers change, but the hospitality shown to the Greek god Aesculapius in the time of the Roman republic usually extends to these new-old gods, who find indifference or devotion throughout the vast empire. This unselfconscious polytheism, which of course does not celebrate itself as such, seems appropriate to the great heterogeneity, the complicated mixture of peoples who made up the Roman Empire. It is only with the growing power of Judaism and Christianity, the increasing numbers of those who worship only one god and deny the existence of the many gods, that this multiplicity comes to be challenged.

PREMATURE MONOTHEISM

If Rome has been seen recently, in popular culture, as dominated by the presence of martyred or soon-to-be-martyred Christians, and Sappho as a worshipper of the one goddess Aphrodite, these are examples what I would call "premature monotheism," the tendency of contemporary monotheists, scholars as well, who inhabit a Western civilization which has long seen itself as monotheist, retrospectively to rehabilitate antiquity. It is difficult for scholars, and has been for centuries, to think their way back into polytheism, even though it is all around them. The French psychoanalyst Jacques Lacan, in his seminar on Sophocles's *Antigone,* concurred:

> We no longer have any idea what the gods are. Let us not forget that we have lived for a long time under Christian law . . . If you read the *Phaedrus,* . . . which is a reflection on the nature of love, you will see that we have changed the very axis of the words that designate it (Lacan, 259).[32]

And further:

> Plato tells us that those who have undergone an initiation to Zeus do not react in love in the same way as those who were initiated to Ares. . . . This whole sphere is only really accessible to us from the outside, from the point of view of science and of objectification. For us Christians, who have been educated by Christianity, it doesn't belong to the text in which the question is raised. We Christians have erased the whole sphere of the gods (Lacan, 260).

Although not one of the "us"—the Parisian Christians whom Lacan was addressing in 1960—still I agree that even in the twenty-first century U.S. and U.K., diverse as they may be, we often unconsciously inhabit a monotheist, Abrahamic paradigm and project it on to other histories, other traditions, including that of the ancient Greeks and Romans.

In the final pages of this chapter I point briefly to sites in studies of ancient Greece and Rome where a recognition and exploration of polytheism may have been difficult, where the mysteries of the world of many gods may have escaped readers and students of antiquity, as we have forgotten how to think "the gods." We haven't always come to terms with what polytheism was to the ancient Greeks and Romans, in my view, although scholars of ancient religion have much to say on the subject. Most classical scholars have come of age within monotheism, whether they are believers or not, post-Enlightenment agnostics, atheists, or those who consider religion an opiate, obscuring class struggle.

The image of all things stuffed, full, bulging with godhood, might need to be insisted upon, not just in our present communities, but also in our appreciation of the ancient world and its aftermath, its survival into the present. Political scientists study ancient Greek politics, literary scholars study ancient Greek literature, religious studies experts study ancient Greek religion, as if they were separate and distinguishable categories.[33] As Jan Assmann has argued, echoing Lacan, in *The Price of Monotheism:*

> What the divine world of a polytheistic religion might be—this we cannot even begin to fathom, let alone believe in it. We must first recognize that after over two thousand years of monotheism, such an understanding has been lost to us.[34]

Assmann too easily accepts a model of inevitable progress, the discarding of polytheism in the name of a superior monotheism, even as he sees the potential for violence in the claims of monotheists for the truth of their one gods. And he completely fails to recognize that there are still polytheists in this contemporary world, that not all human beings on this earth have been participating in the two thousand years of monotheism he numbers. Nonetheless, he points to a crucial blindness in our understanding of the past, even as he ignores the persistence of polytheism into the present.[35]

How do their latent or unconscious assumptions about the transcendent and unique *separateness* of one single, creating divinity affect those who study antiquity? The informing presence of monotheism may trouble our understanding of ancient polytheism, as we try to enter into the world of the ancient Greeks, even affecting our work on such questions as ancient magic. A prejudice against polytheism can obscure the realities of ancient culture, of ancient societies, even as some of us are drawn to study antiquity precisely *because* of its lavish array of gods, who interrupt inherited monotheisms and offer a superb pantheon of rhizomatic *dis*array. My examples of sites of the identification of "premature" monotheism here include the history of philosophy, psychoanalytic interpretations of ancient Greek myth, and readings of Athenian tragedy.

According to Diogenes Laertius, a biographer of the ancient Greek philosophers, the pre-Socratic Thales notoriously "gave a share of soul even to inanimate [lit. soulless] objects, using Magnesian stone and amber as indications" (Kirk and Raven, 94).[36] Aristotle, one of the greatest philosophers of the ancient Greeks, wrote: "Some [say] that it [soul] is intermingled in the universe, for which reasons, perhaps, Thales also thought that all things are full of gods" (*de Anima,* A5, 411a7). In the context in which Aristotle cites Thales, the words seem to be an attempt to describe phenomena we would situate in the domain of physics, expressed in the vocabulary available in sixth-century Miletus. Thales wants to know how the "magnesian stone," a magnet, draws metal to it, how amber can attract, and he resorts to a claim that all is permeated with divinity, that the potency of supernatural forces, gods, omnipresent, inhabit stones and resins and give them life, make them move. The editors Geoffrey Kirk and J. E. Raven commented on the fragment:

> The chief distinguishing marks of the gods are that they are immortal, they enjoy perpetual life, and that their power (their life-force, as it were) is unlimited, it extends both over the animate and over the inanimate world. Thus the assertion may well imply (since even apparently dead things like stone may possess soul of a kind) that the world as a whole manifests a power of change and motion which is certainly not even predominantly human, and must, both because of its permanence and because of its extent and variation, be regarded as divine, as due to the inherence of some form of immortal ψυχη (Kirk and Raven, 95).

The editors turn Thales's statement into an observation for physicists, attributing to him a proto-scientific perspective, identifying an abstract, amorphous, that is, shapeless embodiment. Is it possible that historians of philosophy and science are too quick to assume that Thales did not mean "gods" here, that he was referring to "soul," or "life," rather than gods, and that Aristotle as well prematurely interprets and dismisses this language, moving it toward abstraction and physicist observation, not letting the presence of these gods, their filling up of the cosmos, be felt?[37] Thales says "gods:" θεων, *theon*.

Thales's statement about "all things full of gods" has been *rationalized* and translated into another, more scientific language, even in the text of Aristotle. A French scholar, Clémence Ramnoux, in an essay on "a" Greek monotheism, finds in lines of another early Greek thinker, Xenophanes, "the origin of an archaic monotheism, protesting against the popular and civic polytheism of Greece," and an implication in Xenophanes's formulations of "the existence of a learned monotheistic tradition, developed alongside the popular or civic cults and traditions, and in dialogue with the onto-logy and/or heno-logy of the Eleatic school."[38] But fragment 173 of Xenophanes says: "One god, greatest among gods and men, / not at all like to mortals in body nor in thought."[39] Here too, not monotheism, just one "greatest god," that is, one among the many. [40]

As the Freudian tradition of psychoanalysis reads ancient Greek culture, turning the Greek gods from polytheism into "myth," it sets their stories within the monotheistic, patriarchal family. Richard Armstrong, in his valuable and exhaustive examination of Freud's relationship to the Greeks and Romans, *A Compulsion for Antiquity: Freud and the Ancient World,* sees Freud's resort to Oedipus as fitting into a pattern in his reasoning:

> What ever his reasons were for aligning psychoanalysis so closely with Empedocles, [Freud's] recourse to this figure fits a pattern we have seen: a disturbance in his theorization leads him to adopt a figure of antiquity as he works toward his solutions. When his seduction theory of the neuroses collapses, he adopts Sophocles (or at least his Oedipus) . . . The recourse to figures of antiquity often hides a more troubling and proximate relation. Sophocles' Oedipus, as some suggest, came along in time to save Freud from troubling doubts concerning Wilhelm Fliess, his own father Jakob, or even his mother Amalie.[41]

For whatever reasons, if indeed as a technique of avoidance, Freud selected Oedipus out of a vast array of ancient mythological characters. Oedipus, isolated from a Sophoclean discourse concerning traditional, polytheist piety, against a secularizing tendency in the fifth century BCE, came to haunt the twentieth century, and we see little of the many gods of the ancient Greeks in Freud's work.

In the realm of Athenian tragic drama, the work of Henk Versnel on the *Bacchae,* for instance, seems to me prematurely to locate a Hellenistic "henotheism," or devotion to one god in particular among many, in fifth century BCE Athens. He writes: "The Dionysos of the Bacchae is pictured as a Hellenistic god *avant la lettre*" (Versnel, 205).[42] It seems to me that, while Versnel illuminates the historically specific occasion of the introduction of a new cult into the classical city, he misreads the *Bacchae* as calling for henotheism, or even for an exclusive cult, for a type of religiosity typical of later periods "in the cults of the new type of gods," who "manifested themselves as autocratic rulers to whom a mortal could only respond with an attitude of humble subservience or even slavery" (Versnel, 204).[43] In the *Bacchae,* in contrast, we hear the names of Zeus, Rhea, Cybele the Mother,

Hera, Aphrodite, again and again Aphrodite. Pentheus complains: "I am
. . . told a foreigner has come to Thebes / from Lydia, one of those charla-
tan magicians, / with long yellow curls smelling of perfumes, / with flushed
cheeks and the spells of Aphrodite in his eyes" (lines 233–237).[44] We hear
of Demeter, Earth, Ares, Apollo, Artemis, and more of Aphrodite. The chorus sings: "O let me come to Cyprus / island of Aphrodite, / home of the
loves that cast their / their spells on the hearts of men! Or Paphos where
the hundred / -mouthed barbarian river brings ripeness without rain" (lines
402–408). We hear of the Muses, the Graces, Eros, the goddess Peace. The
messenger who reports the Bacchantes' revels begs: "Whoever this god may
be, / sire, / welcome him to Thebes . . . if there is no god of wine, / there is
no love, no Kypris [i.e., Aphrodite] either, nor other pleasure left to men"
(lines 768–775). We hear of Hades, the nymphs, Pan, Dike, the goddess
Justice. The chorus of Bacchantes sings:

> Slow but unmistakable
> the might of the gods moves on.
> It punishes that man,
> infatuate of soul
> and hardened in his pride,
> who disregards the gods.
> The gods are crafty:
> they lie in ambush
> a long step of time
> to hunt the unholy. . . . (lines 882–890)

The last chorus of this tragedy begins: "The gods have many shapes. / The
gods bring many things / to their accomplishment . . ." (lines 1388–1389).
Dionysos, though he may be called "god" or "the god," is but one of many,
not the object of a "henotheistic," proto-monotheistic focus, just one of the
many gods we have seen earlier in this chapter, all objects of the manifold
worship of the Athenians.

Greek tragedy exceeds the individual character, the tragic hero, the great
man or woman dear to the tradition, and even the individual divinity, in
its haunting by the slaves, born as possessions in the homes and farms of
Greeks, or sold or captured and made part of the households of ancient
Greek society; in its access to mourning, the lamentations over loss central
to the genre; in its presentation of choral song, necessarily collective and

diverse, and also and perhaps especially, in the *multiplicity* of divinities that fill the drama.

In the study of Roman religion as well, there is at times an unseemly rush to find monotheism in pagan culture, as if to redeem the pagans, the ancient Romans, from superstition and backwardness. Recent work in the field of late antiquity has explored the question of so-called pagan monotheism. It was argued that "monotheism, for the most part quite independently of Judaism and Christianity, was increasingly widespread by the time of late antiquity, certainly among the educated and in particular in the Greek east."[45] The contributors to *Pagan Monotheism in Late Antiquity* find monotheistic ideas in philosophy, in the idea of one divine essence, in the address to "the god," as opposed to a named divinity, in worship of one "highest god," in Gnosticism, not yet Judaism nor Christianity, but tending in these writers' views to monotheism. In the later volume entitled *One God: Pagan Monotheism in the Roman Empire,* the editors Stephen Mitchell and Peter van Nuffelen note in their introduction: "Monotheism today seems not only to have triumphed historically but also to be morally superior to polytheism. This is one of the reasons why the study of paganism is often segregated from historical work on early Christianity or Judaism" (Mitchell and van Nuffelen, 1).[46] The editors of this text find more nuance and subtlety in the pagan writers and call into question a pagan embrace of monotheism, before the Abrahamic religions came to dominate. In general, while they attempt to explain the difficult transition from paganism to Judaism and Christianity, seeing not an abrupt break but a gradual evolution, as is fashionable today, as Mitchell and van Nuffellen stress, scholars raised within monotheism also have a tendency to "view ancient religion through a filter of assumptions, experiences, and prejudice" (Mitchell and van Nuffelen, 1). Some may even be said to want to rescue their ancient Greeks and Romans from what they see as the intellectual, spiritual, and social untidiness of polytheism, perhaps unconsciously imposing a teleology, a shape to the inevitable progress to history, and discovering monotheism where it does not exist. There is definitely pressure from some schools in the philosophical tradition towards unity, or monism. The Stoics advocated a unity of the cosmos; the Neoplatonists, especially Plotinus, produced a synthesis among the Platonic forms, the good, the "One," and intermediary emanations, in a monism that was integrated with Abrahamic monotheism by Christians such as Augustine. Yet in popular culture and practices, certainly, the polytheism of ancient Greece and Rome persists for many centuries, even though it is difficult to approach it from within a horizon of hegemonic monotheism. I myself, as noted earlier, am guilty of characterizing Sappho as a worshipper of Aphrodite, the one goddess, when in fact she, like others in her culture, worshipped many gods.

Although I don't advocate return to the worship of the ancient gods, as some do, we might think more about the ways in which our residence in a predominantly and dominant monotheistic cultural setting, one that has been defensively, even militantly attempting to patrol and police monotheism for millennia, has had its effects on obscuring the nature of ancient societies. We can overlook their pleasures and their practice of polytheism, the intricate links between those institutions of Western civilization most valued today, such as democracy and republicanism, with ancient polytheism, occluding as well, perhaps not incidentally, our perceptions of those polytheistic religions thriving in the present.

CHAPTER THREE

The Polytheism of Monotheism

IN EXPERIENCING EVERYDAY LIFE in the U.S. and the U.K., in Europe, in the West, one encounters both the claim that these are "Christian nations," with their one god, and the quite evident truth that in fact polytheism in these places continues to flourish. And not only in those religious communities, such as those with ties to India, immigrants of recent or long standing, who profess polytheism, but also among people who might consider themselves to belong to the Abrahamic tradition, that is, from the religious groups that trace their descent from the patriarch Abraham of Ur—Jews, Christians, and Muslims. In 2010, for example, then-Cardinal Bergoglio, later elected Pope Francis in 2013, called a law supported by the Argentinean government to legalize adoption and marriage by same-sex couples "a maneuver by the devil."[1]

In this chapter, I concentrate on the polytheism evident in the beginnings of these religious communities, as well as the persistence of polytheism in official and unofficial circles in the present. And I consider also the one so-called monotheism that does not look back to Abraham, Zoroastrianism, the religion of ancient Iran, which still survives in the Parsi communities of Iran and India and in a wider diaspora. Popular religion is often polytheist, even when official theology is not.

Peter Brown, the great scholar of late antiquity and early Christianity, criticizes a "two-tiered model" of religious studies looking back to David Hume's *The Natural History of Religion* of 1757, which makes a strong distinction resembling that between today's "official" and "folk religion." Hume differentiated between the beliefs of the vulgar and those of the intelligent and enlightened elite; the vulgar were prone to superstition and polytheism, while the rational and intellectual, a rare few, could see the order in the universe and posit a single divinity.

> It is remarkable that the principles of religion have had a flux and reflux in the human mind, and that men have a natural tendency to rise from idolatry to theism, and to sink again from theism to idolatry.[2]

I am concerned here not with "flux" and "reflux," with a supposed natural ebb and flow between monotheism and polytheism, nor with the decline and corruption of what is imagined as an original pure monotheism, but rather with the persistence of polytheism which, given the history of the development of human societies, seems to me to be inevitable. In the consolidation of these societies, many families, tribes, villages, towns, and cities came together eventually to form larger groups, bound often by religious ideas that incorporate the many gods of the many smaller groups.

Hume here is concerned not with the developments from "pagan" polytheism to Abrahamic monotheism, but rather with the decline from an original monotheism into ignorance and superstition among the vulgar. Peter Brown sees the division between elite and vulgar preserved in modern scholarship on religion as leading scholars to neglect the ways in which an institution such as the cult of the saints in the Middle Ages met the needs of ordinary people in popular religion. And I would add that polytheism, and its many objects of belief, survive in popular religion in the present. There are vestiges, remnants, traces of the many gods, even in the most orthodox of monotheist communities. And the persistence of polytheism, even its resurgence in these circles, may indicate the intrinsic difficulties of a strict monotheism, whether the single god is transcendent, in a realm outside the cosmos, or immanent, dwelling in every aspect of the material world. Many monotheists resort to belief in saints with supernatural powers, to a virgin who resembles a goddess, or a god, a supernatural power, who embodies evil and whose existence accounts for the sufferings and conflicts of human being. All of the so-called monotheisms, historically and in the present, to some degree or other teem with supernatural beings—not just their one god, but other gods, male and female, angels, saints, jinns, and demons.

THE MANY GODS OF ANCIENT ISRAEL

Early Christians may not have been in agreement on whether the god of the Hebrew Bible should be their god, but before the consolidation of Judaism in the rabbinic period (70 CE to sixth century CE), the question of God and gods vexed the community of ancient Israelites. There are many indications that the commandment to worship only one true god was arrived at after centuries of conflict and division, and there are traces not only of different notions of the one divinity, but also of a time when the people who became ancient Israel themselves worshipped many gods. Scholars of the Hebrew Bible and of ancient Israel acknowledge and present with great erudition these features of ancient Israelite society, and I rely on their scholarship here.[3] But I note that frequently narratives concerning the history of ancient Israel focus on the development of monotheism, rather than on the persistence of polytheism in this world and that some readings actually ignore the evidence for Israelite worship of many gods, suggesting by omission that the polytheism apparent in the texts is the exclusive practice of the "pagans," or "heathens," the Canaanites understood to be unreconstructed neighbors of a purely monotheistic Israel. If there is backsliding, as in the case of the desert worship of the golden calf in *Exodus* 32, a representation of Ba'al worship anachronistically presented as occurring before the conquest of Canaan, it is seen as a deviation, a moment of weakness that is only a temporary turn away from inevitable monotheism.

GOD, OR GODS?

But, as is often noted, the god of the book of *Genesis* exhibits a variety of characteristics that reveal the textual layering and meeting of different traditions and interests in its final version. For example, in the very first books of the Hebrew Bible, the god manifests himself in various forms. Modern

Biblical scholars, rather than seeing the first books of the Bible—the Pentateuch or "five scrolls," the Torah, or "instruction"—as dictated by "God" to Moses (whose death is in fact described in *Deuteronomy* 34.5), identify different strains of composition: the "J" source, the "P" source, "E," and "D." "J" and "E" are so called after the names of the god(s) used in *Genesis,* "J" using the name Jahweh, "E" Elohim (which is itself actually a plural form, *"gods"*). "P" refers to the priestly source and "D" to Deuteronomy. All these sources were edited, or redacted, together, intertwined to yield the canonical or accepted text of the present.

The expert commentator of *The New Oxford Annotated Bible* describes the various manifestations of the god in the first five books of the Bible:

> The J source is well-known for its highly anthropomorphic God, who has a close relationship with humans, as seen in Gen 2.4–3.24, which includes, for example, a description of God "walking in the garden" (3.8) and says that God "made garments of skins for the man and for his wife, and clothed them" (Coogan, 5).[4]

The God of the Elohist source is "more distant from people, typically communicating with them by dreams via intermediaries, such as heavenly messengers . . . or prophets" (Coogan, 5). The "P" or priestly source, a later hand or hands, closer to the moment of synthesis of the varied versions, exhibits "a strong interest in order and boundaries (see *Genesis* 1), as well as an overriding concern with the priestly family of Aaron and the Temple-based religious system" (Coogan, 5). The God of *Deuteronomy* "cannot be seen," and "insists that God does not physically dwell in the temple or tabernacle" (Coogan, 6) and that he must only be worshipped in one place, presumed later to be Jerusalem.[5] Thus, even in this earliest document of monotheism, the conceptions of divinity vary so widely as to suggest at the very least that the one god has many faces.

Evidence of other gods worshipped by the people of this text crops up everywhere in the Hebrew Bible. For example, the voice of God uses the first person plural: "Let us make humankind in our image" (*Genesis* 1.26). The commentator suggests that the plural "probably refers to the divine beings who compose God's heavenly court" mentioned in *1 Kings* 22.19, when Micaiah says: "I saw the LORD sitting on his throne, with all the host of heaven standing beside to the right and to the left of him." In the so-called "Song of Moses" in *Deuteronomy* 32, Moses recalls the god "Elyon," "Most High," which is, as the commentator notes, "the title of El, the senior god who sat at the head of the divine council in the Ugaritic literature of ancient Canaan."[6] He "fixed the boundaries of the peoples according to the number of the gods" (Deuteronomy 32.8). And later, in the book of *Job,* we find: "One day the heavenly beings (or sons of God) came to present themselves before the LORD, and Satan also came among them" (*Job* 1.6). This "satan" seems to be "the adversary," "the accuser," resident in heaven, rather than the later personal name for the devil. *Genesis* also refers to "the sons of God," who married human women and produced legendary warriors (*Genesis* 6.2–4).

And there is evidence of the traces of these other supernatural beings throughout the Hebrew Bible. Psalm 29 refers to "the heavenly beings," "sons of God." (The commentator suggests that this may have been "a Canaanite hymn of praise, appropriated by Israel.") Even clearer is Psalm 82, which begins: "God has taken his place in the divine council; in the midst of the gods he holds judgment." He speaks, calling for justice, and demotes these gods at the end of the psalm: "You are gods, children of the Most High, all of you; nevertheless, you shall die like mortals, and fall like any prince." The subordinate divinities are found wanting, and punished.

GODDESSES

There are vestiges of the presence of female divinities as well in the Hebrew Bible. In a passage cited earlier, Jeremiah denounces the polytheist practices of the Jewish people living in Egypt in the sixth century BCE, in the diaspora that occurred after the Babylonian destruction of Jerusalem and its temple in 586 BCE:

> The children gather wood, the fathers kindle fire, and the women knead dough, to make cakes for the queen of heaven, and they pour out drink offerings to other gods . . . (*Jeremiah* 7.18).

The people defend themselves against Jeremiah, and refuse to give up their worship of the goddess, claiming that she brought benefits to the community:

> We are not going to listen to you. Instead, we will do everything that we have vowed, make offerings to the queen of heaven and pour out libations to

her, just as we and our ancestors, our kings and our officials, used to do in
the towns of Judah and in the streets of Jerusalem. We used to have plenty of
food and prospered, and saw no misfortune. But from the time we stopped
making offerings to the queen of heaven and pouring out libations to her,
we have lacked everything and have perished by the sword and by famine
(*Jeremiah* 44.16–18).

The women of the community are especially emphatic about their plans to
continue worship of the goddess, and point out that they were not alone in
their offerings, that their husbands knew, of course, of their devotion. In
Elephantine, a Jewish settlement in Egypt, archaeological evidence shows
that worshippers made offerings not only to Jahweh, but also to the goddess
Anat-Yahu (Anat of the Lord).[7]

The neighboring cultures, Mesopotamian and Near Eastern, worshipped
goddesses, and they are hauntingly present, barely effaced, in the canonical
Bible. The *asherah,* object of cultic devotion, seems to have been some sort
of pole made of wood, probably a stylized tree; these were worshipped until
they were destroyed and denounced as Canaanite.[8] Asherah was the name
of a Canaanite goddess, and under the name Athirat at Ugarit was counted
with Anat and Astarte as a principal divinity. Athirat was the queen of El,
the highest god of the pantheon. As Tikva Frymer-Krensky notes: "Asherah has been the subject of much attention since the discovery of Kun-
tillet Ajrud." Here were found storage jars dating to the end of the ninth
century BCE with inscriptions reading "I bless you by YHWH of Teman
wl'srth" (Frymer-Krensky, 156).[9] She asks: "How should this be translated:
is this YHWH and the Canaanite goddess Asherah? Is this YHWH and
an Israelite goddess Asherah, conceived as YHWH's consort ('his Asherah'), or is this the well-known Israelite cult image ('his/her *asherah*') . . ."
(Frymer-Krensky, 156).[10] Phoenician-born Jezebel, when she was Ahab of
Israel's queen, encouraged his subjects to embrace her polytheism, and
Ahab "made a sacred pole" (*1 Kings* 16.33), even though this was a surrender
to the goddess and to polytheism.

The monarchic period was especially rife with polytheistic variety and
excited the outrage of such prophets as Elijah and the reforms of *Deuteronomy,* in Greek "the second law": "You shall not plant any tree as a sacred
pole beside the altar that you make for the LORD your God; nor shall you
set up a stone pillar—things that the LORD your god hates" (*Deuteronomy*
16.21–22). In the reforms of Josiah, in the seventh century BCE:

> The king commanded the high priest Hilkiah, the priests of the second
> order, and the guardians of the threshold, to bring out of the temple of the
> LORD all the vessels made for Baal, for Asherah, and for all the host of
> heaven (*2 Kings* 23.4).

The priest is made to burn these and to depose those priests who had been
making offerings to Baal (the Canaanite fertility god, represented in the
form of a bull), the sun, the moon, the constellations, and "all the host
of the heavens." And the high priest obeyed this command: "He brought
out the image of Asherah from the house of the LORD" (2 *Kings* 23.4–5).
And he slaughtered on the altars all the priests of "the high places," sites
of sacrifice.

King Solomon was notorious for his openness to and even participation
in the cults of other gods: he had "loved" many foreign women, and he
"followed Astarte the goddess of the Sidonians, and Milcom the abomination of the Ammonites" (*1 Kings* 11.5). There were offerings to Molech;
King Solomon had also built "high places," sites of worship and sacrifice,
"for Astarte the abomination of the Sidonians, for Chemosh the abomination of Moab, and for Milcom the abomination of the Ammonites" (*2
Kings* 23.13). Although the tradition of interpretation tends to emphasize
the thoroughness of the reforms of Josiah and the establishment of a pure
monotheism centered in Jerusalem, the evidence points to centuries during
which polytheism continued to be very difficult to eradicate among this
people. These passages reveal the persistence of polytheism, its presence in
ancient Israel, and indeed, in the text of the Bible.

Raphael Patai, in *The Hebrew Goddess,* summarizes these phenomena in
the earlier parts of the Bible:

> It is from Biblical sources that we know the names of the three goddesses
> who were worshipped by the ancient Hebrews down to the days of the Baby-
> lonian exile: Asherah, Astarte, and the Queen of Heaven, who was probably
> identical with Anath (Patai, 36).

Patai discusses the female divinities named here, but also the Cherubim, "in
their last version a man and a woman in sexual embrace" (Patai, 67), whose
representation was in the innermost sanctuary of the temple.[11]

OTHER GODS

The first commandment, or "word"—"you shall have no other gods before (besides) me" (*Exodus* 20.3)—assumes the existence of other gods, and although they may be worshipped, they should defer to the priority or supremacy of *this* god. It is not a command to practice strict monotheism. The second commandment forbids the making of idols, the bowing down to or worshipping of them, but also does not suggest that there are no other gods. The song of Moses, earlier in the book of the exodus, a hymn of thanks for rescue from the Egyptians in the Red Sea, says: "Who is like you, O LORD, among the gods?" (*Exodus* 15.11).

Violence emerges in the condemnation and sometimes even annihilation of the practices and the practitioners of polytheism in ancient Canaan and Israel. The priests of Baal and the prophets of Canaanite polytheism are eventually killed. Yet, as Patai notes:

> The cult of the Asherah escaped the popular anti-Baal and pro-Yahweh upris-
> ing which, led by the prophet Elijah, took place under Ahab. Several years
> later, when all the Baalists were massacred and Baal's temple in Samaria
> destroyed by Jehu, the Asherah of Samaria again escaped unharmed, and
> her worship survived down to the end of the Israelite monarchy (Patai, 45).

The devotion to the goddess, or goddesses, remains for a long time part of ancient Israel's religious practices. Jan Assmann suggests that it is the assertion of the proposition that there is only one true god, that all other gods are false, which produces the violence that erupts in the history of the establishment of monotheism.[12]

GODS OF THE NEIGHBORS

There are many examples of borrowing from polytheistic Mesopotamian and Near Eastern religious traditions in the Hebrew Bible, as in the flood myth, written down in the *Epic of Gilgamesh,* in a Sumerian account, and in the Babylonian and Assyrian text *The Atrahasis Epic,* all of which feature a flood sent to punish and destroy humankind, with a surviving hero. Psalm 104 begins:

Bless the Lord, O my soul.
O Lord my God, you are very great.
You are clothed with honor and majesty,
wrapped in light as with a garment.
You stretch out the heavens like a tent,
you set the beams of your chambers on the waters,
you make the clouds your chariot,
you ride on the wings of the wind,
you make the winds your messengers,
fire and flame your ministers.

There are distinct resonances here with the Egyptian hymn to Aten, the god of the sun-disk, composed in the fourteenth century BCE during the time of Akhenaten, who focused worship on this divinity among all the gods of the Egyptian pantheon, claiming to be going back to the time of the great pyramids:

Splendid you rise in heaven's horizon,
O living Aten, creator of life!
When you have dawned in eastern horizon,
You fill every land with your beauty . . .
How many are your deeds,
Though hidden from sight,
O Sole god beside whom there is none!
You made the earth as you wished, you alone,
All peoples, herds, and flocks;
All upon earth that walk on legs,
All on high that fly on wings . . . [13]

Sigmund Freud believed that the brief period of imposed monotheism of Akhenaten led eventually to the monotheism of ancient Israel, transferred at the time of Israelite enslavement to the Egyptian Pharaoh.

FROM POLYTHEISM TO MONOTHEISM

The process of arriving at true, albeit shaky monotheism requires many centuries. Like other tribal cultures, that of ancient Israel began by see-ing their god as particularly theirs, then, as superior to the gods of others, other tribes, other nations, that surrounded them. Finally a radical break occurred, in which the claim became: your gods are false, not gods at all; only *our* god is a true god (and we are his chosen ones). Such a move is foreign to other societies in the vicinity; the ancient Greeks, for example, as noted above, seemed to regard the gods of others with interest, and tried to ascertain if the names used for divine beings in other societies referred to deities identical to their own. As Tikva Frymer-Krensky puts it:

> As time went on, the religious thinkers of Israel developed a more refined monotheism and redefined the cosmos. They emptied the heavens of lesser deities and progressively rid Israel of all elements in their ancient traditions that no longer fit their new religious sensibilities. These they denounced as idolatrous and foreign (Frymer-Krensky, 84).[14]

In the song of Moses in *Deuteronomy,* the character Moses recounts some of this history, as noted above, referring to "the number of the gods" (*Deuteronomy* 32.8), and then going on to denounce the people of Jacob, who "abandoned the God who made him . . . and . . . made him jealous with strange gods . . . They sacrificed to demons, not God, to deities they had never known, to new ones recently arrived" (*Deuteronomy* 32.15–17). "They made me jealous with what is no god, provoked me with their idols" (*Deuteronomy* 32.21). The sacred, founding text of monotheism, of the monotheisms that trace their ancestry back to the patriarch Abraham, the so-called Abrahamic monotheisms, is rife with many gods; they haunt the texts, they survive and persist in the text, even though the constant effort to eliminate them also persists. Still the many gods cannot be effaced, even here.

And the later history of Judaism records the appearance of Sophia, "Wisdom," a goddess-like entity who seems to stand alongside Jahweh-Elohim-Adon, the one god with many names. In the postexile text of *Proverbs,* attributed to Solomon, Wisdom is personified and has qualities that link her to the ancient Near Eastern goddesses of wisdom. She speaks:

> The LORD created me at the beginning of his work,
> the first of his acts of long ago.
> Ages ago I was set up,
> at the first, before the beginning of the earth . . .
> When he established the heavens, I was there . . .
> then I was beside him, like a master worker;

and I was daily his delight,
rejoicing before him always (*Proverbs* 8.22–30).

The feminine entity, there at the first, had a hand in the creation and has
qualities of a goddess, of a supernatural mediator between human beings
and their one god. Wisdom is said to bear "Long life" in her right hand; "in
her left hand are riches and honor" (*Proverbs* 3.16), in an image that connects her with the Egyptian Ma'at, goddess of truth and justice, who carried
"the symbol of life in one hand, wealth and dignity in the other."[15] The
Bible's Sophia, a personification treated allegorically, nonetheless represents
a feminine and divine participation in what is sometimes seen as the starkly
masculine monotheism of the later books of the Hebrew Bible.

Raphael Patai in *The Hebrew Goddess* considers the appearance of a naked
female figure in the synagogue of Dura-Europos, built in what is now Syria
as late as 245 CE, a representation which has been interpreted variously,
perhaps as the goddess Anahita. Patai traces other female presences in later
Judaism, including the Talmudic Shekhina, the Daughter of the Kabbalis-
tic tetrad, the Matronit, or the Matron, the Sabbath herself, personified as
a female being, and Lilith, the Talmudic she-demon, who began as the first
and failed wife of Adam (Patai, 282–294). In addition to the various female
manifestations of divinity in rabbinical and later Judaism, the Jewish tradition also includes what are sometimes called saints, the patriarchs of the
Bible. The fourth century CE rabbi Pinhas ben Hama speaks of "the fathers
of the world," the patriarchs: "when they died and the rock closed on their
tombs here below . . . they deserved to be called 'saints.'"[16] The translation of
the term may be disputed, but these patriarchs are still honored as especially
pious mortals and their tombs revered.

Jan Assmann refers to the dramatic change in the history of Israelite religion, from polytheism, to a contested polytheism, to a sometimes unstable
"revolutionary," that is, imposed, monotheism. Assmann designates this as
the shift from primary to secondary religion, and sees two religions in the
Hebrew Bible:

> One scarcely differs from the primary religions that coexisted with it at the
> time in its adoration of a supreme god who dominates and far excels the
> other gods, without, however, excluding them in any way . . . The other
> religion, by contrast, sharply distinguishes itself from the religions of its

environment by demanding that its One God be worshipped to the exclusion of all others, by banning the production of images, and by making divine favor depend less on sacrificial offerings and rites than on the righteous conduct of the individual and the observance of god-given, scripturally fixed laws (Assmann, 8).

For Assmann, the difference is produced by what he calls "the Mosaic distinction." Beyond honoring one's own tribe's god above other tribes' gods, beyond arguing that one's own god should be honored above other gods, beyond translating one's god into equivalents in other cultures, the new religion insists that the gods of others are *false,* that only one's own single god is, in fact, a god. Assmann stresses the implications for individuals of such a distinction:

> to which Sigmund Freud, in particular, has drawn our attention: the shift to monotheism, with its ethical postulates, its emphasis on the inner self, and its character as "patriarchal religion," brings with it a new mentality and a new spirituality, which have decisively shaped the Western image of man (Assmann, 2).

Of course, millennia of other developments, social, economic, philosophical, have had their effects on the production of the modern and postmodern subject. Yet this "emphasis on the inner self," the axis on a patriarch, do seem to have immense implications for how we live in the twenty-first century and how inhabitants of predominantly monotheistic societies, whether believers, agnostics, or atheists, think about their subjectivity and how they encounter polytheisms. Guilt and abjection accompany the command to abhor polytheism, idolatry, and polytheists.

THE DIFFICULTIES OF MONOTHEISM

Throughout the Hebrew Bible, the founding text of the Abrahamic monotheisms of Judaism, Christianity, and Islam, there is a wavering, unsteady commitment to monotheism, to one god, while goddesses, sons of god, and other gods continue to resurface in the representation of ancient Israelite society. Although lapses into polytheism are fiercely denounced by the prophets, the ferocity of their denunciations is a measure of how persistent polytheistic worship is. In particular, the effacement of female divinities, be they *asherahs* or the queen of heaven, seems particularly difficult to achieve. This text, the Bible of monotheism, is in part the record of a conflict, a struggle to focus belief and worship on one god, a masculine patriarch, but his dominance is always read against the background of another story, the subversive presence and persistence of polytheism.

The Hebrew Bible is replete with many gods, and the pious Jews, Christians, and Muslims who regard it as a holy book encounter in their readings and recitations of its verses these many gods, who survive to be named and accounted for in its pages. Although the commandment, once "you shall have no other gods before me," develops into the claim "there is no other god," these other divinities haunt the pages of the text and cannot be effaced, even into the twenty-first century, which is reminded daily of the existence of the Canaanite god Ba'al in temples and churches throughout the land. The narrative of the Hebrew Bible, called eventually the "old" testament by the Christians, is not in fact, as it is usually interpreted, the narrative of the triumph of monotheism, but is rather the account of at least a millennium of conflict, of struggle and oscillation between monotheism and polytheism, and of the many unsuccessful, faltering attempts to crush and eradicate idolatry and the worship of the many gods.

THE POLYTHEISM OF CHRISTIANITY

Sophia, the figure of wisdom who appears in the later books of the Hebrew Bible, is an important character in the Gnostic tradition, which flourished in the first centuries before and after the time of Jesus.[17] Sophia was seen as one of the emanations from the one god of the Gnostics, remote and unknowable, but also the ultimate source of various lesser divinities, creations who established the created world. Among these were Wisdom, who in some versions of Gnosticism gave birth to the so-called demiurge, or "worker," responsible for the production of the material world, which is flawed and deceptive. The elaborate system of emanations from the highest god allowed the Gnostics to account for the existence of evil, always a problem for a monotheist theology. If there is only one god, why is there evil?

In the Hebrew Bible, people disobey their god, but why did he create them with tendencies to disobedience? The later concept of free will, the notion that the god creates his creatures with the capacity to betray him, can seem like a cruel sport invented by the god for his own amusement. Why not create a perfect world, with perfect creatures, if one is a perfect god?

Gnosticism, which is difficult to disentangle from Judaism, Christianity, and even forms of Manicheanism that look back to Zoroastrianism, the religion of the ancient Persians (of which more later), represents a version of polytheism in the midst of the growing enforcement of monotheism in early Christianity and in the creation of the monotheistic Judaism of the diaspora after the destruction of the temple in Jerusalem in 70 CE. Sophia, that divine creature, a goddess, is now paired with Jesus as the lowest of the emanations from the divine one; she is seen by some scholars as an attempt to include some feminine presence in the representation of the universe and its creation, but she is interpreted in the Gnostic tradition, most frequently in a negative light, as the source of the defective material world that human beings inhabit, and by which they are deceived.

MORE VIOLENCE BETWEEN POLYTHEISTS AND MONOTHEISTS

Alongside the developments of Gnosticism, their fusion of Jewish, Zoro-astrian, and Christian traditions, we can find traces of polytheism in what is called the "new" testament, the part of the Bible that treats the middle history of Abrahamic monotheism, after the Hebrew Bible and before the *Qur'an.* The early followers of Jesus, who wrote the books of this text, were themselves Jews and subject not only to all the pressures of the surround-ing Hellenistic and Roman empires, with their extravagant polytheism, but also to the vestiges and traces of ancient Israelite polytheism in their sacred text. The tales of resistance to so-called paganism among the early followers of Jesus draw on such narratives as appear in the fourth book of *Maccabees,* which was never incorporated into the canonical set of scrip-tures of the Jews or the Christians, but which is included in some of the manuscripts of what is called the Septuagint, the Greek translation of the Hebrew Bible. It depicts the resistance of the Jews not to the temptations of ancient Canaanite polytheism, but to the polytheism of the Hellenis-tic Greeks, those Greeks who lived around the Mediterranean in various kingdoms founded by the survivors and heirs of Alexander the Great after his death in 323 BCE. The cruel tyrant Antiochus, descendant of Alexander's general Seleucus, tries to force the Jews "to eat pork and food sacrificed to idols. If any were not willing to eat defiling food, they were to be broken on the wheel and killed" (*4 Maccabees* 5.2–3). Antiochus explains his views on the pig: "When nature has granted it to us, why should you abhor eating the very excellent meat of this animal? It is senseless not to enjoy delicious things that are not shameful, and wrong to spurn the gifts of nature" (*4 Maccabees* 5.8–9). The martyrs, the old man Eleazar and seven brothers, resist and are tortured and killed for their resistance. In *3 Maccabees,* again part of the Septuagint, the Ptolemaic ruler of Egypt, another descendant of one of Alexander's generals, torments the Jews of Alexandria, closing them into the hippodrome, the racing track, contriving to destroy them.

> The king, completely inflexible, was filled with overpowering anger and wrath, so he summoned Hermon, keeper of the elephants, and ordered him on the following day to drug all the elephants—five hundred in number—with large handfuls of frankincense and plenty of unmixed wine, and to drive them in, maddened by the lavish abundance of drink, so that the Jews might meet their doom (*3 Maccabees* 5.1–2).

But the Jews call upon their god, who averts catastrophe and refuses to let the community be destroyed by the polytheist Ptolemy IV Philopator. These Jewish stories of resistance to polytheism and polytheistic rulers prepare the way for Christian stories of martyrdom, and even of redemption, as in the case of Eleazar and the seven brothers, where there are suggestions of atonement and immortality of the soul, ideas uncharacteristic of the theology of the Torah but current in the Hellenistic world that eventually is the matrix for the teachings of Jesus.

This violence reverses that of the earlier books of the Hebrew Bible, in which the reformers massacred the worshippers of Ba'al. Here the Jews are on the verge of mass martyrdom, although their god protects them from destruction. There is certainly violence in the ancient world, in the possibly mythic conquest of Canaan, in wars among Assyrians, Babylonians, and others, but the appearance of a strict monotheism, according to some scholars, begins the long sequence of religiously motivated violence. This is violence not motivated by a desire to conquer others' land, to expand territory or repel invasion, but is rather aimed at the conversion of others to one's monotheistic religious beliefs or, on the other side, to compel monotheists to commit acts that are forbidden by their one god, or to convert to polytheism. These scenes from the books of the *Maccabees* resemble those of later Christian martyrs, many of whom are the victims of violence enacted by so-called pagan or polytheistic Greeks and Romans.

SATAN

There are polytheistic vestiges even within the Christian Bible, although the Jews, those who follow Jesus and those who do not, strive to adhere firmly to the evolved interpretation of the commandment to worship the one god. Yet "a highly developed angelology was a feature of several monotheist groups in Late Antiquity. Early Christian polemic against Judaism included the accusation of angel worship . . ."[18] And there were demons and other supernatural creatures perceived in the everyday life of Jesus and his first followers. Although the canonical interpretation of these beings denigrates them, they are clearly supernatural creatures, the manifestations of Satan, the devil, and part of a polytheistic map of the cosmos. Calling such phenomena "polydaemonism," "many-demonism," simply obscures the fact that these superhuman, supernatural beings, i.e. deities, were vestiges of a more fully realized polytheism in earlier religious practices. Though they might not be worshipped, they were and remain, for many, objects of belief.

It is perhaps unnecessary to note once more that in a polytheistic world, not all of the many gods, the supernatural beings, that are believed in, if not worshipped, are benevolent. The presence of malevolent minor gods, spirits, and demons is not an indication of a convinced monotheism, but a sign that there is at least a dualistic struggle between divine forces, both good and bad. As William Dever points out in his book *Did God Have a Wife?* "We want religion to be 'nice': beautiful, aesthetically appealing, uplifting, ennobling, 'spiritual,' and above all tidy."[19] Although Dever, when he points to the messiness of religion, is referring to the ancient world and does not specify to whom he refers when he uses the word "we," his statement seems pertinent to the climate of monotheisms in the present. Many people still believe in Satan and even demons, and these are gods, not nice, messy, but still "superhuman being(s)," that is, elements of a polytheist religion.

Satan, especially, is a god of evil, rival of the other god, god the father. Matthew recounts the temptation of Jesus by the devil, where the supernatural tempter tries to seduce him into performing miracles, turning stones into bread, throwing himself from the pinnacle of the temple; the devil offers him "all the kingdoms of the world and their splendors . . . if you will fall down and worship me" (*Matthew* 4.1–11). When Jesus is tempted by Peter to forgo his trip to Jerusalem, to his death, he says to Peter: "Get behind me, Satan!" (*Matthew* 16.23; *Mark* 8.33).

The word "satan" appeared in the Hebrew Bible, but as mentioned earlier, scholars insist that it should in many passages be translated as "the/an adversary, the opposer" rather than as the proper name of a deity.[20] In the Hebrew Bible, the satan resembles a divine prosecutor, a son of god who sometimes challenges the authority of his father, but who belongs in the pantheon of gods, in the heavenly company (*1 Chronicles* 21.1). Translators must decide whether to translate the word as "adversary," or Satan with a capital S, which lends specificity to this character in the Bible. A "satan," as obstructer or adversary, actually appears as a benefactor in the story of Balaam and his donkey (*Numbers* 22.22), appearing with a drawn sword in the road and forcing the donkey out of his way; after the donkey speaks to Balaam, who has been ordered to curse the Israelites by Balak, king of the Moabites, the angel, or messenger, says: "I have come out as an adversary, because your way is perverse before me" (*Numbers* 22.32).

In the book of *Zechariah,* "Satan" appears in the author's vision as a member of the divine entourage to accuse the high priest Joshua (*Zechariah* 3.1). The satan, his S capitalized here by the translator, appears most prominently in the book of *Job:*

> One day the heavenly beings came to present themselves before the LORD, and Satan also came among them.[21] The LORD said to Satan, "Where have you come from? Satan answered the LORD, "From going to and fro on the earth, and from walking up and down on it" (*Job* 1.6–7).

Satan argues that Job, who lives in the land of Uz and is not an Israelite, remains God-fearing only because he prospers, and that when he loses everything, he will curse God "to his face." God takes up the challenge and allows Satan to ruin Job. The adversary, the "prosecutor," here clearly has supernatural powers, inflicting "loathsome sores" and other grievous troubles on the innocent man. Satan is eventually thwarted in his efforts to convince Job to repudiate his god, who not only restores Job's fortunes, but doubles his wealth (*Job* 42.10).

In addition to the satan and Satan, there are nameless supernatural beings in the New Testament. In the gospel of Mark, Jesus casts out demons from a man who comes to him "out of the tombs" with an unclean spirit who says his name is "Legion: for we are many" (*Mark* 5.9). A Roman legion, like the ones that occupied Judaea, consisted of about five thousand soldiers; these spirits *are* many. They ask not to be sent out of the country and to be cast into a herd of nearby pigs. "The unclean spirits came out and entered the swine," who rush down the bank and are drowned in the sea (*Mark* 5.13). The people witnessing these events beg Jesus to leave their neighborhood. This same episode is also recounted in the gospel of Matthew (8.28–34). Jesus exorcises a demon in the synagogue at Capernaum (*Luke* 4.33–36), and he is accused himself of harboring a demon by the Jews in the Jerusalem temple (*John* 8.48–52).

According to Matthew, the Pharisees, when confronted with Jesus's power to cast out demons, responded: "It is only by Beelzebul, the ruler of the demons, that this fellow casts out demons" (*Matthew* 12.24). Jesus points out that "if Satan casts out Satan, he is divided against himself" (*Matthew* 12.26), and then, "If I cast out demons by Beelzebul, by whom do your own exorcists cast them out?" (*Matthew* 12.27). This name recurs in the gospels of Mark (3.22) and Luke, where someone in the crowd watching Jesus cast out a mute demon says: "He casts out demons by Beelzebul" (*Luke* 11.15). The accusations are denied by Jesus, but the name of this character refers back to a god. In the Hebrew Bible, Ahaziah king of Israel, said to serve and worship Ba'al (*1 Kings* 53), invokes this deity.

> Ahaziah had fallen through the lattice in his upper chamber in Samaria, and lay injured; so he sent messengers, telling them, "Go, inquire of Baal-zebub, the god of Ekron, whether I shall recover from this injury" (*2 Kings* 2).

The name Baal-zebub, the commentator points out, means "Baal/lord of the flies," a taunting Hebrew play on the name Baal-zebul, "Baal the exalted." Ahaziah is punished by death for consulting the god of Ekron. The Christian books use the correct name of the god, Beelzebul, to refer to Satan, the god, ruler of the demons.

Satan—god, devil, demon, king of demons—was held responsible for the betrayal of Jesus. As Luke writes, "Satan entered into Judas called Iscariot, who was one of the twelve" (*Luke* 22.3). The possession of one of Jesus's disciples by Satan is a breaching of the gates, entry into the circle of the faithful, and bodes ill for Jesus's future. Although Jesus himself had resisted the temptations of Satan earlier, the possession of Judas the Iscariot demonstrates the vulnerability of his followers to demonic entry. These themes of a world of Christians besieged not only by "pagan" polytheists, but also by malevolent demons and spirits, become important preoccupations of the early Christians in cities like Antioch, Jerusalem, and Milan, where the fathers of the church such as the fourth-century John Chrysostom, archbishop of Constantinople, repeatedly warned his community about the invisible dangers that encircled them.[22]

The conflation of the god of Ekron, Beelzebul, with the serpent who deceived and possibly seduced Eve in the garden of Eden (*2 Enoch* 31.6), with Satan the son of god, the accuser, the devil (Greek *diabolos,* "the accuser or slanderer"), and the king of the demons, the king of death (*John* 12.33) is confirmed in the last book of the New Testament, *Revelation,* sometimes called the *Apocalypse.* This fusion of all the different entities, each of them malevolent, may have occurred in books not contained in the canonical Hebrew Bible, such as *2 Enoch,* where "Satanael" is described as a prince cast out of heaven. A passage in the work of the prophet Isaiah that refers to Canaanite divinities may have sparked this understanding. Isaiah writes, taunting the king of Babylon:

> Your pomp is brought down to Sheol,
>   and the sound of your harps;
> maggots are the bed beneath you,
>   and worms are your covering.
>
> How you are fallen from heaven,
>   O Day Star, son of Dawn! (*Isaiah* 14.11–12).

The commentator notes that this reference "draws on a Canaanite myth of the gods Helel and Shahar (Morning Star and Dawn), who fall from heaven as a result of rebellion. In Christianity the myth reemerges as the fall of Lucifer and his attendant angels."[23] The taunt in Isaiah ends: "And I will make it [Babylon] a possession of the hedgehog . . ." (*Isaiah* 14.23).

Jesus had referred to the transformation of the satan, according to the evangelist Luke, when he received seventy returning followers bearing the news that even the demons had submitted to them: "'I watched Satan fall from heaven like a flash of lightning'" (*Luke* 10.18). In *Revelation* the author John, writing his visionary text on the Greek island of Patmos, describes the defeat of the enemies of the good, and includes this figure among them: "The great dragon was thrown down, that ancient serpent, who is called the Devil and Satan, the deceiver of the whole world—he was thrown down to the earth, and his angels were thrown down with him" (*Revelation* 12.9). Later in his immense and elaborate vision:

> I saw an angel coming down from heaven, holding in his hand the key to the bottomless pit and a great chain. He seized the dragon, that ancient serpent, who is the Devil and Satan, and bound him for a thousand years, and threw him into the pit, and locked and sealed it over him, so that he would deceive the nations no more, until the thousand years were ended. After that he must be let out for a little while (*Revelation* 20.1–3).

This is not good news, since the thousand years have surely passed since the author wrote in the first century CE. The text continues: "When the thousand years are ended, Satan will be released from his prison and will come out to deceive the nations at the four corners of the earth, Gog and Magog, in order to gather them for battle; they are as numerous as the sands of the sea" (*Revelation* 20.7–8). This time, though, a fire from heaven consumes these enemies, and "the devil who had deceived them as thrown into the lake of fire and sulfur" and he and the "beast and the false prophet will be tormented day and night forever and ever." (*Revelation* 20.10). These events occur at the end of time, Jerusalem descending as a bride out of heaven, in contrast to the whore of Babylon, the image of Rome.[24]

In the letter to the Galatians attributed to Paul, written between the late 40s and early 50s of the so-called Common Era (CE), the author rebukes the Galatians for backsliding: "Formerly, when you did not know God, you were enslaved to beings that by nature are not gods. Now, however, that you have come to know God, or rather to be known by God, how can you turn back again to the weak and beggarly elemental spirits *(stoikheia)?* How can you want to be enslaved to them again?" (*Galatians* 4.8–9). These "elements" are referred to again in *Colossians:* "See to it that no one takes you captive through philosophy and empty deceit, according to human tradition, according to the elemental spirits of the universe . . ." (*Colossians* 2.8). It is unclear whether the phrase refers to some spiritual entities or the four physical elements: earth, air, fire, and water. In either case, enslavement to them entails a turning away from monotheism. The "ruler of the power of the air, the spirit that is now at work among those who are disobedient" (*Ephesians* 2.1) has come to dominate the Ephesians, according to the letter sent to them, probably written in the late first century CE, not by Paul himself. They are exhorted not "to make room for the devil" (*Ephesians* 4.27), to "stand against the wiles of the devil. For our struggle is not against enemies of blood and flesh, but against the ruler, against the authorities, against the cosmic powers of this present darkness, against the spiritual forces of evil in the heavenly places" (*Ephesians* 6.11–12). Although these demons are condemned, they are nonetheless supernatural powers, aligned with Satan, the devil, called son of god in the Hebrew Bible, and populate a polytheist universe.

Thessalonians 2.9 refers to "Satan, who uses all power, signs, lying wonders, and every kind of wicked deception"; in *2 Corinthians* Paul says he forgives "so that we may not be outwitted by Satan, for we are not ignorant of his designs" (*2 Corinthians* 11). Satan has "blocked his way" (*1 Thessalonians* 2.18). In the letter to the Romans, Paul writes: "The God of peace will shortly crush Satan under your feet" (*Romans* 16.20). Satan is a god who embodies evil, who is in conflict with the good god, and who has a god's supernatural powers. "Even Satan disguises himself as an angel of light" (*2 Corinthians* 11.14). In this letter of Paul, Satan is called "the god of this world" (*2 Corinthians* 4.4), "Beliar" (*2 Corinthians* 6.15), and "serpent" (*2 Corinthians* 11.3).

Official Christianity labors to suggest that only one god exists, the good god, but in fact it acknowledges the existence of this other divine presence in opposition to him, or them, Jesus and his father the god. Elaine Pagels in her *Origin of Satan,* discussing the story told in the New Testament about Jesus and his enemies, points to the evangelists' correlation of this story with "the supernatural drama the writers use to interpret that story—the struggle between God's spirit and Satan":

> Because Christians as they read the gospels have characteristically identified themselves with the disciples, for some two thousand years they have also identified their opponents, whether Jews, pagans, or heretics, with forces of evil, and so with Satan (Pagels, xxiii).

Satan, for these believers, is alive and well; pagans, polytheists, are satanic.

TRINITY (1 + 1 + 1 = 1)

And although the teachings of Jesus focus on the one god, he himself is the son of the one god, as is Satan, leading to intense theological debate concerning the question of whether Jesus himself is a god, another god, whose worship would require deviation from the pure monotheism of the Jews. These are questions that preoccupied the theologians of early Christianity. In the introduction to this book I discussed the arguments of Marcion, who contended that the god of the Hebrew Bible was not the same god as that of the followers of Jesus, the people who became "Christians," and that they should establish as their scripture not the Hebrew Bible with the added portions of the Gospels, Letters, etc., that concerned Jesus, but restrict themselves to those books that invoked what he saw as a new god.

In the evolved Christian theology of late antiquity, which has guided the worship and belief of the Christians of Europe and their diaspora, the mystery of the trinity was developed in a polytheist form. God, the holy spirit or holy ghost, and Jesus are three divinities. Although they are mystically understood to be one, this is a logical paradox that attempts to resolve the problem of Jesus, who is neither the one god nor holy spirit. The obvious conclusion here is that the trinity is in fact a polytheist element of Christianity, which evolved from monotheist Israelite religion but had to incorporate a new divinity, Jesus son of the god, and resolved this question with a synthesis of three elements into a single entity. The end of the book of Matthew has Jesus using this phrase: "Go therefore and make disciples of all nations, baptizing them in the name of the Father and of the Son and of the Holy Spirit" (*Matthew* 28.19). The nature of this "spirit" remains a matter of debate. This formulation of Jesus was adopted in official Christian theology, after some struggle in the early church concerning differing points of view.

The third-century Church father Tertullian is said to have been the first to use the word "trinity," Latin *trinitas,* to refer to this tripartite god, one in essence but not in person, in *Against Praxeas* Chapter 3. The council of Nicaea, called in 325, made the trinity official doctrine and asserted that the son was of "the same substance" as the father god. Other conceptualizations of divinity had previously vied with this finding, but were eventually condemned as heretical. Arianism, for example, established a hierarchy, with the father eternally existent, superior to the son, who was created by the father, the son himself superior to the spirit; and there were intense conflicts between the advocates of Arianism and those of what became the orthodox view. Other heresies that emerged over the centuries included so-called adoptionism—claiming that Jesus only became divine at the moment of his baptism—Ebionism, Docetism, Basilidianism, Alogism or Artemonism, Patripassianism, Sabellianism, Apollinarianism, Nestorianism, Eutychianism, Monophysitism, and Monothelitism, referring to the "one will" of Jesus. These are debates that touch on the question of monotheism, and the difficulties inherent in Christianity's claim to be a monotheistic religion when there are at least two, possibly three deities at stake.

MARY, MOTHER OF GOD

The mother of Jesus, said to be a virgin, partakes of many of the attributes of goddesses of the ancient Mediterranean. In her masterly work *Alone of All Her Sex: The Myth and Cult of the Virgin Mary,* Marina Warner traced the history of reverence and even worship of the mother of Jesus and emphasized its continuity with the goddess worship of classical antiquity.[25] Warner discusses the cult of Mary as virgin, queen, bride, mother, and intercessor, with extensive discussion throughout of the long history of Mariolatry, devotion to Mary. She explores Mary's links with the virgin goddesses of classical antiquity. Mary's sash, her belt, for instance, was treated with special devotion and was treasured as a sacred relic in the Italian city of Prato. Warner notes: "the girdle that encircles the loins of a goddess has direct mythological antecedents in the west" (Warner, 279). She recalls the so-called girdle of the Greek goddess Aphrodite, which when untied gives her victory over the other goddesses Athena and Hera in the judgment of Paris; this belt was borrowed by the wife (and sister) of Zeus, Hera, to enhance her desirability to her husband as she sought to distract him from the battlefield of the *Iliad.* "Another cult of a magic girdle existed at Ephesus in classical times. For Ephesus was the centre of the worship of the Amazons, who, it was believed, had founded the city" (Warner, 279). The belt of Hippolyta, queen of the Amazons, sacred to the god Ares, was taken from the queen by the hero Herakles. "The cult of the Amazons flourished in Cappadocia, where Diana of Ephesus was still worshipped in Christian times" (Warner, 289). Her temple in Ephesus, an architectural marvel, was one of the seven wonders of the ancient world. Called Artemis by the Greeks, Diana the virgin god of wilderness and the hunt, and much more, was the object of special reverence for the Amazons, and Warner describes her ancestry:

> In the figure of Diana of Ephesus a number of different divinities were con-flated: by the reign of Artaxerxes II (404–358 BC), the Iranian goddess of the waters, Anahita, had been coalesced with the Greek goddess of the moon, Artemis. By Roman times, Artemis had in turn been identified with Diana, an Italian maiden goddess of springs and fruitfulness who was invoked with Juno to bless marriages with fertility and ease childbirth (Warner, 280).

The silversmiths of Ephesus worshiped this goddess, represented in their works with breasts, eggs, or testicles attached to her body; she is the divinity celebrated when Paul, the follower of Jesus, arrived in the city to preach in hopes of converting its residents. The author of *Acts* detects mercenary motives in their devotion:

> A man named Demetrius, a silversmith who made silver shrines of Artemis, brought no little business to the artisans. These he gathered together, with the workers of the same trade, and said, "Men, you know that we get our wealth from this business. You also see and hear that not only in Ephesus but in almost the whole of Asia this Paul has persuaded and drawn away a considerable number of people by saying that gods made with hands are not gods. And there is danger not only that this trade of ours may come into dis-repute but also that the temple of the great goddess Artemis will be scorned, and she will be deprived of her majesty that brought all Asia and the world to worship her" (*Acts* 19.23–28).

When Paul came into the theater at Ephesus, an open-air space that could hold 25,000 people, ready to address the crowd, "for about two hours all of them shouted in unison: 'Great is Artemis of the Ephesians!'" (*Acts* 19.34). And Paul left for Macedonia.

Although these followers of Artemis were eventually succeeded in the city by Christians, and later by Muslims, Warner suggests that there was some synthesis of beliefs in the genealogy of Artemis/Diana and Mary:

There could be, therefore, a chain of descent from Hippolyte to Diana to the virgin, for one tradition also holds that Mary was assumed into heaven from Ephesus, where she spent the last years of her life, and where St. Thomas, according to the legend, received her heavenly girdle as proof (Warner, 280).

Devotion to Mary replaces worship of the goddesses of antiquity in a form of masked polytheism characteristic of early and medieval Christianity that endures in current interpretations of her place in Roman Catholic Christianity. Theologically, "God is owed *latria* (adoration) and the saints *dulia* (veneration), but Mary occupies the principal mediating position, as a creature belonging both to earth and heaven" (Warner, xxii). Mary requires a special veneration, unique to her, *hyperdulia,* "super-veneration." A sixteenth-century former Catholic and newly Protestant critic of the worship of Mary wrote about an idolatrous shrine that resembled the Santa Casa, the house of Mary that had miraculously flown through the air from Nazareth to Loreto, in Italy:

> What do you think that the construction of that temple of Diana of Ephesus, which the papists call Madonna of Tirano, has cost? . . . How many tablets, painted with thousands of falsities and dreams have been attached there? How many statues of paper, clay, wax, and even silver? How many heads, how many eyes, arms, hands, legs, candles, and torches? How many of those idolatrous masses they ordered to be spoken and sung . . . ? (Miladinov, 301).[26]

The Protestant Reformation returned to the themes of the Hebrew Bible, with its protests against idol worship and polytheism, which here link Mary, mother of god, to the virgin goddesses of pagan antiquity. Michel de Montaigne visited the Holy House of Loreto for three days in 1581, offering a silver votive tablet in an unrepentant show of what others might call idolatry.[27]

SAINTS

The cult of the saints is another domain in which Christianity resembles a full-fledged polytheism. Some of the saints, of Christian Italy and Greece especially, bore the names of ancient Greek and Roman gods and were associated with former sites of appearance or worship of these gods. And some of the Christian saints were thinly disguised survivals of these "pagan" divinities, worshipped in practice as "supernatural beings," that is, as gods in their own right. Dionysos, for example, one of the most important gods of the ancient Greeks, known as Bacchus to the Romans, discussed earlier, god of wine and theater, did not disappear with the triumph of Christianity over so-called paganism, the polytheism of ancient Greece and Rome.[28] The folklorist Rennell Rodd listed various manifestations of Dionysus and other Greek gods that survived in nineteenth-century Greece. "The numerous churches and chapels scattered over the country in Greece, and frequently in spots far removed from human habitation, are again and again found to have been built upon the foundations as well as with the materials of early pagan temples" (Rodd, 140).[29] He argues that the great number of little, ruined churches testifies to the desire that "the worship of their saint might replace some Artemis of the crossways . . ." (Rodd, 141). A church dedicated to the so-called Virgin of Fertility sat on the site of a temple of the ancient Eileithyia, goddess of childbirth. Saints who are patrons of medicine were worshipped in a chapel that replaced a temple of the ancient healing god Aesculapius. The twelve apostles occupy an altar of the twelve gods of the ancient pantheon. St. Demetrius churches replace shrines to the goddess Demeter, and stories feature St. Demetria as well. "In the island of Naxos, once devoted to the worship of Dionysus, popular tradition ascribes to Saint Dionysius the introduction of the grape" (Rodd, 142). The saint carries the grapevine sprig in the bone of a bird, then of a lion, then of an ass:

> The plant grew and prospered and bore magnificent grapes, and from these they made the first wine, and the saint gave it men to drink. And then the wonder of it was that when they had drunk a little they sang like birds, when they drank more they grew strong as lions, but then if they drank yet more then became like asses (Rodd, 143).[30]

Although tracing these connections is less fashionable, and less possible today, in a world that is becoming homogenized in the twenty-first century, there are still traces of these ancient forms of worship, and of the ancient gods, in Greece and in the parts of Italy once colonized by the Greeks.

The scholar of late antiquity Peter Brown discusses the cult of the saints and insists on the differences between pagan worship of the gods and heroes, and the Christian saints. Saints die. While the heroes of pagan, that is, polytheist antiquity had once lived as mortals and were worshiped, prayed to, and made offerings at their tombs and shrines by devotees, Brown insists that the cult of the Christian saints was a different matter, breaking down pagan oppositions between the living and the dead, between tombs and altars, between public and private (Brown, 5–9). He wants to cast aside the "two-tiered model" discussed earlier in this chapter, a model that separates elite from popular religion, and to see the presence of the saints in the lives of worshippers as belonging to new forms of power, dependence, and hope in late antiquity and early Christianity (Brown, 22). Yet in discussing "Latin" Christianity, developments in Western Europe, "the Latin-speaking countries of the Mediterranean and their northern extension in Gaul" (Brown, xiv), Brown may have overlooked the extent to which worship of the saints in some areas of Italy, Greece, and further east often incorporated former sites of devotion to the ancient, so-called pagan gods.

In *The Clash of Gods: A Reinterpretation of Early Christian Art,* Thomas Mathews argues that the earliest representations of the Christian god Jesus were based not on the imagery of the Roman empire, the iconography of imperial power, but rather on the polytheist images of the gods of the ancient Greeks and Romans. Mathews analyzes the use of icons representing the saints in early Christian households:

> Some Christians . . . were known to be using icons in a domestic situation the way pagans used painted images of their gods in the third century (Mathews, 178).[31]

The "pagans" had a tradition of panel paintings of the ancient gods, some of them recording "religious and miraculous phenomena, such as Parrhasius' painting of Herakles done from a vision . . ." (Mathews, 179). Mathews demonstrates that there are formal parallels between these images and the early representations of Christian deity. "Half- and full-length figures are represented in frontal poses holding symbols of their divine power" (Mathews, 180). The very construction of pagan icons is consistent with that of the Christian images. Icons of Jesus imitate the facial type of representations of Jupiter, which was also used for other powerful male gods, including Neptune, Asklepios, and Serapis. Jesus is shown not with the more likely and historically accurate short curly hair of the first century

BCE, but rather with the broad forehead and hair style of Jupiter, father of the Roman gods. Mathews sums up the resemblances and adds: "Still other correspondences are in particular features of iconography: the engaging gaze, the halo, the throne, the Zeus-type face, and the military or equestrian garb. Even the inscriptions invite comparison with inscriptions on Christian icons" (Mathews, 190). The ancient gods survive in these forms, in the now canonical versions of the imagery associated with Jesus.

Anne Marie Yasin shows how the presence of saints in the late antique Mediterranean did affect practices of worship:

> In the interior of the church the saints' memorials and their perceived "presence" provided greater visibility and accessibility to the divine. . . . Since saints could intervene to help bring about . . . everlasting salvation, increasing the frequency and earnestness of prayer directed toward them became a primary objective of commemorative monuments.[32]

The saints had supernatural powers, and received what might be considered worship.

The word *dulia,* discussed by Marina Warner, denoting the attitude of the pious toward the saints, is in Catholic doctrine opposed to *latria,* "adoration," the worship owed to God, presumably in the tripartite unity of the trinity. But *dulia* is a transliteration of the ancient Greek word for "slavery" and seems to indicate more than simple "veneration" in the case of the thousands of saints of the Catholics. For many worshipers, Mary and the other saints take priority over Jesus and his father and are presented with votive offerings and prayers for assistance, as well as gratitude for acts of beneficence. In what may seem a trivializing reference, scholars of religion, as noted earlier, sometimes make a distinction between popular and elite religion, "folk religion" and "official religion," especially when referring to antiquity or to societies that they perceive as more primitive than their own. But in many neighborhoods in the U.S. and the U.K., as well as in the predominantly Catholic countries of southern Europe, the chapels of the saints are abundantly furnished with gifts from their devotees. Is this "folk religion," popular religion, or simply the persistence of polytheism in the circles that disregard or disobey or flourish in ignorance of or resistance to official doctrine that prescribes a difficult tight-rope adoration of the three elements of the trinity, father, son and holy ghost, none of them the virgin or the male and female saints so dear to millions of believers?

A single saint can proliferate into a multiplicity of objects of devotion. Henk Versnel describes Mariolatry in contemporary Italy:

> Five Madonnas are honoured in Montegrano, a little village in South Italy. They are differentiated according to principles of topography or quality, and for many of the inhabitants the connection between them and the biblical mother of Christ is opaque to say the least (Versnel, 66).[33]

And he notes that during the Spanish Civil War, "local 'reds' from Santander refused to destroy their shrine image of Our Lady of Mt. Carmel, by arguing that 'Our Virgin is Communist'" (Versnel, 66–67).

POLYTHEIST CHRISTIANITIES

Mormonism, one of the forms of contemporary Christianity, founded in the nineteenth century in the U.S., can also be seen as a polytheism. Among believers are those who cite the founder Joseph Smith, who seems to have, late in his life, led followers to believe that the god, the heavenly father, had a heavenly mother as wife, consort, or queen. Some feminist Mormons have urged the recognition of this heavenly mother, although official doctrine skirts the issue. When a feminist professor at Brigham Young University, a Mormon institution of higher learning in the state of Utah, was denied tenure, one of the issues cited was her publicly advocating prayer to the female partner of the god. "While the Mormon hymn 'O My Father' and other texts refer frequently to a mother in heaven and parents in heaven, the BYU administration concluded that Professor Houston's comments constituted 'public affirmations of the practice of praying to Heavenly Mother that contradict fundamental church doctrine that we should pray only to Heavenly Father.'"[34] Mormonism also suggests that human beings who spend well their time on earth will live eternally as gods and goddesses, reunited with their families.

And in many zones into which Catholicism was imported by missionaries, or where slaves or other workers were transported from polytheist religious contexts to officially Christian countries, syntheses of indigenous or imported polytheisms with allegedly monotheistic religious practices became very common. The sort of fusion that Samuel Purchas lamented became the norm, for example, around the Caribbean and in Brazil, where traditionally polytheist indigenous peoples and slaves brought from West Africa and Christians invented new forms of polytheism that incorporated elements of many traditions for their practices. In such religions as Santeria, the practice of Vodou in Haiti, Louisiana, Florida, and elsewhere, in Brazil's Umbanda and Candomblé, and in other belief systems that fused different traditional practices, to be discussed more fully in the next chapter, worshippers adopted the Catholic saints, or at least the images of the saints, sometimes changing their names and attributes, and recognized their ancestral divinities in these new forms. Such gods can be worshiped in churches (where they often appear as "saints") and in religious festivals, in versions of full-fledged polytheism, sometimes condemned, sometimes tolerated by official Catholic Christianity.

And even in contemporary Northern American Christianity, especially in evangelical Protestant communities, we encounter the persistence of polytheism, especially the presence of that supernatural force of evil, Satan. A conservative Tea Party Republican candidate in the presidential race of 2012, adamantly opposed to same-sex marriage on the basis of her interpretation of the Hebrew Bible, demonstrated continuing belief in this deity of evil. Condemning what she called "the homosexual agenda," citing the inevitable misery of the "choice of the same-sex lifestyle," she argued that to call homosexuals "gay," that is, using the definition of the adjective that denotes light-heartedness, pleasure, and happiness, is "a part of Satan."[35] Although the grammar of this phrase is somewhat mysterious—what does "a part of Satan" mean, precisely?—it is clear that Satan survives in her world-view, as in that of many of her co-believers.[36] In *How to Stay Christian in College,* the author advises students: "What can you do about ridicule? In the first place, stay calm; anger gives Satan a foothold."[37] This god of the Canaanite city of Ekron, the "adversary," son of the god of the ancient Israelites, the "accuser, slanderer," the *diabolos* who became the devil, is alive and well in the imaginations of many Americans, demonstrating the survival of polytheism even in the most fundamentalist Christian circles and, in the same context of condemnation of same-sex unions, in the imagination of Pope Francis as well.

POLYTHEISM IN ISLAMIC MONOTHEISM

The question of polytheism in ancient Arabia, and its vestiges in Islam itself, excites a great deal of controversy. A very strict prohibition on polytheism governs traditional, purist, fundamental Islam, with interpretation of the *Qur'an* as directing believers to resolutely resist, oppose, and exterminate the heresies associated with polytheism and idolatry. The prophet Muhammad was a prophet, not a god, the prophet Moses was not a god, the prophet Jesus was not a god. Yet, "the Ka'ba in Mecca is reported to have contained a picture of Jesus and Mary, a picture which the Prophet commanded to be preserved when he ordered the obliteration of others."[38] And there are Sufi saints, the object of some controversy concerning this very question of idolatry: "For the Muslim masses in general, shrines of Sufi saints are particular objects of reverence and even veneration. In Baghdad the tomb of the greatest saint of all, 'Abd al-Qadir al-Jilani, is visited every year by large numbers of pilgrims from all over the Muslim world."[39] These shrines sometimes become targets of other Muslims, Islamists who destroy them as remnants of idolatrous practices.

IDOLATRY

Islamic teachings concerning polytheism focus on the question of "idolatry," worship of idols, denoted by various words connected with the word *shirk*.[40] The historical period into which Muhammad was born is called the *jahiliyya*, "the age, or condition, of ignorance," and that ignorance is associated historically with polytheist Arabia in the centuries before his birth in the seventh century CE. Scholars debate the matter of whether Islam defined itself originally as a monotheism against contemporary polytheisms. This is the traditional and orthodox interpretation of many passages in the *Qur'an* that refer to idolatry. Other scholars argue that the energy directed against unbelievers and heresy is aimed not at contemporary polytheism at the time of Muhammad, at worshipers of the ancient Arabic goddesses, for example, but rather at other monotheists, Christians and Jews in the environment of early Islam, even in the diaspora after Arab conquests in Palestine, Damascus, and Baghdad, where the invaders encountered Christians and Jews who were seen to practice an impure version of monotheism.[41] The debate concerning whether the condemnation of idolators refers to Arab polytheists or Jews and Christians in Arabia is less important for us here than the concern expressed in the *Qur'an* and in later Islamic texts concerning polytheism. Whether the idolators were worshipers of Arabic goddesses, the god of ancient Israel, or the god of the Christians, they are present in the *Qur'an* and a constant preoccupation of the messages traditionally understood to have been transmitted to Muhammad by the angel Gabriel.

THE GODDESSES

One of the most important passages in this regard is Surah 53, "The Star," which refers to idols of the unbelievers:

> Have you thought on Al-Lat and Al-Uzza, and on Manat, the third other?[42]

It is at this point that the so-called satanic verses were inserted, verses that called the idols "exalted" and hoped for their intercession, verses that were subsequently attributed to Satan (see Surah 22: "Never have We sent a single prophet or apostle before you with whose wishes Satan did not tamper. But God abrogates the interjections of Satan and confirms His own revelations.")[43] The passage from Surah 53 continues in the canonical text with a new revelation to Muhammad that replaced the "satanic verses." Although difficult of interpretation, like the other sacred texts from centuries past that we look at here, these passages are often thought to refer to female deities worshipped at the Ka'ba, the sacred site of Mecca which Muslims believe to have been established by Abraham, the patriarch of the three monotheisms practiced by Jews, Christians, and Muslims. The orthodox view is that Abraham came to Mecca, bringing his son Ishmael and his son's mother, Hagar, and then later founded the Ka'ba as a site of monotheistic worship of the one god. Subsequently, deterioration of strict monotheism occurred, and the Arabs set up other idols in the Ka'ba and elsewhere in Arabia. One traditional interpretation is that Al-Lat, Al-Uzza, and Manat were among the idols worshipped in the Ka'ba, the shrine that Muhammad purified, destroying the 360 idols that had resided there after Abraham had, long before, built it to honor his one god. Other idols are named in Surah 71, called "Noah"—Wadd, Suwa, Yaghuth, Ya'uq,

Nasr—but the names of the goddesses have been the subject of special historical interest and speculation.

The "satanic verses," expurgated from the canonical text, suggest a falling away from monotheism, according to the orthodox view; this perceived slackening was denied and erased with the further revelation that constitutes the remaining portion of the citation given above, in which the goddesses were belittled by the angelic messenger to Muhammad. These goddesses, represented as idols, may have taken various forms: rocks, sanctuaries, and steles in Arabia and were under the protection of different tribes. And they had affinities with Aphrodite, with Venus, identified with a heavenly body, and even with the Greek goddess Athena.

> There is no reason to doubt that names related to those the Koran says were given by the opponents to beings whom they regarded as "daughters of God," and which Muslim tradition identifies as those of goddesses, idols, or sanctuaries, were in common use with reference to deities or other supernatural entities in the Near East, including Arabia, before Islam.[44]

Like believers in surrounding societies, the Arabs had worshipped female as well as male divinities.

ANGELS

Angels play in important part in Islam, as they do in the other Abrahamic monotheisms. Part of the heavenly host, they serve as messengers from the god, who is not anthropomorphized, that is, not imagined to have human form, in Islam. Allah is not visualizable and exists without a plural form, without gender. The prohibition on images, or aniconism, is based on the view that the only creator is Allah, and that only he can create creatures; a tradition is preserved that the Prophet said whoever makes an image of a living being will be asked on the day of judgment to infuse life into it— Allah is the sole creator, such a person seeks to rival Allah. In addition, with the representation of animate beings, it was thought that there was the possibility of idolatry, worship of the image as an idol, which is strictly forbidden. Yet there were private images, in the beginning kept not in mosques but in homes, and in the Persian Islamic world, more tolerant of such forms of representation, a tradition of miniatures that did depict human beings and angels.

Islam certainly, while adamantly opposed to polytheism, does include angels in the divine company, angels who are understood to be messengers of god, without the free will attributed to other created beings, humans and jinn. One of the six articles of faith is to affirm faith in God's angels (*malak*); among the others are faith in god, in his books, in his messengers. The angels are the messengers of Allah, who carry out his commands, communicating revelations from the god, as does the angel Gabriel, Jibril, who dictated the *Qur'an* to Muhammad. A complex array of angels shares various powers and responsibilities. Raphael will blow his trumpet at the end of time, to mark the beginning of the day of judgment; Michael is the angel of mercy, Azrael the angel of death. Angels carry off the souls of the dead, "striking their faces and their backs" (Surah 47). There are angels of the seven heavens, guardian angels for each human being, one to record her good, the other her evil deeds. "Our angels, who are at their side, record it all" (Surah 43). The angels Harut and Marut were somehow implicated in the devils' teaching of witchcraft in Babylon (Surah 2). Over time, there is an extensive record of other angels, including Malik, the chief of the angels who govern hell, supervising those who torment sinners. Surah 66, "The Prohibition," says: "Believers, guard yourselves and guard your kindred against a Fire fuelled with men and stones, in the charge of stern and mighty angels who never disobey God's command and who promptly do His bidding" (Surah 66). "We have appointed none by angels to guard the Fire, and made their number a subject for dispute among the unbelievers . . ." (74). The evil-doers call out to Malik in hell, asking to be relieved of their suffering, but he replies: "Here you shall remain!" (Surah 43). The angel Radwan watches over paradise (*Jannah*). The angels are mentioned frequently, as in Surah 2, "The Cow," where God says to Adam, of the angels, "tell them their names" (Surah 2). And the angels prostrate themselves before Adam, all but Satan. In the Surah called "The Imrans," the angels announce the birth of Jesus to Mary and call him the Messiah (Surah 2). Surah 35, "The Creator": "He sends forth the angels as His messenger, with two, three or four pairs of wings" (Surah 35). It is said elsewhere that the archangels Gabriel and Michael have thousands of wings, while the lesser angels are less be-winged. And animals, wonderfully, can see the angels. The pagan Arabs erroneously "regard as females the angels who are God's servants" (Surah 43).

The French scholar of Islam Henry Corbin makes the case for angels in a book called *The Paradox of Monotheism,* and his arguments in fact pertain to *all* the monotheisms.[45] He argues that in the Abrahamic tradition, especially in Islam, the one god is unknowable by means of perception and reason, and he is "transcendent," that is, beyond the range of normal, physical human experience, apart from and not subject to the limitations of the material universe. And if monotheism imposes itself as an alternative to earlier polytheisms, then the god cannot assimilate himself to any created being in this world. Although his light is comparable to that of a niche enshrining a lamp from a blessed olive tree (Surah 24), this god can reveal himself to human beings only through holy books and by his messengers, or prophets. Corbin argues that such beliefs recreate, at the heart of monotheism, the very idolatry that it strives to eradicate. Christianity is a special case, in that it produces a second god, son of the one god, who mysteriously, in the trinity, is considered still to be one god. But Islam rejects the divinity of Jesus, seeing him as a prophet, not a god, like Adam, Abraham, Moses, and other prophets who preceded Muhammad, the seal of the prophets, the last messenger of the one god.

In a fascinating chapter entitled "The Necessity of Angelology," Corbin stresses the inevitable and indispensable creation of a body of angels, who are the objects of belief, and who trouble the emphatic insistence on monotheism of this tradition (Corbin, 97–210). The transcendent god must be revealed to human beings and by that revelation loses his absolute transcendence. Without what Corbin calls "angelology," the lore, the intermediation of angels, there would be no monotheism. He argues that Christian, Neoplatonic angelology provided a philosophical model for the Islamic conceptualization of angels, messengers from the god, and that in fact prophetic religion cannot manage without angelology: the revealing angel and the receiving prophet are inextricably linked. If monotheism is to escape from the two dangerous possibilities of agnosticism and anthropomorphism, that is, in the former case, accepting the unknowability of the god, and not knowing, not believing, and in the latter case, imagining the god in the shape of a human being, as Christians often do, then angels become necessary to pass between god and man, to convey the message of the god to human beings, to present to human beings the face of god.[46] He concludes: "monotheism is impossible without angelology" (Corbin, 181).

JINN

The patriarch Abraham had already fought the battle against idols, according to the orthodox view, and established the true monotheism: "Tell of Abraham, who said to Azar, his father: 'Will you worship idols as your gods? Surely you and all your people are in palpable error'" (Surah 6, "Cattle"). Abraham had seen a star, the moon, and the sun, all of which faded and set, and refused to worship them, turning instead to their creator and saying "I am no idolator" (Surah 6). Idolators worshipped "the jinn as God's equals, though He Himself created them, and in their ignorance ascribe to Him sons and daughters" (Surah 6). The jinn are created supernatural beings, neither angels nor devils, below the level of these superior beings. There is a hierarchy among the jinni, including *ghul,* spirits of changing shape; *ifrit,* diabolical evil spirits; and *si'la,* who do not change shape, but are invariably treacherous. The jinn can take human or animal form and live in inanimate objects; they enjoy punishing human beings for any slight and are in popular culture held responsible for misfortunes and accidents. They figure prominently in the marvelous collection of stories known as *The Thousand and One Nights,* and in the decades during which American popular culture was more sympathetic to the Arab world, in the era of the films *Kismet, Sinbad,* and *The Thief of Baghdad,* came to inhabit popular movies, and even American television serials, in the form of "Jeannie" the genie in *I Dream of Jeannie* of the 1960s. In the Surah entitled "The Jinn," these supernatural beings are instructed to say that the god "has taken no consort, nor has He begotten any children" (Surah 72); the jinn are said to have themselves been created from "smokeless fire" (Surah 55). They say in Surah 72 that they "made their way to high heaven, and found it filled with mighty wardens and fiery comets" (Surah 72). And they claim that some of their number are righteous, though others are not, some Muslims and some wrongdoers (Surah 72). There are also "devils," who rebel, who eavesdrop; the god has set the lower heaven with constellations to defend against these devils: "Meteors are hurled at them from every side" (Surah 37).

THE DEVIL

So, although there is but one god, there is belief in and vestiges, foot-prints of the goddesses, of angels, of worship of the heavenly bodies, of jinn, and of devils: "The devils will teach their votaries to argue with you. If you obey them, you shall yourselves become idolators" (Surah 6). There are also saints, as mentioned earlier, especially in the Sufi branch of Islam, where female believers such as Rabia el-Basri, an eighth-century Iraqi who may have been a slave in early life, exemplified a truly monotheistic and mystical approach to divinity, saying when asked if she hated the devil, that she had no room for hating or loving any but god. She herself became the object of devotion. Satan—as we have seen a potent presence in the Hebrew Bible, in Judaism, in the New Testament, and even in contemporary Catholicism and evangelical Christianity—also figures in the *Qur'an*. Surah 7, "The Heights," recounts some of the history of Satan; the god created human beings and told the angels to bow down before Adam, but Satan refused. "I am nobler than he," he says. "You created me from fire, but You created him from clay" (Surah 7). His is a story repeated several times: Surahs 2, 15, 17, 18: "Satan was a jinnee disobedient to his Lord" (Surahs 20, 38). Satan tempted Adam and his wife in paradise, and lured them into trans-gression (Surah 2). "Satan tempted them, so that he might reveal to them their shameful parts, which they had never seen before" (Surah 7). Satan is the deceiver, the seducer, who leads human beings into the worship of idols. "God will not forgive idolatry . . . Rather than to Him, they pray but to females: they pray but to a rebellious Satan" (Surah 4). This Satan will say to the damned on the judgment day: "I never believed, as you did, that I was God's equal" (Surah 14). But, although he is not God's equal, he has supernatural powers.

The Hajj, the pilgrimage to Mecca required of every devout Muslim able to perform it, "the fifth pillar" of obligations, includes a ritual stoning of the devil, once represented by pillars but now by walls. These walls are said to stand for the devil's assaults, first on Abraham the patriarch, tempted not to sacrifice his son Ishmael although commanded by the god to do so, second on Hagar, the mother of Ishmael, to resist the sacrifice, and finally, on Ish-mael himself, tempting him to forego being sacrificed. The devil was repu-diated at each of these temptations; the stoning is symbolic of the rebukes hurled at him for these efforts, and is performed also to rid the devout pilgrim's self of internal and external demons or despots that attempt to control him. The devil, or Satan, very much present in the verses of the *Qur'an,* is then still active, symbolically and perhaps for some believers literally, in contemporary Islamic practice.

ZOROASTRIANISM

The polytheism of monotheism may be usefully examined through the traditions of Zoroastrianism, a religion of ancient Iran and the Persians, which survives to this day, and which some would argue is the only non-Abrahamic monotheism. Yet, as we will see, in fact Zoroastrianism posits a kingdom of light and one of darkness and a great struggle between the forces of good and evil. Although there is finally one good and triumphant divinity, the power and malevolence of the gods of evil make this a polytheism, one that illuminates the Abrahamic tradition of so-called monotheisms as well. In fact, the Abrahamic monotheisms—Judaism, Christianity, and Islam—may have influenced and been influenced by Zoroastrianism, with its monotheistic, polytheistic, and dualistic aspects.[47]

While there is a great deal of debate and even controversy within this religious tradition, it is often said to have been founded by Zarathushtra, whose dates of birth and death are disputed, but who received the divinely transmitted *Gathas,* "songs," from the god Ahura Mazda. Before the time of Zarathushtra, the people of the Iranian plateau, connected by some scholars with Indo-European migrations, the travels of the people who eventually inhabited Europe and India, shared some religious views with the Aryans who may have eventually entered the Indian subcontinent, although this too is matter of heated argument. The first sacred texts, the *Gathas,* which have some affinities with the Sanskrit *Rig Veda,* were probably composed in the mid-first millennium BCE and transmitted orally. Eventually, there were other gods noted in sacred texts beside the greatest Ahura Mazda, among them Mithra, a god of fire sacrifice, and a sacred liquid akin to the Sanskrit Veda's *soma,* a divine hallucinogen. The people who arrived on the Iranian plateau seem to have divided their supernatural world between the *daiva,* later *daeva,* the "heavenly ones," and *asura* (later *ahura*), another group with occult power. Reversing the valuation of these entities in the Sanskrit tradition, the Iranians reduced

the *daeva* to the status of demons, while honoring the *ahuras*. Zarathushtra was said to be the priest of one of the *ahura,* called "wise," later Ahura
Mazda, the greatest god worshipped by the Persians of the Persian empire
in the sixth century BCE. In the sacred hymns the great god, accompanied
by a host of lesser deities, engages in a combat with the forces of evil,
the *daevas.* "The Gathas introduce the construct of a vertical separation
between the world of living beings, who sustain and strengthen order
in the cosmos, and those who are fueled by the principles of chaos and
deception" (Rose, 16).[48] Over time, these concepts develop into a dualist
theology in which the god is confronted with a sort of anti-god, the force
of darkness and evil. "Young Avestan" hymns, that is, from 1000 to 500
BCE, mention "beings worthy of worship (Av. *yazatas*), such as Mithra,
Anahita and Tishtrya, while still upholding the supreme status of Ahura
Mazda" (Rose, 23).

THE GODDESS

Phiroze Vasunia describes the goddess Anahita, mentioned earlier, "an Iranian divinity of water and fertility whose name in Avestan means 'unde-
filed' or 'immaculate'" (Vasunia, 221). He cites *Yasht* 5, "a lengthy and
well-preserved Avestan hymn":

> she is a beautiful maiden, powerful and tall, her girdle fastened high,
> wrapped in a gold-embroidered cloak, wearing earrings, a necklace, and a
> crown of gold, and adorned with thirty otter skins (Vasunia, 221).

Statues were erected in honor of the goddess throughout the Persian empire;
she was associated by the Greeks with their goddess Athena, because of her
martial aspect, and through her links with fertility, with their Aphrodite.
But she was especially seen as the Persian Artemis, or Diana, and had temples in Asia Minor, in the neighborhood of Ephesus, already mentioned
in this chapter as an important site of virgin goddess worship, sacred to
Artemis, the Amazons, and even the virgin Mary. Vasunia notes that the
high priest of the great Artemis temple in Ephesus—as noted, one of the
seven wonders of the ancient world—had at the time of the Persian emperor
Darius a name associated with the Persian god, Megabyxos.[49]

SAVIOR

Thus Zoroastrianism exhibits the complex layering of the other religions we have looked at so far, original polytheism overlaid with a monotheism that is actually a duotheism, a struggle between *two* forces. The great wise god created "a good place" for the Iranians, but that good place, its settlements, were initially destroyed by the evil Angra Mainyu, "the Lie," a separate entity. In later developments in the middle Persian period (300–1000 CE, during the Sasanian empire), Ahura Mazda, now Ohrmazd, was believed to have created the world, but as a battlefield in which to engage the evil Ahriman over the course of 9,000 years, at the end of which light and life and good would overcome the demons of darkness, death, and evil.

Zoroastrianism also conceives of a savior, descended from Zarathushtra himself through the preservation of his semen in Lake Kansaoya, producing three sons born a thousand years apart, the last of whom would be Ast-vat-ereta, incarnated justice, that is, the Saoshyant, "the savior." It is he who brings about the end of time:

> The activity of *frashegird*—"the making wonderful or perfect"—begins with the resurrection of the dead, the reuniting of the soul with the body and the judgment of the whole person, which involves walking through molten metal, representing one's own deeds . . . Ahriman and the *devs* are rendered power-less. The *devs* are destroyed by their good counterparts, Ahriman is flung back through the hole in the sky into darkness as Ohrmazd chants the *kusti* prayer of exorcism, and the hole is sealed up with molten metal (Rose, 111).

The victory of the forces of light over those of darkness inaugurates an eter-nal reign of the benign Ohrmazd with a healing and revitalization of the cosmos. Present-day Zoroastrians, in Iran, India, and in the greater dias-pora, whether descended from other Zoroastrians, Parsis (for Persians, the Zoroastrians of India), converts from Islam, people returning to a Zoroas-trian family heritage, Neo-Zoroastrians who convert to the religion, and so-called "ara-Zoroastrians, who "emphasize belief and commitment rather than birth" (Rose, 226) as in Russia, in the Saint Petersburg community, debate among themselves the centrality of Zarathushtra, of the *Gathas,* and differ concerning the question of whether Zoroastrianism is a monotheism (Rose, 217–232).

Parallels with Zoroastrian texts and the Hebrew Bible, noted by Morton Smith, can be seen in *Isaiah* 40–48, where the juxtaposition of light with good and evil with darkness seems to recall sections of the *Gathas*.[50] This section of *Isaiah* is sometimes called "the consolation of Israel" and looks to the Persian emperor Cyrus, the sixth-century founder of the Achaemenid empire, who freed the Israelite exiles from captivity in Babylon after his conquest of the Babylonians, allowing the exiles to return to Jerusalem. In the biblical verses, the god of the Israelites takes credit for the victories of Cyrus, here called a "messiah," an anointed ruler. Not Marduk, god of Babylon, to whom Cyrus attributed victory, but the Israelite god reminds his listeners: "I am the LORD, and there is no other. I form light and create darkness, I make weal and create woe" (*Isaiah* 45.6–7).

The idea of a savior, which appears in the Zoroastrian tradition, has significance for both Judaism and Christianity. The term "anointed" is used here in *Isaiah*: "Thus says the LORD to his anointed, to Cyrus, whose right hand I have grasped . . ." (*Isaiah* 45.1).[51] This passage was read as preparation for later appearances of the messiah in Judaism of the Hellenistic and Roman periods, when there were many contenders for this role of the king of the Jews, designated by the honorific which had been used of Solomon (*1 Kings* 1.34), among others. The term "messiah" refers to mortals, human kings, in the Hebrew Bible; the supernatural element enters with the Zoroastrian idea of the "savior." The term is also then transferred to the idea of a supernatural being, a savior, and used of Jesus, the *khristos,* that is, in Greek, "the anointed," the one rubbed with oil as a sign of sovereignty.

In the period of the Arsacid or Parthian empire (247 BCE to 224 CE), the influence of Zoroastrianism was felt on other religious traditions, including the Judaism of the period, which "display a growing emphasis on the struggle between the forces of good and the forces of evil" (Rose, 88). As a symptom of the interpenetration of these religious traditions, in translations of the Hebrew Bible into Greek, the Persian word *paradeisos* was used to convey not just the idea of a garden, orchard, or vineyard, but also a restoration to the garden of Eden (Rose, 59).[52]

MANICHEANISM

Manichaeism, named for the Persian prophet Mani, born in 216 CE, has elements of Zoroastrianism, as well as Judaism, Christianity, and Buddhism. Like the religion of Zarathushtra, it posits a struggle between a good world of light and an evil world of darkness, the result of a fall into the world of matter. Manichaeism differs from Zoroastrianism in positing a final destruction of the world at the end of time, rather than a renewal in perfection after the destruction of all evil. The religion of the Manichaeans is significant not only because Manichaeist heresies cropped up in the history of Christianity, as in the case of the Cathars of southern France, who were persecuted and eliminated by official Christianity. In addition, and even more significantly for the development of Christian theology, Augustine (354–430 CE), who came from Hippo in North Africa, in 387 converted to Christianity from Manichaeism. The Roman emperor Theodosius I had condemned all Manichaeans to death in 382; he later declared Christianity to be the sole true religion in the Roman empire. According to the *Confessions,* after nine or ten years of adhering to the Manichaean faith as a member of the group of "hearers," Augustine became a Christian and a committed opponent of Manichaeism. One of his principal objections to the dualistic understanding of the universe taught by Manicheanism was that it permitted an individual to deny his own responsibility for sin, as he or she could blame the darkness, the evil, as a separate force, just as later Christians have come to identify Satan as the cause of their wrongdoing, seeing temptation as an *external* and embodied supernatural creature who attempts to seduce.

> I still thought that it is not we who sin but some other nature that sins within us. It flattered my pride to think that I incurred no guilt and, when I did wrong, not to confess it . . . I preferred to excuse myself and blame this unknown thing which was in me but was not part of me. The truth, of course, was that it was all my own self, and my own impiety had divided me against myself. My sin was all the more incurable because I did not think myself a sinner. I believed that evil, too was some similar kind of substance, a shapeless, hideous mass, which might be solid, in which case the Manichees called it earth, or fine and rarefied like air. This they imagine as a kind of evil mind filtering through the substance they call earth (*Confessions* 5.10).[53]

Augustine repudiated Manicheanism, yet scholars see traces of its dualism in his later theological writings, which have in turn found their way into the mainstream of official Christianity, and into popular ideas of the dangerous presence of Satan in the everyday life of believers. Augustine shows the influence of Manichaeism in his thinking concerning the nature of good and evil and in a denigration of the material world, especially with regard to carnal life and sexual activity. These features of Christian doctrine, which became orthodoxy in some currents of Christianity, are not necessarily part of the New Testament teachings of Jesus, but may be very much influenced by the complex dualistic polytheism of the teachings of the prophet Mani, themselves affected by the religious concepts of Zoroastrianism.

The official, orthodox advocates of all of these monotheisms, Abrahamic and not, present arguments for a single divinity. The identity of that divinity is in question——is he Yahweh, Eli-Kurios, Adon, Father-Son-Holy Spirit, Allah, Ahura Mazda—? Do all these names refer to the same being? Do even the Abrahamic monotheisms share the same god? And in the popular, folk, everyday practices of these religions there has always been a strong undercurrent of belief in other supernatural beings—in angels, in a son of the god, a savior, in a female consort of the great god, in the mother of the god, in goddesses, in saints, and in a god or gods of evil, who are recognized, who are the objects of intense belief if not worship. Although the story is often told of a triumph of monotheism, of the inevitability, logical development, and ethical superiority of monotheism, in fact in all these monotheisms, Abrahamic and not, we find a multiplicity of gods and other supernatural beings, a persistent and ineradicable current of polytheism, from the time of their beginnings into the present.

CHAPTER FOUR

The Politics of Polytheism

JACQUES DERRIDA, although caught up in the restricted world of the Abra-hamic monotheisms and the contemporary war of brothers among Chris-tians, Jews, and Muslims, pointed to the political dimension of religious affiliations: "Wars or military 'interventions,' led by the Judaeo-Christian West in the name of the best causes (of international law, democracy, the sovereignty of peoples, of nations or of states, even of humanitarian imper-atives), are they not also, from a certain side, wars of religion?"[1] How has polytheism figured in such conflicts over the centuries?

There have been many polytheisms, both extinct and flourishing, and they do not, as some fundamentalist monotheists might suggest, fail any more than monotheisms in the domains of ethics, theological sophisti-cation, and a politics engaging tolerance of others. Polytheism is char-acteristic of many traditional cultures, and a loyalty to many gods can mark resistance to colonization and its demand to convert, to accept the conquerors' one god and abandon the deities, the ancestor-gods, and the ancestors. The prejudice against conquered peoples' religious practices, be they animism or polytheism, has often been linked to forms of racism, the view that phenotypically different human beings are racially inferior, their skin color along with their religions markers of primitivism and backwardness. Conquest and sometimes brutal and relentless religious conversion are justified as means to rescue such benighted souls from their darkness, to draw them into the security of the imperial embrace, sometimes named "democracy." Yet to map the history of polytheism and earliest democracy, for example, is to see that polytheism has on some occasions been more consonant with democracy than has monotheism, which in some ancient societies was associated with monarchy, the imposed rule of one: an emperor, a king, a single sovereign.

DEMOCRACY AND POLYTHEISM

In her encyclopedic work on Hinduism, Wendy Doniger calls it "the Ellis Island of religions; the lines between different beliefs and practices are permeable membranes."[2] Ellis Island was the point of entry of millions of immigrants to the U.S. from the "old" world of Europe in the nineteenth and twentieth centuries, from 1892 to 1954. Refugees, political and economic, arrived in huge waves from Eastern Europe, from Ireland, from Italy, to seek their fortunes in North America, and supposedly, today, a third of the U.S. population can trace its family's arrival to Ellis Island. These Americans brought their traditions with them—anarchism, socialism, Greek Orthodox Christianity, Judaism, Hasidism, Roman Catholicism of various stripes, from Sicilian to Irish, Huguenot Protestantism like that of my grandparents. Ellis Island stands for the diversity of the American population, for its pluralism and its polytheism, which has been even further enriched by further waves of immigration from Latin America and Asia.

The word democracy, "rule of the people," the much-vaunted governmental system of the U.S. and of other developed, developing, and deliberately *under*-developed nations, including India, comes from polytheist ancient Athens. After being ruled by aristocrats and monarchic tyrants, the ancient Athenians decided in the sixth century BCE to rule themselves. In a radical experiment, they began entrusting the roles of government to fellow citizens. At its most democratic moment, the city chose most of its magistrates by lottery. It paid its citizens to attend the theater. It offered the choice of service on juries that provided a living wage for citizens. The only elected office in the city was that of general or admiral, in recognition of the special skills required to wage war. Otherwise, the citizens trusted one another to govern. After service in one of the allotted positions in Athens' administration, the city conducted an audit of the finances concerned, so that no office-holder could cheat his fellow citizens. The great historian Thucydides puts into the mouth of Pericles, an exceptional figure among the citizens, this assessment of Athens:

> We have a form of government that does not emulate the practices of our neighbors, setting an example to some rather than imitating others. In name it is called democracy on account of being administered in the interest not of the few but the many, yet even though there are equal rights for all in private disputes in accordance with the laws, wherever each man has earned recognition he is singled out for public service in accordance with the claims of distinction, not by rotation but by merit, nor when it comes to poverty, if a man has real ability to benefit the city, is he prevented by obscure renown (Thucydides 2.37).[3]

Often being "singled out for public service" entailed the provision of funds for public benefit in the form of theatrical subsidies or ships for the navy and, as noted earlier, generals were elected. But most public offices were occupied by men chosen by lot to carry out their duties. And of course, as noted in Chapter 2, the Athenians were polytheists.

In 415 BCE, at war with the Spartan coalition, when they were about to set out on an ill-advised attempt to conquer their enemies' friends on the island of Sicily, the Athenians suffered a rude shock. On the eve of the departure of the expedition, they found that the "herms"—the pillar-like boundary markers dedicated to the god Hermes, often adorned with the god's head and an erect phallus—had been cut, mutilated by unknown persons. In addition, while the city's councilors carried out an investigation into this sacrilege, the citizens learned of other crimes. The sacred rites of the Eleusinian Mysteries, performed to initiate worshippers into the mystery cult of the goddesses Demeter and Persephone, had been profaned. Some of the city's most prominent men had apparently been performing or parodying them, revealing secrets never to be revealed, not at the sacred sites in Eleusis, near Athens, but in their own homes. The panic and uproar in the city were tremendous; people feared the wrath of the gods and also an oligarchic conspiracy bent on overthrowing the democracy. The desecration of the gods' rituals and votive offerings went along with possible plotting to end the experiment of democracy and restore rule by the few, the elite, the aristocrats or the wealthy. This is part of the later defense speech of one of the alleged conspirators, who had been arrested by the councilors and put in the stocks:

> They called up the generals and told them to proclaim that Athenians living in town were to go armed to the Agora, those in the Long Walls to the Theseum, and those in Piraeus to the Agora of Hippodamus, and that a trumpet-signal should be given before daybreak for the cavalry to come to the Anaceum [temple of Castor and Pollux, the twins], and that the Council was to go to the Acropolis and sleep there . . . The Boeotians had heard what was going on and were out in force on the frontier (Andocides, "On the Mysteries,"45).[4]

The threat to the gods was a threat to the democracy, and the citizens rallied to protect both. Andocides was accused of sacrilege against "the two goddesses" Demeter and Persephone.

Athens' democracy was intertwined with its worship of its many gods. In the course of his defense, Andocides cited Athenian law: "If anyone subverts the democracy at Athens or holds any office when the democracy has been subverted, he shall be regarded as an enemy of the Athenians and may be killed with impunity, and his property shall be confiscated and a tenth part of it devoted to the Goddess" (Andocides, 95). Athenians swore an oath to kill anyone who subverted the democracy and vowed that they would consider a killer of such a person "pure in the sight of gods and divinities."

The oath of initiation of the young citizen-soldiers, the ephebes, cited earlier, was sworn over sacrifices before the festival of Dionysos. As Robert Parker notes in *Polytheism and Society at Athens*:

> Religion in Greece was not, in chemical language, a volatile substance. It was stable partly, to continue the metaphor, because it did not react explosively to other polytheistic systems, but could blend or coexist with them. There were no wars of religion in the ancient polytheistic world because there was nothing for such a war to be about. But it was a stabilizing and conservative factor above all because its organizational structures tracked so closely

those of Greek society as a whole . . . Every individual's primary and shaping experience of religion was within exactly the structures through which he or she first experienced the existing social order. One's identity as a worshipper of the gods was also one's identity as a citizen (Parker, 453).[5]

In ancient Athens, even though it was also the site of challenges to belief in the gods made by the sophists and by later philosophers, democracy and polytheism went hand in hand, even though, as we have seen, this link has been disregarded, effaced in Western civilization's narrative about itself. The prejudice against polytheism and an almost messianic devotion to democracy appear somewhat contradictory, held in a cognitive dissonance in the ideology of modernity.

MONOTHEISM AND MONARCHY

As detailed earlier, many Biblical scholars date the beginnings of exclusive monotheism in ancient Israel not to origins in a garden in Eden, nor to a revelation to Moses, but rather to the later reign of King Josiah of Judah in the seventh century BCE. It was at this time, in 622, during the period of Deuteronomy or "second law" reform, that the people of Judah were commanded to give up their "high places" of sacrifice, to abandon any idolatry or worship of the *asherahs,* to worship only in the temple of Jerusalem, the capital of Josiah. The "second law" of this period, supplementing the law of the tablets of Moses and the covenant of Sinai, was said to have been found among the scrolls of the Torah in the Jerusalem temple: "The high priest Hilkiah said to Shaphan the secretary, 'I have found the book of the law in the house of the Lord'" (*2 Kings* 22.8). Josiah tore his clothes when he realized that these laws, put into the mouth of Moses, had not been known and not been obeyed. And he took out of the temple vessels made for Ba'al, for Asherah, and "for all the host of heaven" (*2 Kings* 23.4). He deposed the idolatrous priests who had been making offerings in the high places, to Baal, to the sun, the moon, the constellations, and all the host of heavens. He removed the image of Asherah from the temple, "beat it to dust and threw the dust of it upon the graves of the common people" (*2 Kings* 23.6). "He broke down the houses of the male temple prostitutes that were in the house of the LORD, where the women did weaving for Asherah" (*2 Kings* 23.7). He defiled the high places and ended the practice of making children pass through fire as an offering for Molech. He burned the chariots dedicated by the kings to the sun and then destroyed all the "high places," sites of sacrifice, and "slaughtered on the altars all the priests of the high places who were there, and burned human bones on them" (2 *Kings* 23.20). "Josiah put away the mediums, wizards, teraphim [household gods], idols, and all the abominations . . ." (2 *Kings* 23.24). Jerusalem and its temple became the center, the only site of worship, of the first nationally celebrated passover festival under the sponsorship of its king.

Historians have interpreted these acts not only as a theological ordering of the practices of the Judaeans, but also as a consolidation and centralization of the monarchic power of King Josiah. The convenient discovery of a new law allowed him to impose his sovereign will and his administrative authority over all his subjects and to center the religious life of his people in his city. The northern kingdom of Israel had been conquered by the Assyrians in 722 BCE, but Josiah attempted with his reforms to claim these territories as well and to establish autonomy from the Assyrians for both kingdoms. When the Egyptian pharaoh Neco killed him at Megiddo, the body of Josiah was brought in a chariot and buried in Jerusalem. The earlier narratives of the history of the people had been refashioned to lead inevitably to the perfected rule of Josiah, who attempted to (re)establish absolute monotheism in his reforms. Looking backwards, the Bible attempts to show any deviance from monotheism as a falling away from a previous devotion to a single god, but as I argued earlier, the picture is less clear, and it is more likely that this reform of Josiah is in fact the beginning of a truly monotheistic commitment, although even so, the people continued to worship their many gods.

The consolidation of monarchic power in this case fits neatly with the imposition of monotheism. Similarly, in his struggle to assert the worship of the one god, the Aten, and to disempower the priests of the many cults of the Egyptians of his day, the pharaoh Akhenaten may have been attempting to consolidate his sovereignty over all of Egypt. With his strenuous efforts to eliminate other centers of power, including the powerful cult territories of the priests, Akhenaten reduced the multiplicity of challenges to his authority. The priests of the various gods of Egypt possessed extensive holdings of land, valuable temples and votive offerings, slaves, and dependents, and at times threatened the pharaohs in their supremacy. With the ascension of Akhenaten and his one god, monarchy marched with monotheism in Egypt. As Cyril Aldred put it:

> Instead of incorporating all the old gods in his sole deity, he rigidly excluded them in an uncompromising monotheism. Where this idea came from in a world which tolerated so many diverse forms of god head is unknown. They were presumably Akhenaten's own, the logical result of regarding the Aten as a self-created heavenly king, whose son, the pharaoh, was also "unique, without a peer."
>
> Other gods, particularly the influential Amun and Osiris, were abolished, their images smashed, their names excised, their temples abandoned, the revenues impounded. The plural form of the word for god was suppressed. At the same time, however, the prayers to the Aten were usually addressed through the intermediary of the king . . .
>
> This increase in the power and glory of the kingship, in conformity with the spirit of the time, was the inevitable outcome of Akhenaten's religious ideas.[6]

The temples were closed, and their property and income transferred to the pharaoh. Tutankhamun, successor to Akhenaten, reported that before his inheritance of the throne, all the temples of Egypt had been deserted, and their sanctuaries were full of weeds. He and subsequent pharaohs attempted to repair the damage and to win back the favor of the many gods who had been offended by Akhenaten's attempt to establish absolute monarchy accompanied by absolute monotheism.

As Jan Assmann describes these changes, he emphasizes the correspondence between monarchy and monotheisms.

> Comparable forced unions are also to be found in early Jewish, Christian, and especially Islamic monotheisms, whether in the form of theocracy, Byzantine caesaro-papism, or the usurpation of profane authority by spiritual leaders. Time and again, whenever monotheism ceased being a political resistance movement and established itself as the ruling order, its political theology easily shifted from criticism of the state to legitimation of the state.[7]

Monotheism has at times served monarchs; it centralizes power, focuses worship in the hands of those authorized by the monarch, and allows him or her to control the finances and the politics of religious life.

However, there are situations in which the links between one god and one ruler do not apply. And of course, although religion may be one factor in the political arrangements of any given society, it is not determinate, and there are many other currents, historical, geographical, economic, social, among others, that have come to bear on the shape of political arrangements of ancient and contemporary cultures. In the Roman Empire, the many gods of the Romans and of the many peoples conquered and drawn into the empire created a vast landscape of difference and polytheism. Although the cult of the emperor himself, living or dead, a symbol of allegiance to the Roman state, eventually served as a sort of umbrella for many kinds of worship, one of the issues that troubles this imperial history is the conflict between monotheists and polytheists, which surfaced in the resistance of the Judaeans, their guerilla warfare against Rome, and their eventual defeat. The temple of the Judaeans was eventually razed and its people scattered in diaspora. The great Italian historian Arnaldo Momigliano, in an essay entitled "The Disadvantages of Monotheism for a Universal State," discussed the relationship between the Roman empire and polytheism: "The gods provide models to the emperors; they do not explain the Empire" (Momigliano, 145).[8] Momigliano finds general indifference by Romans to the "actual religious structure of the Roman Empire" (Momigliano, 147) until the second century anti-Christian polemicist Celsus, who defended the Roman pantheon only in the context of arguments that the Christians "abandoned the laws of the Jews in order to disobey the emperor and refuse military service" (Momigliano, 148). It was the Christians who formulated the political argument for "one god—one empire" (Momigliano, 151). They argued that the Roman state was preparing the way for Christianity by ending the diversity of governments in the wider Mediterranean world and interpreted the empire as "a providential instrument for the Church" (Momigliano, 152).[9]

Scholars of late antiquity and early Christianity differ concerning the motives of Constantine, the first Roman emperor to "convert" to Christianity in 312 CE. Was he an autocrat who saw advantage to his empire in conversion? Or was he caught up in belief in the new monotheistic religion? Although he did not force conversion on his subjects, nor did he persecute "pagans," Constantine adopted a conscious policy of encouraging Christianity and of discouraging especially the animal sacrifices of the older polytheism, eventually condemned as paganism and idolatry. The effects of his policies were long lasting. At the point of his conversion, the Christian population of the empire is thought to have been only 5–10% (Veyne, 1).[10] As one scholar wrote: "It must never be forgotten that Constantine's revolution was perhaps the most audacious act ever committed by an autocrat in disregard and defiance of the vast majority of his subjects."[11] The title of French historian Paul Veyne's 2007 *When Our World Became Christian* brings up many questions, particularly in light of my arguments here. Who is the "we" referred to in the title? What is "our" world? France and the French, one assumes, perhaps a limited perspective. But Veyne claims that "without Constantine, Christianity would have remained simply an avant-garde sect" (Veyne, 3). "Without Constantine's despotic decision, it could never have become the regular religion of the whole population" (Veyne, 42). Veyne compares Constantine to Lenin in Saint Petersburg in 1917 (Veyne, 47–49). This particular congruence of an emperor and a monotheism, their symmetry, their correspondence, the eventual consequences of Constantine's conversion, may have allowed the Roman Empire to survive and to resuscitate itself within the catholic church, to persist as a "holy" Roman empire.

Yet the transition was not without interruptions. The emperor Julian, a committed advocate of polytheism who emerged from Constantine's Christian family in the fourth century CE, tried to return the empire to "paganism," to polytheism, arguing that the many gods better served the diversity of the many peoples subsumed in the empire:

Ares rules over the warlike nations, Athena over those that are wise as well as warlike, Hermes over those that are more shrewd than adventurous, and in short the nations over which the gods preside follow each the essential character of their proper god. ("Against the Galileans"115e)[12]

In this interesting development in the history of late antiquity/early Christianity, the return to polytheism, to paganism, becomes a form of resistance against the domination of the Christians, with their one god, an enforced theological monotheism, and a Christian emperor. Julian, called "the apostate," was committed, for example, to rebuilding the temple at Jerusalem for the Jews, to reestablish other traditions besides the Christian in the empire. The Christians had interpreted the destruction of that temple as a sign that their one religion was destined to dominate the reformed empire, and the monarch Julian wanted to restore not just polytheism, but also diversity, beginning with the temple.[13] His efforts failed.

In the history of Western Europe, monarchy has sometimes enforced a monotheist form of religious worship. In England, Henry VIII imposed Protestantism on his people and violently persecuted those who continued to define themselves as "Roman" Catholics, looking to the pope rather than to their sovereign, the king of England. The religious conflicts that followed speak to the difficulties of monarchy faced with a diversity of religions. In Europe too, there were conflicts between Holy Roman emperors and popes, as well as between French Protestants and the absolute monarchy. Eventually, the European monarchs settled down with their one official church, as in the case of the Church of England, a compromise formation between puritan Protestantism and Catholicism. Nonetheless, resistance continued, and new forms of protest and Protestantism arose, as well as tenacious and unyielding pockets of Catholics, who were often persecuted well into the modern era, as can be seen in such incidents as the Gordon riots of the late eighteenth century, depicted in Charles Dickens's 1841 novel *Barnaby Rudge.* In the annual Guy Fawkes bonfires in England, effigies of the Catholic plotter Fawkes and the pope are still burned in the twenty-first century (in Lewes, in 2001, Osama bin Laden was added to the mix).

James C. Scott describes similar practices, the attempt to ally monarchy with a single religion in Southeast Asia:

> Theravada Buddhism, as a would-be universal creed, was very much the religion of a centralizing state compared with the local deities *(nat, phi)* that predated its spread. Despite their syncretism and incorporation of animist practice, Theravada monarchs, when they could, proscribed heterodox monks and monasteries, outlawed many Hindu-animist rites (many of them dominated by females and transvestites), and propagated what they took to be "pure," uncorrupted texts.[14]

Theravada Buddhism can be seen as an atheism, a polytheism, or simply as a universalizing monotheism that serves to consolidate monarchy.

POLYTHEISM AS RESISTANCE

In the U.S. and the U.K., popular narratives tend to stress a polemical version of the history of Judaism and then of Christianity, representing Abrahamic monotheism as the oppressed, its adherents the persecuted minorities who valiantly survive persecution. And of course this has often been the case, as in the history of the Roman empire, as in the terrible history of anti-Semitism in Europe into the present. Yet in fact, in Europe and the Americas, official religious discourse supports the claim that "monotheism today seems not only to have triumphed historically but also to be morally superior to polytheism."[15] Although Biblical epics such as *Ben Hur,* still popular, appeal especially to children's sense of Christians as a persecuted minority, in fact monotheists are the majority in the West now, and are in a position to dominate, if not persecute, polytheists.

In many cases historically, clinging to polytheist traditions has been part of an overt or covert resistance to power. We see it in the case of the First People, the Native Americans threatened with extermination and extinction, who continue to fight for sacred lands and rights to traditional secret rituals in a world that has little patience for their claims to priority in the Americas. Scott, in *The Art of Not Being Governed,* describes forms of resistance to hegemonic power in what he calls "Zomia," upland southeast Asia:

> Most, if not all the characteristics that appear to stigmatize hill peoples—their location at the margins, their physical mobility, their swidden agriculture, their flexible social structure, their religious heterodoxy, their egalitarianism, and even the nonliterate, oral cultures—far from being the mark of primitives left behind by civilization, are better seen on a long view as adaptations designed to evade both state capture and state formation (Scott, 9).[16]

Although the forms of religious heterodoxy Scott describes include prophecy and millennarianism, the pattern of resistance to hegemonic states has at times taken the form of polytheism.

The history of the Virgin of Guadalupe in Mesoamerica presents a fascinating example of the persistence of polytheism in the form of goddess worship, which has a strong presence also in the U.S., wherever there are immigrants from Mexico. The invasion by Cortes and the conquest of Mexico brought Christian missionaries in its wake, and the military order of the New Spain enforced a religious order in Christianity. The Catholic Church exerted intense effort to eradicate what the missionaries condemned as idolatry in the polytheism and the veneration of many gods in religious ceremonies that disturbed the invading priests. There were some exceptions to the brutal imposition of colonial power, the Franciscan Sahagun and the Dominican Bartolomé de las Casas, among others, who sometimes tried in their writings to align native beliefs and gods with those of the ancient Greeks and Romans and who began to some extent to attempt to defend the indigenous people against the military. More commonly the conquered peoples were drawn into a compulsory worship of the Catholic god(s).

The virgin of Guadalupe appeared to the Aztec Juan Diego on December 9, the day of the Christian feast of the Immaculate Conception of Mary, in 1531, on a hill in the Tepeyac desert; she asked him to build a church on the site. The apparition came just ten years after the conquest, on a site where the Aztecs had worshipped their Tonantzin, "revered mother," a name ascribed to various female gods. Juan Diego had announced the request for a church to the bishop of the region, who wanted proof of the virgin's appearance. So Juan Diego returned to the spot, told the apparition that he needed evidence, and she told him to turn around. He found roses growing in the desert behind him, roses that he cut and took to the bishop. When he opened his cloak to deliver them, it bore an image of the virgin among the flowers. When confronted with a church honoring the virgin Mary, which had replaced their temple to Tonantzin, the inhabitants continued to address her by the name of their goddess. According to the tradition, the apparition had told Juan Diego her name in Nahuatl, Coatlaxopeuh, "the serpent-crusher"; her blue-green garment is said to be of the color reserved for the divine couple Ometecuhtli and Omecihuatl. But the Spanish interpreted her name as "Guadalupe," an echo of the name of the Extremadura Mary from the Spanish region of Hernan Cortes himself. This dark-skinned virgin, said to have been carved as a statue by Luke the evangelist himself, dug up by a peasant in the fourteenth century, had been credited with aiding the Christians' efforts in the Reconquista, the expulsion of the Muslims from Spain. She was then enlisted to help in the conversion of the native Americans encountered by the Spanish invaders of the sixteenth century. Although doubts sprang up about the very existence of Juan Diego, doubts that persisted for centuries, Saint Juan Diego Cuauhtlatoatzin was canonized by the Roman Catholic Church in 2002.[17]

In 1981 members of the French archaeological and ethnological mission in Mexico wrote:

Among the Maya in the south of Yucatan, fierce resistance to the invaders and their religion was sustained until the end of the seventeenth century and left scars still visible today. The superficial character of the evangelization, which spread rapidly throughout the Americas, led to inevitable rearrangements.[18]

The authors point to permeability between the sun god of the Huichol people and Jesus and resistance among the Maya, who preserve their cycle of rain gods into the present. "The open confrontation between the two religions is still at issue, resulting in situations of rejection . . . or precarious equilibrium" (*Mission archéologique*, 46). We see the vestiges of this resistance in the autobiographical text of the Nobel Prize winner Rigoberta Menchu who, although a practicing Catholic, writes in a veiled way about still-secret practices of her transnational Maya people, who continue to protect their ancient religious beliefs from the domination of the colonizers' religion and the genocidal attacks of their descendants in Guatemala.[19] In Mexico, "in the present-day indigenous cosmologies, the vision of the sun-moon duality is an extension of the tradition of a couple with antagonistic and complementary principles, characterized as Grandfather and Grandmother (Quiche), Father and Mother (Tarascan), Son and Mother (Tzotzil) or more conventionally Husband and Wife (Yucatan, Oaxaca, central high plateau)."[20] There is intense resistance to abandoning the female divinity. Goddess worship persists in the syncretism, the mixture, between indigenous religious beliefs and Catholicism: "the lines between the religion of the Indians and the popular faith of the *mestizos* (whose worship of the Virgin of Guadalupe is a living symbol of syncretism) are very often difficult to recognize. Mexican Catholicism is an institution impregnated with Indian religious feeling, and its effects can be felt even in the urban world."[21]

The figure of Jesus was early on, as mentioned above, assimilated to the sun god, and the virgin Mary to the moon, and in the virgin of Guadalupe scholars find "a receptacle of pre-Columbian beliefs about fertility, rain, and the mountains . . . The cult of the saints succeeded the polytheism of earlier times . . ."[22] The male saints were oriented around the sun god, the female saints around the moon goddess. The Matlalzinca people address the moon and the virgin Mary as "our revered mother, the Otomi call the moon "our mother Guadalupe" (*Mission archéologique*, "The Sky," 62).

Another tradition of American belief and worship that includes female divinity goes back to West Africa, including a huge diaspora around the Atlantic Ocean and beyond, of people transported largely by early modern slave trading. As in the case of the preconquest Americas, invasion by colonizers and the need to preserve ancient traditions orally, to protect them from outsiders, resulted in complex fusions of indigenous beliefs and monotheisms, especially proselytizing Islam and Christianity. A vast array of African societies and spiritual practices—including the Yoruba religion, for example, which made its way into the Americas with the captured, sold, stolen people brought in the Middle Passage—recounted in such narratives as that of Olaudah Equiano, published in 1789 in England. Here Equiano tells of his early life in what is now Nigeria (although his birthplace has been subsequently disputed and might have been South Carolina, in the U.S.) and his baptism as a Christian in London.

Many of the religions of Africa posit a single creator god, who made the earth but then withdrew and remains remote; intermediary supernatural beings, divinities, and intercessors provide contact between the creator and human beings. In Nigeria, believers in the Yoruba religion recognize the primacy of the god Olorun, but this creator is said to govern lesser beings, the *orisha,* among them female powers. In the *vodun* (divinities) ceremonies of Benin, worshippers are possessed by supernatural beings who "mount" and "ride" them; these practices accompanied the diaspora and created a fusion of African, Catholic Christian, and indigenous worship in Haiti, as well as other places around the Caribbean, most notably in New Orleans in the southern U.S.

The Yoruba *orishas* are said to line the way to heaven; an individual is linked to a particular *orisha,* who mediates with the higher power(s). The anthropologist Judy Rosenthal describes the flourishing of female spirits in Africa in her wonderful book *Possession, Ecstasy, and Law in Ewe Voodoo.*[23] She visited Mamisi Kokoe in Lome, a priest of Mami Wata, deity of the snake and the rainbow, a white female water god often represented as a mermaid, associated with the arrival of northern peoples to the West African coast, with the virgin Mary, and with "an Indian woman called the woman snake-tamer":

As the years have passed, African, European, and American researchers and friends have complemented her already crowded altars and mirrors with additional images of magical and beautiful women, mermaids, spirits, virgins, Hindu snake tamers, and photographs of the priest with her anthropologists (Rosenthal, 117).

Rosenthal relates a Mami Wata celebration where the worshippers preened themselves, putting on lipstick and powder, pouring on cologne; she likens the *passio* ("ravishment") to that of Yoruban Yemoja, Cuban Yemaya, and other Haitian divinities. The *orishas* traveled with West African slaves to the Caribbean, and their worship there has been called Vodou, and also Santeria, "the way of the saints," the version first established in Cuba.

Santeria connects the Yoruba *orishas* with Roman Catholic saints, *santos,* at times as a form of resistance to official Catholicism, which long sided with a racist and oppressive state. Santeria was often a subversive, underground protest against that state and a preservation of traditions brought with slaves from Africa. In pre-Revolutionary Cuba:

> Folk Catholics, church Catholics, people who practiced the different African religions at home and went to church, people who practiced mixed Afro-Catholic rites exclusively, as well as those who went to church and practiced Espiritismo, or Afro-Catholic-Spiritist religion, all claimed to be Catholic.[24]

The persistence of Santeria became part of the Black Power movement in the African diaspora to North America, and the traditions fragmented, with anti-Castro, black nationalist, and Puerto Rican strains, among others.

In the widely practiced Ifa oracle, the priest divines the future through the examination of sacred palm nuts; other divination processes involve sacrifice to the *orishas,* and often a particular relationship between one *orisha* and an individual, seen as a child of that god. Initiation into the devotion of the *orisha* includes a coronation of the devotee and sometimes produces a trance in which the worshipper becomes a medium for the god as an *olorisha.* The devotees of Santeria also establish relationships with the *orishas,* who guide them in times of trouble, through practices of divination, initiation, possession, and sacrifice. As part of the diaspora of Cubans throughout the U.S., especially to New York City and southern Florida, Santeria has become a significant element of the polytheism of the U.S., with thousands of adherents and chaplains in the U.S. Army and prison systems. As an indication of this polytheist tradition, in a U.S. Supreme Court case handed down in 1993, the right to animal sacrifice was upheld for believers in Santeria (Church of the Lukumi Babalu Aye v. Hialeah). The African heritage of the Yoruba, through Santeria and Vodou, is thus scattered throughout the Caribbean and into the metropolis, in major cities of the U.S., and goddess worship and female *orishas* are central to this tradition.[25]

These female spirits are part of the vast diaspora of West African peoples in the early modern slave trade and persist, thrive, and change throughout the Atlantic world and beyond, having their impact on religious beliefs in Africa as well. Among them is the supernatural being, goddess, spirit, divinity called variously Yemoja in Africa; in Brazilian Candomblé and Umbanda Yemanjá, Iemanjá, Janaína; in Uruguay Iemanjá; in Cuba Yemaya, Yemayah, Iemanya; in Haitian Vodou La Sirène, LaSiren; in the U.S. Yemalla, Yemana, Yemoja. Among the Yoruba in Africa, she is worshipped as a mother goddess, sometimes source of all the other *orishas*, associated with water, especially the river Ogun, and with women, particularly when pregnant.

The worship of the goddess in Brazilian Candomblé and Umbanda illustrates the fusion of her cult with that of the Catholic virgin Mary. She is one of the seven gods of the pantheon, queen of the ocean, sometimes celebrated on the same day as the Catholics' Nuestra Senhora dos Navegantes, "our lady of the sailors," the sailors' saint. In Salvador, in Bahia state, there is a great festival of the goddess, or goddesses, when offerings are left at her shrine in Rio Vermelho. Flowers and cosmetics are taken out to sea by fisherman and cast upon the waters of the Atlantic Ocean. The New Year's Eve celebration in Rio de Janeiro includes a similar celebration on the beach at Copacabana, with fireworks and, again, the casting of flowers into the sea in hopes of a blessing for the year to come from Iemanja. Jorge Amado, who died in 2001, published his novel *Mar Morto* in 1936, depicting the worship of Jemanja by the fishermen of the state of Bahia, Amado's birthplace. In a chapter called "Iemanja of the Five Names," Amado invokes the goddess:

> Iemanja, who is mistress of the docks, of the sloops, of the lives of all of them, has five names, five sweet names that everybody knows. She is called Iemanja, she has always been called that and it is her real name, as mistress of waters, lady of the oceans. Canoemen, however, like to call her Dona Janaina, and the blacks, who are her favorite children, who dance for her

and fear her more than any others, call her Inae, with devotion, or they make their entreaties to the Princess of Aioca, queen of those mysterious lands hidden behind the blue line that separates them from other places. The women of the docks, however, who are simple and valiant, Rosa Palmeirao, women of the evening, married women, virgins awaiting their betrothed, call her Dona Maria, because Maria is a pretty name, it's even the prettiest of them all, the most venerated, and so they give it to Iemanja as a gift, the way they take boxes of soap to her stone by the Dike (Amado, 69).[26]

The goddess is "a siren, mother-of-waters, the mistress of the sea" (Amado, 69).

Amado describes a feast for Iemanja held every year, when she is called by all her names, given gifts, and sung to. All the seas are hers, so her worship is everywhere on the seas. "In ancient times she lived on the coasts of Africa . . . , but she came to Bahia, . . . and she stayed" (Amado, 70). She lives there in a sacred sea stone, and in a grotto at Monte Serrat, and on her feast night, she spreads her hair over the sea. She can be wrathful, accepting human sacrifice, or benign, calming the waters and bringing sailors safe home from their voyages. Raped by her son, she fled, her breasts broke open, and the seas and the bay, Bahia, resulted. Turning their backs on the church at Monte Serrat, the sailors go out in their boats to call Iemanja to them. Amado describes the sacrifice of a blind black horse, driven into the sea as an offering to the goddess; at the *candomblé,* the goddess enters her priestesses and they dance. At the end of the novel, the women are at the helm of the ship, the heroine Livia sailing away to find the body of her beloved Guma, lost at sea, and an old sailor sees Iemanja with them. Decades later, in 1995, Jorge Amado published the novel *O Compadre de Ogum* (the companion of [the god] Ogum), referring to another of the *orixas* who appears in other of Amado's novels (such as *Os Pastores da Noite* [*Shepherds of the Night*], 1964). The transported and transformed gods and goddesses of West Africa continue to survive in the practices and the imagination of the present; in 2011 the popular U.S. vampire television series *True Blood,* set in Louisiana, made reference to "Yemaya" in one episode, when the character Lafayette healed his boyfriend Jesus, nurse and witch, with a blessing from the goddess.

Polytheism persists in the rites of Vodou, Santeria, and Candomblé in which African Americans, now very far, very long removed from West

African roots, have actively created new religious syntheses, preserving polytheism and fusing it with indigenous and Roman Catholic practices. J. Lorand Matory discusses Brazil in the present in his masterly book *Black Atlantic Religion* and describes, not a hermetically sealed Candomblé, the religion once seen as a vestige or remnant of the slave culture of West Africa transferred by the slave trade, but a far-ranging network of dialogue involving Cuba, Manhattan, and Nigeria as well as the eastern coast of Latin America. Slaves were carried across the Atlantic, but even as they developed hybrid, complex fusions of African Yoruba polytheism, in consonance or resistance to Roman Catholicism, after slavery was ended, former slaves and their descendants traveled back to Africa. Merchants, diplomats, and travelers carried on a rich and various set of exchanges in encounters in Africa with British and French colonialists. In the so-called Lagosian Renaissance, forms of nationalism and invented heritage produced discourses that transformed religion and politics in Africa as well as in Brazil and elsewhere in the Americas.

> In functioning diasporic communities (i.e., those whose social order is actively shaped by communication with the "homeland"), religion is the typical social glue, and it can be elaborated in a way enhancing forms of solidarity, hierarchy, and economic interest that would otherwise—under the reign of the multiple, ethnically plural nation-states across which these diasporas are dispersed—be unenforceable. Perhaps religion is the least common denominator among the ties that bind and guarantee the endurance of transnational communities.
>
> Moreover, in secular or constitutionally pluri-religious states, religions are not just a space of allowance that the authorities do not care about controlling; they are the typical symbolical representation of the private organization and reproduction of the diverse classes that necessarily make up the capitalist nation-state and of their profitable connections to the world beyond the nation-state. Yet religiously coded diasporas do not serve the interests of the nation-state alone, and they are often shaped by priorities at odds with those of the nation-states, such as the value that the Jejes and Nagôs of Bahia gave to "African purity" amid elite Euro-Brazilians' embrace of mestiçagem, or "hybridity." Such contradictions reveal that diasporas often possess a relative autonomy of interests, interests that are economically, politically, and socially conditioned.[27]

Matory argues against those who claim that transnationalism is a new phenomenon, the result of a twenty-first century globalization, pointing out that travel back and forth across the Black Atlantic, from Africa to Brazil and the Caribbean and the U.S., has been carried on for centuries, affecting religious, political, and social ideas on all sides of the ocean. He presents arguments, too, against the notion of "diaspora," suggesting that such a model posits a fixed and unchanging point of origin from which dissemination occurs, while in fact "dialogue" better reflects a constant flow in both directions, as in the case, for example, of South Asia and South Asians in Africa, the U.K., and the Americas. One might consider other such networks of translation, mobility, and exchange across vast geographical terrain—the Mediterranean, the silk routes, the Islamic Umma—as networks that become more and more visible as our attention is drawn to such possibilities through the heterogeneity of the present. Often these networks continue to preserve, transform, and enrich traditional polytheistic religious practices.

In the diaspora of East Asians to the U.S., prominent among many goddesses is the Chinese Guanyin (or Guanshiyin), known as Kannon in Japan. She has an extraordinary history, living through a gender transformation, having begun as a masculine avatar of the Buddha, Avalokiteshvara. She is the one who hears the cries of the world, a goddess of compassion and mercy; the bodhisattva in the Indian tradition was an awakened being who postpones nirvana, and obliteration and comes to earth, compassionately, in order to assist suffering human beings. The Tibetan savior goddess Tara is sometimes seen as the female counterpart of Avalokiteshvara. The change in gender of Guanyin from masculine representations to feminine occurred in China, as Buddhist missionaries carried the new religion eastward; after a period in which the bodhisattva was shown as masculine, then either male or female, she became a female entity, probably in the twelfth century. She is portrayed as a mother goddess, a guardian of mothers and of sailors, and is often today shown in white robes. She is said to escort the dead to the "pure land" in the Pure Land sect of Mahayana or "great vehicle" Buddhism, brought by missionaries north and east from India. Pure Land adherents believe in salvation, that worshippers can achieve release from suffering in a single lifetime. The goddess of mercy and compassion can assist them in their efforts to escape from the turning wheel of *samsara,* or rebirth. The goddess was incorporated into Chinese Taoism as well.[28] In the Philippines, the goddess Guanyin has been identified by devotees with the Roman Catholic virgin Mary.

Although the Greek Titan Prometheus is not part of a pantheon of living gods, many other such tricksters, or benefactors of human beings at the expense of the other gods, do receive recognition and offerings, if not worship, from believers. In Africa, the god Legba is a trickster or culture hero like Prometheus, who stole fire to aid human beings. Legba makes trouble, disrupts harmonious situations, and is regarded as a divinity with transformative powers, like the Greek Hermes, a guardian of boundaries and frontiers. As a translator, he communicates what are otherwise seen as indecipherable messages of the great god and benefits human beings through these acts of mediation. Like the angels of Islam, he is a necessary feature of the supernatural world.

Legba survived the Middle Passage, the horrific transport of Africans across the Atlantic Ocean to slavery in the Americas. As Papa Legba, he is a central figure in Haitian Vodou, preserving his position as a mediator between human worshippers and the world of the gods. Speaking in all the languages of human beings, he guards the entrance to the *loa,* the "spirits," and allows the living to communicate with the dead. He is the gatekeeper, god of the crossroads. The great blues artist Robert Johnson was said in one version of the story to have met Legba at a crossroads in Mississippi, and to have sold his soul to the god, in exchange for musical genius; Papa Legba is invoked in the great film *I Walked with a Zombie,* produced by Val Lewton and released in 1943, during World War II.[29] The science-fiction writer William Gibson, in his *Sprawl* trilogy, uses the figure of Legba to guard the portal to cyberspace.

In the Vodou tradition, Baron Samedi, "Baron Saturday," god of the cemetery, mediator between the living and the dead, resembles a satanic god, with a great potential for mischief. He is the *loa,* the *orisha* of the dead; another name he bears is "Baron Kriminel." The Baron appears nattily dressed, as if ready for burial, with a skull for his head, wearing a top hat and a tuxedo, sometimes in dark glasses. He is not only the god who accepts the dead into the underworld by digging their graves, but he is also a god of sex, associated with the phallus, and of healing, the escape from death. He protects corpses in the earth, allowing them to rot so that they are not resurrected as zombies. He smokes cigars, drinks rum, cheats on his wife

Maman Brigitte, and is rowdy, obscene, and debauched. In Neil Gaiman's novel *American Gods,* the baron appears as Mr. Saturday.

In northern America, despite the many centuries of willed destruction of their polytheist traditions, native peoples, the records of observers, and other evidence reveal a vast network of polytheist beliefs. Scholars estimate that there may have been as many as three hundred indigenous languages at the time when Europeans invaded the North American continent, belonging to thirty to fifty distinct language families, and each of these language groups had its own relationships with the supernatural. These are often what might be called "pantheistic," in that the whole of nature—the earth itself, its plants and animals, including human beings—is seen as sacred. Even more sacred are the spirits of the dead, of animals, and sometimes of specific divinities, often seen in the guise of animals or birds. The role of gods is very different from that in some other traditions; this is a more holistic understanding of the divinity of all reality, but also of another reality beyond that accessible in the ordinary course of life.

One such god, sometimes seen as the first human being, but with supernatural powers, both ridiculed and honored in some native American communities, is Coyote. The trickster as culture hero is among the most popular characters in north American mythology, appearing not only as the coyote, but also as a crow, mink, jay, or magpie. This supernatural being takes on the mission of traversing the whole world and has numerous adventures, some of them erotic. Coyote is an ambiguous character, both dupe and trickster, humble and pretentious, altruistic and selfish, a creator and destroyer, and the stories told of him contain riotously comic moments. One Winnebago trickster has a long conversation with a tree branch, which he thinks is a man's arm.

Coyote has captured the modern imagination and appears in many forms in popular culture, in animated cartoons as the character Wile E. Coyote and as a character in novels. The passers of people across the border from Mexico to the U.S. are called "coyotes"; they exhibit the inventiveness and duplicity of the trickster and culture hero of the gods of the American Southwest. In one story collected from the Blackfoot tribe in North America, recounted in *American Indian Trickster Tales,* Old Man Coyote and Coyote Woman meet and discover that they are carrying compatible genitals in their medicine bags. They decide the most convenient place to put them is between their legs, and then that they fit together very nicely. Maybe this would be a way to make human beings, they agree, since the two find the world rather boring. Together they concoct the shape of human faces, eyes and mouths going crosswise, and the allotment of tasks, the men hunting, the women cooking. Coyote Woman says, "I think that the men should pretend to be in charge and that the women should pretend to obey, but that in reality it should be the other way around." Old Man Coyote disagrees, so they decide to wait and see. The story ends, neatly, with Coyote Woman saying to Old Man Coyote, "And why don't you stick that funny thing of yours between my legs again?"[30]

There were often courageous and resistant underground rites performed at great risk to honor traditional gods in the face of violent attempts to conquer indigenous American peoples, to convert Africans to Christianity and to enforce monotheism on slave populations. The continuity with the African polytheist past is part of the African diaspora, or "dialogue," to use Matory's preference, a form of resistance to homogenization, a powerful sign of allegiance to a lost world and to the creation of alternatives to assimilation. The adoption of beliefs tied to the polytheism of Africa has figured in black power movements in recent times, and the return to these beliefs persists in African and Caribbean communities and in sites of resistance, such as the many prisons of the U.S., where African Americans represent a hugely disproportionate number of prisoners, not only in the southern states, but throughout the country. The persistence of traditional forms of worship in indigenous American contexts has also met with tremendous obstacles, as the conquering power continues to limit and eradicate native Americans' access to their ancestral lands and sacred spaces, and has refused to surrender precious relics now housed in museums. Native children have been taken from their families, and placed in orphanages and schools; there have been long-lasting policies of forced conversion to Christianity. Yet polytheistic forms of worship and belief have survived.

INDIA

Another case of polytheism as resistance concerns the people of India. In the face of Islamic invasion and domination of the subcontinent in the Delhi Sultanate beginning in the thirteenth century and in the Mughal empire from the seventeenth to the nineteenth centuries, many polytheists of various tendencies held on to traditional beliefs and practices. Although the Muslims were not bent on missionary work and conversion, it was often politically, socially, and economically advantageous for "Hindus" to convert to Islam. The sometimes inchoate, highly various, and regionally diverse beliefs of the indigenous people of India are sometimes said to have coalesced into "Hinduism" in part because of the invasion of the Islamic monotheists, whose forms of religious worship contrasted with the tolerance and openness of the Indian world. It was through contact with these invading monotheists that the people of India came to see themselves most definitely and defiantly as polytheists, and even as Hindus, holding on resolutely to their Vedic, Vedantic, Saivist, Vaishnavist, and local diversity in the face of a more monolithic imperial presence. The sultans and the emperors of Islamic India, although they tolerated and even patronized some cults, such as the Jains, and married into Indian families, nonetheless found the monotheism of Islam more compatible with imperial rule.

In the face of subsequent invasions, commercial and then military, the people of India again braced themselves in resistance to monotheism. The early missionaries, Jesuits, for example, who arrived on the west coast, sought to convert "Hindus" to Christianity and, according to Samuel Purchas, as noted in the introduction to this book, from the Protestant perspective exposed the intrinsic paganism and polytheism of Catholicism with their indulgence of Indian analogies to their form of Christianity.

Paul Axelrod and Michelle Fuerch, in their account of sixteenth-century Hindu resistance to Christianity, list

> several well-known and oft-told lessons about Hinduism in Goa. Like those Muslim rulers in India who pursued policies of forced conversions, the Portuguese mistakenly believed that they could eliminate Hinduism by destroying the temples, implementing draconian conversion policies, and systematically discriminating against Hindus. But more than 450 years after the Portuguese attempted to remove every vestige of Hinduism from Goa, it remains, in transformed but remarkably vibrant form (Axelrod and Fuerch, 391–392).[31]

Axelrod and Fuerch note how the *Konkanakhyana,* an eighteenth century Marathi language chronicle of the Saraswat Brahmans in Goa, celebrates the escape of the Hindus' deities from the areas of Portuguese control. It

tells of the "calamitous happenings in Goa's most important villages" at
the hands of the "filthy Europeans" and the ensuing relocation of the gods
from their sacred places (Axelrod and Fuerch, 392). The gods were taken to
Muslim or Hindu areas and protected from the Christians, "the defiled for-
eigners" (Axelrod and Fuerch, 392). Festivals still performed in the temples
of West India commemorate the escape and survival of the deities. A semi-
circle of these temples surrounds the terrain of Goa, in which the Portuguese systematically destroyed the Hindus' temples and attempted to force
conversion. A letter from the viceroy of Goa, from 1580, relates that "Hindus set a bad example for new converts by worshipping idols and causing
them to return to their old ways and rituals. The Hindus persevere in their
idolatry and abominable errors. Anyone who impedes the work of conversion should be seriously punished. They cannot be allowed to have idols nor
carry out festivals in their honor" (Axelrod and Fuerch, 412). The authors
note the irony that a decree insisting on these prohibitions and punishments
was reissued in 1633. Using language that recalls the struggle in the Hebrew
Bible between idolators and monotheists, the Portuguese king continues
to ban polytheist temples, ceremonies, rituals, and festivals. Hindus were
forced to conduct wedding rituals on boats, in the dark of night. And the
Hindus fled, with gods and rituals, to "the land of the Moors." Two hundred fifty persons attacked by tigers while marching south in 1566, when
asked why they were leaving the security of Goa, replied that "nothing was
more dear to them than their religion and that they would never leave their
dearest and the best Hindu religion. It did not matter if they had to die
for this" (Axelrod and Fuerch, 417). Although there is syncretism between
Catholicism and Hinduism in Goa today, the struggle of the polytheists
to maintain their religious practices resulted in a truce rather than in the
triumphalist victory narrated by the Catholics concerning this period and
their successful conversion of the region.

Later British missionaries, military personnel, and civil servants arrived,
also with conversion to Christianity in mind, and again, Hinduism became
a form of national resistance to domination by the British.[32] Current-day
Hindu nationalists of India have at times encouraged the violent persecution of Indian monotheists, Muslims and Christians, yet in the past, multireligious nationalism was a crucial instrument of resistance to colonialism
and occupation by the British. Gandhi, the Mahatma, for example, born
in British India, led the Indian independence movement of the twentieth

century as a Hindu and a nationalist, yet always insistent on the need to promote the ancient principles of *ahimsa,* "nonviolence," and *satyagraha,* "devotion, holding to the truth," to other Indian sects, including the Jains, Sikhs, Buddhists, Muslims, and Christians. Late in his life, when he was asked whether he was a Hindu, he replied, "Yes I am. I am also a Christian, a Muslim, a Buddhist and a Jew."[33] Gandhi's movement for Indian independence was, in this sense, an imagination of cohabitation, profoundly polytheist, and equally resistant to the continuing presence of the colonial British government in India.[34]

Dipesh Chakrabarty locates the prejudice against polytheism in the history of India and its troubled relationship to waves of colonizers:

> My contention is that scientific rationalism, or the spirit of scientific enquiry, was introduced into colonial India from the very beginning as an antidote to (Indian) religion, particularly Hinduism, which was seen, both by missionaries as well as by administrators—and in spite of the Orientalists—as a bundle of "superstition" and "magic." Hinduism, wrote the Scottish missionary Alexander Duff in 1839, is "a stupendous system of error" (Chakrabarty, 259).[35]

The greatest, most populous and thriving polytheism of the present is this religion of South Asia, often called "Hinduism," a name given by others to the texts, rituals, and beliefs transmitted from the seers of the Vedas. Hindu is merely the name first used by Persian geographers to refer to people living on the "other" side of the Indus River.[36] A handy instrument of colonialism, which sought to divide up communities of monotheists from polytheists and convert the latter if possible, it is nonetheless often used by adherents themselves, worshippers of the many gods, and the few gods, and the one, of the surviving Vedic tradition.

It is impossible in such a short space to take in, to describe, to appreciate the vastness of the history of these beliefs. But for those who argue that so-called monotheism, or even ethical monotheism, is the *telos,* the goal, the final end of religious developments from the primitive to the enlightened, one only has to point to Hindu polytheism, the complex, sprawling, incredibly rich practices and beliefs of the people of India and their diaspora. India is the most populous democracy on earth, the site of extraordinary technological development, full of contradictions, village slaves as well as global billionaires, but not by any stretch of the imagination at an "earlier" stage of religious development than the Abrahamic monotheisms. The most sophisticated metaphysical, theological speculations, advanced mathematics, cosmological reflection on earth have taken place, and continue to take place in the great cosmopolis of Hinduism.

There are many sacred texts in the Hindu tradition, dating back to the *Rig Veda,* the hymns of praise to the earliest gods. These magnificent hymns were communicated to the *rshis,* the seers, and record the beliefs of the Aryan people who shared aspects of their culture with the Iranians, and who may have entered the Indian subcontinent around 1500 BCE. The hymns speak of devotion to many gods, and to ceremonies and sacrifices performed in their honor. In this magnificent hymn to Usas, goddess of the dawn, for example, she is asked to bring abundance to those who worship her, as she harnesses horses or cows to her chariot:

> See how the dawns have set up their banner in the eastern half of the sky,
>   adorning and anointing themselves with sunlight for balm. Unleashing
>   themselves like impetuous heroes unsheathing their weapons, the tawny
>   cows, the mothers, return.
> The red-gold lights have flown up freely; they have yoked the tawny cows
>   who let themselves be yoked. The dawns have spread their webs in the
>   ancient way; the tawny ones have set forth the glowing light . . .
> Like a dancing girl, she puts on bright ornaments; she uncovers her
>   breast as a cow reveals her swollen udder. Creating light for the whole
>   universe, Dawn has opened up the darkness as cows break out from
>   their enclosed pen.
> Her brilliant flame has become visible once more; she spreads herself
>   out, driving back the formless black abyss. As one sets up the stake in
>   the sacrifice, anointing and adorning it with coloured instruments,
>   so the daughter of the sky sets up her many-coloured light (*Rig Veda,*
>   179–180).[37]

The hymn goes on to describe the rich gifts of the goddess, and asks for more: "Harness your red-gold horses now, O prize-giving Dawn, and bring all good fortunes to us" (*Rig Veda,* 180). This hymn exhibits the Vedic qualities of heat generated, of bounty and excess and proliferation, of eroticism and joy in the natural world that the Dawn brings with her, reborn each day. Another hymn: "Sky and earth that stream with honey, that are milked of honey, that have honey for their vow, let them soak us with honey, bringing sacrifice and wealth to the gods, great fame, the victory prize, and virility to us" (*Rig Veda*, 206). Other gods are invoked, among them: Agni the fire of sacrifice; the hallucinogenic drink Soma; Indra, releaser of the trapped waters; gods of the storm; Surya, the sun; Varuna, sky god like the Greek Ouranos, watcher and judge; Rudra, kept outside the sacrifice, a predecessor to the non-Vedic god Shiva; Vishnu, connected to the power of the sun, benign, a benefactor of human beings, much more important in later worship than at the time of the Vedas. Some of these gods, like Varuna, recede into the background, never lost in this tradition, but added to in a great dynamism of accretion. There are other Vedas, and later texts that modify and elaborate on these earliest songs.

Some of the *Upanishads,* subsequent spiritual treatises, may go back as far as 800 BCE; they represent further developments from the time of the *Rig Veda,* meditations on the nature of reality that transcend the performance of ritual sacrifices to particular divinities, although the many gods are present in these texts as well. The *atman,* the individual spirit, is akin to, part of, *brahman,* the transcendent reality, like salt dissolved in water. The sage Yajnavalkya, when asked by a seeker after truth how many gods there are, responds:

> "Three and three hundred, and three and three thousand."
>
> "Yes, of course," he said, "but really, Yajnavalkya, how many gods are there?"
>
> "Thirty-three."
>
> "Yes, of course," he said, "but really, Yajnavalkya, how many gods are there?"
>
> "Six."
>
> "Yes, of course," he said, "but really, Yajnavalkya, how many gods are there?"
>
> "Two."
>
> "Yes, of course," he said, "but really, Yajnavalkya, how many gods are there?"
> "One and a half."
>
> "Yes, of course," he said, "but really, Yajnavalkya, how many gods are there?"
>
> "One."[38]

Hinduism can be seen as a monism, in which all the many divinities are seen as but aspects or manifestations of a single transcendent being, as ultimately a monotheism, and/or as made up of what some scholars have termed "heno-theisms," the focus on a single god among many, a "kathenotheism," the shifting and intermittent and temporary centering on one of many gods, and/or as a polytheism, a term that acknowledges the existence, recognition of, and devotion to many gods. The Upanishadic speculations on the nature of reality have also been seen as pantheism, in which everything is god, or "panentheism," in which godhood penetrates the universe but is also greater than that universe (Doniger, 174). As Wendy Doniger points out, from the time of the *Rig Veda,* the "creative tension between monism and polytheism extends through the history of Hinduism" (Doniger, 128).

In the history of this tradition, sacrificial practices performed by Brah-mins, priests of the highest class, were supplemented over time by an inter-nal sacrifice, a belief in individual practice and contemplation. Later there evolved an intense set of devotions directed toward the particular gods, some inherited from the earliest Vedic traditions, others not. There are thousands of gods, children of the gods, different manifestations of the gods, local gods the objects of intense devotion. The principal divinities became the goddess, Devi; Shiva, not part of the Vedic world, although he may have been anticipated in the figure of Rudra; and Vishnu, who notably manifested himself in his avatars (incarnations or manifestations among human beings) Rama and Krishna. Rama is the hero of one of the two great epics of this tradition, the *Ramayana;* he is benefactor of humankind, ruling a golden age, the Rama-raj, and ridding the world of an evil creature, the ten-headed demon-king of Lanka, called Ravana.[39] Rama himself, born to a mortal woman, is deified and worshipped, as is Krishna, another avatar of Vishnu. Krishna appears in the *Bhagavad-Gita,* a passage in the other great epic song of the Vedic tradition, the *Mahabharata.* If the *Ramayana* is a complex tale of rulership, of marital love between Rama and his wife Sita, of conquest over evil, and of the lost perfections of a golden age, the *Mahabharata* tells a darker story, of the end of a cycle in time, of the horrors of war and the killing of one's own kind. In the *Bhagavad-gita,* "the Song of the Lord," perhaps inserted into the longer epic song, the charioteer (and therefore bard) Krishna counsels the warrior Arjuna concerning his *dharma,* his duties, his place in the class system, in a moment that stops time on the battlefield. He leads the human being through a series of teachings, and at Arjuna's request, reveals himself as not just Krishna the charioteer, but as Vishnu himself, in a glorious scene of theophany, the god on earth. Krishna is transformed before Arjuna's eyes into Vishnu; Krishna gives Arjuna a divine eye with which to see reality and reveals to the man the true majesty of the god's form; he is all the gods, Vishnu, Indra, Shiva, "the eternal syllable, OM," Himalaya, "I am the great ritual chant, the meter of sacred song." The battlefield is here not just the literal place of war, but also the self, the plain but also the plane on which all mortal beings must struggle. Krishna reveals not just the duties of the warrior class and the need to accomplish one's actions according to one's class position, without attachment to their outcome, but also the ultimate nature of reality, the multiplicity of gods and their mutual implication, and, finally, anticipating a new understanding of worship that goes beyond sacrifice, the need for human beings to show devotion to their gods.

Dharma, the duties, truth, right path, good life, evolved over time, and also in relation to gender, class, ethnicity, and stage of life. The worship of the gods also developed over many centuries, from the Vedic divinities, to the many gods in the *Puranas,* to a highly elaborated "sectarian" worship of Shiva, Vishnu, Devi, and other, more local gods. Devotees favored particular gods among the pantheon and honored them with pilgrimages and *puja,* sacred offerings. Such devotion increased and became ever more focused in *bhakti,* supremely personal and intense commitment to a god. It is impossible to describe them all, or to give an account of the great proliferation over time. I just want to point to some fascinating features of this polytheism— Tantrism, the worship of the savior-killer Shiva, the ambiguous nature of goddesses, the ways in which Hinduism incorporates and complicates all the examples of divinity listed earlier in this chapter, the goddesses, the trickster-helpers, the gods of evil. Almost anything one says about Hinduism is both true but in other cases not true.

As for *dharma,* the Tantric tradition urges the violation of all the rules. In this "left-hand" practice, devotion requires experimenting with the caste laws in order to achieve nirvana, sensual delight in spiritual release. In the five "M"s, that is, five Sanskrit words beginning with the letter M, worshipers are said to commit prohibited acts, to consume wine, eat meat, fish, and farina, and fornicate. In the five "Jewels," they are said to have consumed semen, urine, feces, menstrual blood, and phlegm, violating the laws of purity and reveling in the forbidden. Although there is some doubt about whether these rules were ever followed to the letter, the Tantric texts nonetheless encourage transgression (Doniger, 419–444).

The worship of the Vedic gods changed with the incorporation of other divinities, and the pantheon shifted over time. Shiva became a major divinity, an ascetic, like the long-haired rider of the wind in the *Rig Veda* (10.136), sitting in the mountain, receiving the goddess Ganga, the river Ganges, in his great mass of hair, to break her fall as she came down from heaven to benefit human beings. He is savior and destroyer, the bearer of skulls. He is associated with forms of asceticism, of renunciation, that accompany and challenge the orderly management of householder life. He is the dark outsider Rudra who becomes a central figure, object of intense devotion in the sectarian opposition between Vaishnava and Shaivist traditions, a god who appears as the *lingam,* the phallus, as lord of the dance, as the braided-haired one, as destroyer and savior, patron of the outsiders, of ashes and cremation-ground asceticism, a great yogi, god of ten thousand names, patron of Varanasi (Benares), where the *lingam* broke through the surface of the earth.

The goddesses emerged as powers in their own right, with their own devotees, in shaktiism. Some consorts of the gods, some not, they have been seen as divided into goddesses "of the tooth" and "of the breast."[40] The great all-encompassing goddess, Devi, has many aspects, some of them benign, generous, maternal, some of them violent, frightening, and intimidating. Parvati is the loving consort of Shiva; Chandika-Durga, a goddess with a great many teeth; Santoshi Mata, a maternal and benevolent force made newly popular by a mythological, or theological, a film from 1975 depicting her birth from the elephant-headed god Ganesha; and Kali, the black outer skin of Parvati, the dark goddess riding on a lion, the ultimate figure of destruction and chaos.

The great Bengali writer Rabindranath Tagore, engaged in a struggle against the partition of his people, wrote nationalist poetry in which he personified the land of Bengal as Durga herself, and as the goddess Lakshmi:

> In your fields, by your rivers, in your thousand homes set deep in the mango groves, in your pastures whence the sound of milking arises, in the shadow of the banyan, in the twelve temples besides the Ganges, O ever-gracious Lakshmi, O Bengal my mother, you go about your endless chores day and night with a smile on your face (Chakrabarty 172).[41]

The land itself is a goddess, several goddesses. As Dipesh Chakrabarty points out, Tagore was not an "idol-worshipper," as he and family belonged to a group called "Brahmos," who had repudiated such practices; yet he used the term *murati* as he represented Bengal as the goddess Durga, meaning not "form," but "a material form of embodiment or manifestation," according to Chakrabarty, who interprets Tagore's gesture as a nationalist "seeing beyond," resistant to historicization, deploying "the real, shared practices sedimented in the language itself" (Chakrabarty, 173). In Chakrabarty's argument, such a use of language goes beyond the Western subject's subject-centered perspective, to a heterogeneous, I would say polytheist imagination, implicit in the vocabulary of a political nationalism.

Eventually, other divinities were assimilated into the Hindus' understanding of the sacred. Wendy Doniger recalls that:

> In a move reminiscent of the ambiguous positioning of the Buddha as an avatar of Vishnu, Jesus became one of the avatars in a Christian tract published in Calcutta (and written in Oriya) in 1837, warning the reader that the deity worshiped in the Jagannatha Temple at Puri in Orissa was a degenerate form of the true Jagannatha and exhorting the pilgrim to Puri to "remain a Hindu and also believe in Christ," who is, by implication, the true Jagannatha (Doniger, 585).

There are important theological strains, the dualist/anti-dualist debates among Vedanta teachers, who in general understand themselves to be worshippers of Vishnu, Shankara (788–820 CE), Ramanuja (1017–1137 CE), and Madhva (thirteenth century CE). And there are many other crucial matters in the study of Hindus' practices and beliefs, including ideas about class, caste, and various yogic traditions, festivals of local divinities as well as the great gods of the pantheon. But in terms of this study of the many gods, Hinduism stands alone with its embrace of multiple divinities, pantheism, panentheism, dualism, monism, all of which coexist in a magnificent luxury of sacredness.

Alain Daniélou, author of the text *Hindu Polytheism,* responded to the assumptions of the West concerning the prejudice against polytheism, and the condescension toward Hinduism in particular:

> In our time monotheism is often considered a higher form of religion than polytheism. . . . In the polytheistic religion each individual worshiper has a chosen deity [*ista-devata*] and does not usually worship other gods in the

same way as his own, as the one he feels nearer to himself. Yet he acknowledges other gods, . . . always ready to acknowledge the equivalence of these
deities as the manifestations of distinct powers springing from an unknowable "Immensity" (Daniélou, 8–9).[42]

He is critical of monotheism, for the "precarious equilibrium" of the monotheist, who projects his own individuality into the cosmic sphere, and thus
locates his own habits, his customs, his ideals, in his god. "Religion becomes
a means of glorifying his culture or his race, or of expanding his influence
. . . We can see all monotheistic religions fighting to impose their god and
destroy other gods" (Daniélou,10). Hindu polytheism, on the other hand,
"acknowledges all gods" as "but aspects of the divine power" (Daniélou,12).
Wendy Doniger, in *The Hindus: An Alternative History,* argues that the
Vedas are "intolerant of intolerance." "The Veda shows a tolerance, a celebration of plurality, even in asking unanswerable questions about the beginnings of all things" (Doniger, 129).

Some Hindus argue that Hinduism is the religion of the Indian subcontinent, the only religion of this place, and that this place is the only site of true
Hinduism. Yet in the great diaspora, or "dialogue," to use Matory's term,
of Hindu people's migration and return to other parts of Asia, to Africa,
Europe and the Americas, the gods accompany the migrants. In 2012, with
my friend Kate, I visited the Sri Swami Swaminarayan Mandir, a temple
compound in Neasden in greater London, a part of the Bochasanwasi Shri
Akshar Purushottam Swaminarayan Sanstha (BAPS) organization, which
organized the construction of a complex of buildings paid for by donations
and inaugurated in 1995. The temple itself, built entirely of stone, rather than
being remodeled from other uses, is an extraordinary structure that dramati-
cally changes the landscape and the skyline of the London borough of Brent.
It is as if a Hindu Taj Mahal had been built, brand new, in the middle of an
old English parking lot. The first site of worship of this group was established
in 1970 in a converted church in the north London neighborhood of Isling-
ton; the community outgrew the space and eventually decided to embark on
this project of construction. The temple, made of Italian marble and Bul-
garian limestone, was carved by artists in India, in a workshop devoted to
the task, and is elaborately adorned with delicate, intricate stonework. It
features seven pinnacles, with golden spires and golden domes. The members
of the community assembled the temple themselves as a giant puzzle. Under

each of the pinnacles is a shrine devoted to a particular divinity, attended to by holy men who live in the complex's ashram. Against the backdrop of gleaming Italian marble, the sacred images of this sect, set in dioramas and colored brilliant red, orange, and green, command the visitor's attention. The shrines resemble caves, the pinnacles the mountains of India, associated with holy ascetics. Intricately carved columns show the traditional gods of Hinduism, including Lakshmi, Ram, Krishna, Hanuman, Shiva, and Parvati. If the many, often immense, and now disused Christian churches of Northern Europe, in the Netherlands, Scandinavia, and Britain, are being repurposed, turned into community centers, and in general no longer welcoming the congregations that supported their construction in the medieval period and later, this amazing religious edifice shows the energy and devotion of a passionately committed community to its sacred traditions.

There is also a restaurant, a souvenir shop, an assembly hall, and a permanent exhibition on "Understanding Hinduism," with crafts, paintings, dioramas, and other instructive material, to introduce visitors to the history and traditions of the Hindus. The magazine *Time Out* listed the temple as one of the seven wonders of London in 2007, along with Kew Gardens, the St. Pancras train station, and the Hoover Vacuum building; it attracts many tourists as well as worshippers from the Hindu immigrant community, thousands of whom live in the vicinity. Hinduism, the greatest polytheism on earth today, is alive and flourishing not only in India, but also in an immense diaspora.

POLITICS OF COHABITATION

To acknowledge the openness of the Hindu tradition to new sites, to difference, to new gods, to the multiplication of divinities as well as to abstract metaphysical speculation is not to say that there is not violence in this tradition—the structural violence of class distinctions, of intolerance of other sects, of resistance to and persecution of the monotheists who seek to judge and identify the Hindus as idolators. But among the most notable of advocates of tolerance in matters of practice and belief is the Indian emperor Ashoka, who attempted to mediate between the Vedic traditions of the world into which he was born and the Buddhist values which he discovered later in life.

Before the time of the great empires, there was little need of pleas for tolerance. Gods were local, acknowledged by all, and there was often an interested, almost anthropological tendency to name the gods of others with the names of one's own gods, to find correspondences among pantheons, to "translate the names." With the growth of archaic empires that conquered and absorbed what had once been distinct societies, with their own gods, ideologies were promulgated that attempted to unify all of the inhabitants of an empire under a monarch, a single ruler whose right to legitimacy was often said to be the sign of the many gods' favor. So the pharaoh of Egypt was a ruler-king, his sovereignty justified by his earthly existence as the embodiment of Osiris, god of the underworld, guarantor of the regular flooding and receding of the great river Nile, one of the deities of an extended pantheon.

Some of these great, god-appointed rulers became proponents of openness, urging the comfortable cohabitation of different peoples with their different gods within empire. One of the first may have been the Persian emperor Cyrus, mentioned in Chapter 1. He appears in the Hebrew Bible, in *Isaiah* 40–48, as "the consolation of Israel." This sixth-century BCE founder of the Achaemenid empire freed the Israelite exiles from captivity in Babylon after his conquest of the Babylonians and allowed the exiles to return to Jerusalem. In the Bible Cyrus is called a "messiah," an anointed ruler. His religious policies seem generous in comparison to those of his predecessors, destroyers of the temple of the Israelites; he vaunts his generosity towards the conquered peoples whose cults, temples, and gods he restored:

> Of Nin[eveh], Assur, and also of Susa, of Agade, of Esnunna, of Zamban, of Meturnu and of Der, up to the borders of Gutium, the cult centers beyond the Tigris, whose [cult] structures had long remained in ruins, I returned to their place the gods who lived there and reestablished them for eternity . . . And the gods of Sumer and Akkad whom Nabonidus, to the wrath of the lord of the gods [Marduk], had transported to Babylon, I had them, on the order of Marduk, the great lord, joyfully installed in their cella, in a dwelling for the joy of the heart . . . (Briant, 43).[43]

Following Cyrus's example, the later Persian emperor Darius showed respect for the Egyptian gods after his ascension to the throne. The classical author Diodorus wrote of him that he was so greatly honored that he alone of all the kings was addressed as a god by the Egyptians in his lifetime (*Library of*

History 1.95). As Lindsay Allen points out in a history of the Persian empire: "Persian religious tolerance was a result of an inclusive imperial ideology, but it was a tactic of domination and could still work well for some, harshly for others."[44] Yet the tolerance has led some to see Cyrus as "the inventor of 'human rights'" (Briant, 47).

The great rock inscriptions of the Persians may have inspired another emperor, Ashoka of the Mauryans, himself an advocate of religious tolerance in India. After bloody conquests, and a conversion to Buddhism, Ashoka issued his own rock edicts after 256 BCE. Some of his proclamations suggest a program of mutual understanding among religious sects:

> Asoka's Dharma is broadbased upon the principle of tolerance. The Asokan idea of tolerance differs, however, from the general Indian idea in that it offers a scheme of active co-operation *(samavaya)* among all sects for their growth in essential matters . . . and does not leave any sect to itself under the comfortable belief that all faiths lead ultimately to one and the same goal. It wants all sects and exponents to come together for frank and free interchanges of their thoughts and ideas in a mutually helping spirit. It urges that men of all sects should listen to and study each other's doctrines so that all may be well-informed *(bahusruta)* and possessed of noble traditions.[45]

Ashoka's rock edict thirteen, inscribed after a great victory, reads in part:

> The Brahmanas and Sramanas [the priestly and ascetic orders] as well as the followers of other religions and the householders—who all practiced obedience to superiors, parents, and teachers, and proper courtesy and firm devotion to friends, acquaintances, companions, relatives, slaves, and servants—all suffer from the injury inflicted on their loved ones. . . . [Moreover, there is no country except that of the Yonas (that is, the Greeks), where Brahmin and Buddhist ascetics do not exist] and there is no place where men are not attached to one faith or another.[46]

Ashoka has remorse for his slaughter and urges forgiveness, even as he gently threatens those who do not fall into line with his concept of *dharma*. In Kalinga edict 2, he expresses his commitment to his people: "All men are my children. Just as I seek the welfare and happiness of my own children in this world and the next, I seek the same things for all men" (53). Romila Thapar summarizes his view: "The plea that every sect desires self-control and purity of mind is that of a man who generalizes thus for the sake of a broader principle. Ashoka must have realized the harm that these sectarian conflicts would produce."[47] One of the most remarkable aspects of Ashoka's relationship to diversity is his call for study and knowledge about difference. Ignorance of others' beliefs, or the assumption that they are beneath the surface identical, are unacceptable. His views go beyond pluralism.

A perspective like Ashoka's, or even Cyrus's, may only have become possible in a world in which great empires, built on conquest and domination, brought together many peoples under one sovereign ruler and state. In these circumstances, the value, even necessity of religious tolerance, and in Ashoka's case, going beyond tolerance to knowledge and understanding, even cohabitation, became essential to the internal peace and security of the empire. These rulers acknowledge that sectarian conflicts, hatreds between religious groups, clashes between monotheists and polytheists, erode the happiness and welfare of subjects; they also distract the sovereign from external conflicts, from further conquest and, of course, more and sometimes ruthless efforts at extending territory and bringing ever more human beings under the control of state and ruler. Yet these boasts, or pleas, made long before the enlightenment of the European eighteenth century, offer models of cohabitation that speak to our contemporary situation, in the U.S. and the U.K., of mixture and "living-with" others, many others, with different skin colors, foods, habits, holidays, prohibitions, pleasures, and religious practices and beliefs, both monotheist and polytheist.

There are no states, any longer, in which authoritarian or monarchic rule can control the proliferation of religious beliefs, the many gods of obedient or disobedient subjects and inhabitants. Even in the most repressive nations, as for example in Saudi Arabia, an absolute monarchy, a theocracy with a single religion, where there are no protections for believers of other traditions and the suppression of worship of other gods, including raids on prayer carried out by the "religious police," there are foreign workers from different sects within Islam, and others who profess various versions of Christianity, Roman Catholics, Eastern Orthodox as well as Protestants, and Hindus. There are half a million Hindus, at least, living in Saudi Arabia, and almost that number in the United Arab Emirates, which has allowed the construction of Hindu temples. Oman has traditionally had a strong Hindu presence, going back to trade with India in the Middle Ages. Hinduism was brought to Muscat in 1507. There was once a Hindu quarter in Muscat, and although the numbers have declined, there are active Hindu temples today: the Muthi Shwar temple in Al-Hawshin Muscat, a Shiva temple in Muttrah, and the Krishna temple of Darsait. Here, as elsewhere, there can be prejudice against polytheism, even active persecution of polytheists.

But no ethnic cleansing, no matter how genocidal in its intentions, can succeed in producing a homogeneous population in this world. The nations include subcultures, regional groups, heretics, atheists, populists of a polytheistic bent under a monotheistic official umbrella, as well as traditionally polytheist immigrants. The U.S. Army manual for chaplains, with its supplement for "Certain Selected Groups," serves as an indicator of the great diversity of beliefs in the U.S. The manual lists "Christian Heritage Groups," including "Children of God," the "Holy Order of Mans," the "Mennonite Church." There are various Islamic Groups, among them the Sufi Order; Japanese Heritage Groups, Buddhist and Zen, as well as the "Church of Perfect Liberty." The manual lists several different Jewish groups, as well as "Eckankar," and the "Healthy, Happy Holy Organization." Then there are the "other" groups, among them the American Council of Witches, the Church of Satan, "Gardinerian Wicca," the Rastafarians, the "Universal Church of the Masters," and the "Universal Life Church." Indian Heritage Groups to be taken account by Army chaplains include Sikhs, the "International Society for Krishna Consciousness," and the Satchidananda Ashram-Integral Yoga Institute. These are the groups significant enough in numbers, or in persistence, to have registered on the huge bureaucracy of the United States Army, and there are many, many groups too small, or too resistant to employment in the army, to appear in this official document.

It is not for me, but for courts and legislators to sort out the various claims of those who insist on imposing their religious beliefs on others. But if we define "polytheist" as an adjective meaning "worshipping many gods," the world, its nations, its populations are already polytheist, and the traditions most valued in the development of Western civilization, consciously or not, incorporate elements from a polytheistic past and present. In fact, as I have argued, polytheism is an integral part of the history of the West, of the two strands, "Jerusalem" and "Athens." Polytheism persists not only in traditionally polytheistic societies and their diasporas, but also in the Abrahamic monotheisms. In fact, polytheism may be more consonant with contemporary life, its mixed populations, its recognition of psychic complexity and interdependence, than a rigorous Protestant monotheism, than a traditional fencing off of public and private spheres. If a true pluralism and the separation of "church" and state are incompatible, if a pluralist separation of church and state is an oxymoron, we need to think more about these questions, to privilege not just one tradition, openly or cryptically, but to strive to know more, to live in truly neutral states, and to "cohabitate." Beyond condescending to polytheists, beyond *tolerating* polytheists, the so-called monotheists, the "Christian nations," the U.S. and the U.K., have a great deal to learn from them.

Epilogue

NEIL GAIMAN, author of the graphic novel series *Sandman,* sets his immensely popular novel *American Gods* in an American continent swarming with gods, those of the indigenous people of the Americas and those brought along with the millions of immigrants. From Russian gods, to Mr. Ibis of Egypt, to Mr. Nancy, the West African god Anansi, to Kali, "with her ink-black skin and her white, sharp teeth," to Odin, god of the Norse, they all eventually come together in a great show-down with new gods, like the god of technology, a wired-up fat boy with prosthetic electronic devices hanging off him, "gods of credit card and freeway, of Internet and telephone, of radio and hospital and television, gods of plastic and of beeper and of neon," led by Mr. World. The blood-thirsty Odin, Mr. Wednesday, stages the confrontation, seeking and failing to create a final massacre and to feast on the slaughtered corpses of all the gods in order that he himself survive. The novel ends with a return to everyday life, to a reality still teeming with gods, with the reader newly alert to this American polytheistic landscape.[1]

I grew up in a small city in California, a river port deep in its central valley, where ocean-going cargo ships loaded up with rice and wheat on their way to far-away places, where tomatoes flourished in the sun, where asparagus planted in the alluvial soil of a great delta made the town, in its own view at least, "Asparagus Capital of the World." I realize now that, although I frequently felt oppressed by the dour, puritanical presence of my Congregationalist grandmother and her Midwestern Methodist husband, I was in the midst of full-on polytheism. My father's family, French-speakers, Huguenots, had left Strasbourg when it reverted to Catholic France at the beginning of the twentieth century. My mother abandoned the faith of her fathers, a severe form of Protestant Christianity, marked by New England and the Middle West, and became a devotee of Ramakrishna, a Hindu saint of the nineteenth century who had blended Christian ideas with traditional Hinduism and created a seductive mix of charity, attention to the poor, and forms of meditation that my mother practiced, "religiously." I learned later that the expatriate Christopher Isherwood, transplanted to Hollywood from Berlin and London, was also a devotee of Ramakrishna. The author of *Berlin Stories,* on which *Cabaret* was based, had become a Hinduizing Californian who worshipped at a Vedanta temple in Hollywood. My mother used to venture out from our home to the Vedanta temple in Berkeley for periodic refreshment, since Vedantists like Isherwood were few and far between in the San Joaquin Valley.

One of my friends was the son of a Taoist herbalist, among the wealthiest citizens of our city, descended from immigrants from China who came to Stockton at the time of the gold rush of the 1840s. His son attended "Chinese school" after our regular school days were done, and we visited him at the mung bean factory where he had a temporary job. The factory was in an old building in the city's downtown, richly adorned with ornate gilded beams and what I thought at the time were pagoda roofs. The old Chinese restaurants in this part of town had teak booths, with doors that closed, a mysterious and seemingly exotic feature, as well as altars burning incense to the gods of good fortune.

My best friend took me with her to St. Luke's, the Catholic church she attended, for an annual ceremony called "The Stations of the Cross." We moved around the modest church, stopping at various sites that stood for points on the route of the via Dolorosa in ancient Jerusalem; I recall being unnerved at the time by the sight of both Jesus and his mother with their hearts outside their bodies, bleeding, pierced by arrows. A great number of saints inhabited the building, and Mary especially seemed to me to be a divinity rather than a subordinate to the trinity of father, son, and holy ghost, who to my childish mind seemed like three additional gods rather than three aspects of a one god. I helped Kathy, now Kate, memorize the profoundly mysterious responses in the Baltimore catechism in preparation for various rituals, perhaps her first communion, or her confirmation. The answers to the questions posed, I realize now, represented hard-fought and deeply considered answers to theologically complex questions once fought over in the streets of Antioch, Milan, and Constantinople on the nature of the Christian god, his incarnation, and possible mortality. In her parent's house were images, shrines, various altars, it seemed to me, to the many gods of the Irish Catholics, although her mother, a heavy, anxious smoker, was whispered to be going to hell for having married a divorced and non-Catholic man.

Another close friend took us to his temple, where I conceived a passionate desire to convert to Judaism, given that the town's few intellectuals, psychiatrists, college professors, and other readers of books seemed all to be members there. My friend's family had returned from a more secular Unitarianism to join the small community of Jews. As a teenager I read Leon Uris's novel *Exodus* and found the struggle for the foundation of a new home for the refugees from the European holocaust to be a thrilling narrative, and was for a time an ardent although quite ignorant Zionist. My passion for conversion, though, was thwarted, as the elders of the synagogue gently dissuaded me from my quest. This friend, and my Catholic friend, and I together attended various riotous Christian church events "on the wrong side of the tracks," unbeknownst to our parents, where people of many colors were in turn possessed by the spirit, fell to the ground, writhed and spoke in tongues, as the assembled congregation sang lustily and magnificently. We once went to a tent meeting where an evangelist traveling from Memphis, Tennessee entranced the faithful with electric guitars, where members of the congregation, as if struck by lightning, were suddenly saved and rushed forward to the front of the tent to testify.

There was a Sikh temple in the town, where the worshipers fed the hungry; they had been enlisted by the city to emigrate from India because of their agricultural expertise, especially in rice cultivation, and they gave great feasts for any strangers who cared to enter their temple. Many of my classmates in school came from families that had come long ago, or very recently, from Mexico and Central America, often as farm workers, speaking Spanish at home and learning English at school. The Filipino agricultural laborers in town had their own interpretation of Catholicism, mediated by indigenous traditions brought with them from distant homes. There were other such communities, Greek, Sicilian, and Armenian, with annual festivals, wonderful traditional food, rituals, and ceremonies particular to their heritage. In sum, this was a world full of gods, far from the homogeneous nation founded by the pilgrim fathers, who of course themselves encountered, challenged, and finally almost entirely eliminated the indigenous people, who themselves had many spirits, and gods, and who continue to worship those many gods in the few tiny communities that managed to survive the invasion and occupation by the Protestant refugees.

Now, my Jewish friend is a friend of the Dalai Lama, an interpreter of Buddhist meditation for Americans. When we meet, we discuss whether or not the Buddha, as discerned with greatest difficulty in the earliest recorded teachings, was an atheist, someone much more concerned with attention to one's everyday life than with gods. The Buddha, the awakened one, is said to have said that a man who seeks to know who created him, where he came from, is like a man wounded by an arrow who, instead of focusing on healing his wound, wants to know from what village the arrow-maker came. My Catholic friend lives in London, where one of her closest friends is a Muslim whose daughter first married a Hindu man, and then left him and became a lesbian. My Chinese-American friend is a psychiatrist, still living in Stockton, where the immigrants are no longer just Chinese, Filipino, Sikh, and Mexican, but include a large number of Hmong people who came there as refugees after the Vietnam War. The Hmong, who may have originated in China, are thought by some to be related to the Miao people encountered by the Han Chinese as early as the third century BCE. As they rebelled against assimilation into the Chinese empire, many, though not all, were pushed into Southeast Asia, into the countries now known as Burma, Thailand, Laos, and Vietnam. After they were recruited to support the American invasions of the twentieth century, and after the defeat of these invasions, some Hmong spent time in Thai refugee camps and were eventually resettled, many in Stockton, where they have a flourishing farmer's market and a strong presence in the city. Though some have converted to Christianity, sometimes an implicit condition of support from missionary groups that help refugees, others continue to practice their traditional forms of worship, often alongside Christian observances. Their traditions include reverence for ancestors, animism, and shamanism, in which the spiritual practitioner or healer mediates between the world of the living and the underworld, or spirit world, of the dead. Anne Fadiman's book *The Spirit Catches You and You Fall Down,* set in Merced, California, near Stockton, records the tragic collision of Hmong spirituality and shamanism with the interventions of American medicine.[2]

I now live in Southern California and like many of my friends and neighbors practice yoga, and meditate, read and teach the *Bhagavad-Gita,* see a Taoist acupuncturist from Taiwan, and am in general surrounded by a very great variety of worshippers and their gods. My husband and I eat in restaurants in the San Gabriel Valley just east of Los Angeles, one of the most fertile grounds for Chinese cuisine in the world. A favorite is an Islamic Chinese restaurant, which serves the lamb dishes and wheat breads of Western China to a highly varied and appreciative public. My students are Buddhists, Hindus, Muslims, Latino Catholics, Korean-American evangelical Christians, Jews, and atheists, and represent many ethnicities, just as back in Stockton, my sister's children attended a high school in which the students came from fifty-eight different linguistic traditions; one of her children became a Mormon and has two Latino children, and the other married a Chinese-American woman. One of my favorite students comes from Stockton, daughter of a Filipino mother and a Persian father; her mother converted to Islam, her father cooks lavish Persian feasts. I married an Irish Catholic American who grew up worshipping, as far as I can tell, the virgin Mary and the saints. One of my favorite friends is an African American priestess in a West African polytheist religious tradition. My husband and I live in an Orthodox Jewish-show business-gay neighborhood, with parish churches, synagogues, and temples all crowding together. When we drive north on the I-5, from Los Angeles to San Francisco, passing by Stockton, we stop at an Indian restaurant at a truck stop in the Central Valley called Buttonwillow, where the owner and his wife offer beautiful meals for travelers and for local farmers, Hindu, Sikh, and not.

The vastly intriguing heterogeneity and religious diversity of the world I inhabit seems to me to represent precisely the wonder of the present age, and also the threat to homogeneity that excites such fear and anxiety in many sites in our culture. There are intense debates about whether we live in "Christian nations," whether the founders of the U.S. were Christians, theists, and monotheists, and, on the extreme fringes of our society, whether evolution is a so-called failed theory.

Religious questions are insistent today and can inform and trouble other issues of class, race, genders, and brutal exploitation, the violence of a transnational economic system that relegates many in the world to poverty. Polytheism informs not only the religions of many peoples of the world, but also the psyches, traditions, and institutions of the West. When arguments about "religion" reassure some in an imaginary position of ethical superiority and rightful dominance, even conquest, economic or military, we need to think more and again about the separation of "church" and state and about how atheists, agnostics, monotheists, and polytheists might all inhabit the world together.

NOTES

ACKNOWLEDGMENTS

INDEX

Notes

(

INTRODUCTION

1. On the application of the concept of pluralism to the religious landscape of the U.S., see Diana Eck, *A New Religious America: How a Christian Country Has Become the World's Most Religiously Diverse Nation* (San Francisco: Harper San Francisco, 2001). For another view of pluralism, registering contestation, see David Campbell and Morton Schoolman, eds., *The New Pluralism: William Connolly and the Contemporary Global Condition* (Durham, NC: Duke University Press, 2008). "Pluralization" might be preferable to "pluralism," as a counter to universalization: "Equal protection, or, indeed, equality is not a principle that homogenizes those to whom it applies; rather, the commitment to equality is a commitment to the process of differentiation itself." Judith Butler, *Parting Ways: Jewishness and the Critique of Zionism* (New York: Columbia University Press, 2012), 126.

2. *The New Oxford Annotated Bible,* 3rd ed., ed. Michael D. Coogan (Oxford: Oxford University Press, 2001). All subsequent citations of and commentary on the Bible refer to this edition.

3. *Popul Vuh, The Mayan Book of the Dawn of Life,* rev. ed., trans. Dennis Tedlock (New York: Simon and Schuster, 1996).

4. Hans H. Penner, *Impasse and Resolution: A Critique of the Study of Religion* (New York: Peter Lang, 1989), 7, 8.

5. Pascal Boyer, *Religion Explained: The Evolutionary Origins of Religious Thought* (New York: Basic Books, 2001), 9. Supernatural agents seem plausible to people, in Boyer's view, because there are inference systems in the human mind: "the intuitive psychology system treats ancestors (or God) as intentional agents, the exchange system treats them as exchange partners, the moral system treats them as potential witnesses to moral action, the person-file system treats them as distinct individuals. This means that quite a lot of mental work is going on . . ." (Boyer, 314).

6. Richard King, *Orientalism and Religion: Postcolonial Theory, India and "the Mystic East,"* (New York: Routledge, 1999), 35.

7. King, *Orientalism,* 36, citing Lactantius, *Institutiones Divinae* IV.28, trans. by Sister Mary Francis McDonald (Washington, DC: Catholic University of America Press, 1964), 318–320.

8. *The Oxford English Dictionary,* 2nd ed., ed. E. S. C. Weiner and J. A. Simpson (Oxford: Oxford University Press, 1991), s.v. "deity."

9. *The American Heritage Dictionary of the English Language* (Boston: American Heritage Publishing and Houghton Mifflin, 1973), s.v. "god."

10. Scott Atran, "Religion's Social and Cognitive Landscape: An Evolutionary Perspective," in *Handbook of Cultural Psychology,* Shinobu Kitayama and Dov Cohen, eds. (New York: Guilford Press, 2007), 417–453.

11. Saba Mahmood, "Religious Reason and Secular Affect: An Incommensurable Divide?" in Talal Asad, Wendy Brown, Judith Butler, and Saba Mahmood, *Is Critique Secular? Blasphemy, Injury, and Free Speech* (Berkeley, CA: Townsend Center for the Humanities, 2009), 64–100.

12. Peter Danchin, "Of Prophets and Proselytes: Freedom of Religion and the Conflict of Rights in International Law," *Harvard International Law Journal* 49:2 (2008), 275. Cited in Mahmood, "Religious Reason and Secular Affect: An Incommensurable Divide?," in *Is Critique Secular?,* 86.

13. On secularism, see Charles Taylor, *A Secular Age* (Cambridge, MA: Belknap Press of Harvard University Press, 2007); Asad, Brown, Butler, and Mahmood, *Is Critique Secular?*; E. Mendieta and J. VanAntwerpen, eds., *The Power of Religion in the Public Sphere* (New York: Columbia University Press, 2011); Giorgio Agamben, *The Kingdom and the Glory,* trans. Lorenzo Chiesa (Stanford, CA: Stanford University Press, 2011).

14. Andrew Higgins, "A More Secular Europe, Divided by the Cross," *New York Times,* June 17, 2013.

15. Moshe Halbertal and Avishai Margalit, *Idolatry,* trans. Naomi Goldblum (Cambridge, MA: Harvard University Press, 1992), 8.

1. THE PREJUDICE AGAINST POLYTHEISM

1. Jan Assmann, *The Price of Monotheism,* trans. Robert Savage (Stanford, CA: Stanford University Press, 2010 [2003]), 43.

2. Aeschylus, *The Suppliant Maidens,* trans. Seth G. Benardete, in *The Complete Greek Tragedies,* vol. 1 (Chicago: University of Chicago Press, 1992), 185.

3. Fragment C32 (Fr. 20), from Clement of Alexandria, *Miscellanies* 5.110, and fragment C33 (F 22), also from Clement, 7.22, in Daniel W. Graham, trans. and ed., *The Texts of Early Greek Philosophy: The Complete Fragments and Selected Testimonies of the Major Presocratics* (Cambridge: Cambridge University Press, 2010), 109–111.

4. Plutarch, "The Obsolescence of Oracles," in *Moralia,* vol. 5, trans. F. C. Babbitt (Cambridge, MA: Harvard University Press [Loeb]), 1936), 401.

5. Helen Morales, *Classical Mythology: A Very Short Introduction* (Oxford: Oxford University Press, 2007), 5–6.

6. Samuel Purchas, *Purchas, His Pilgrimage, OR Relations of the World and the Religions Observed in All Ages and Places Discovered, from the Creation unto this Present* (London: William Standby for Henrie Fetherstone, 1613), 49.

7. Jordan Paper, *The Deities Are Many: A Polytheistic Theology* (Albany: SUNY Press, 2005), 104.

8. Moshe Halbertal and Avishai Margalit, *Idolatry,* trans. Naomi Goldblum (Cambridge, MA: Harvard University Press, 1992), 237.

9. Michel Danino and Sujata Nahar, *The Invasion That Never Was,* 2nd edition (Delhi: The Mother's Institute of Research, 2000), 32. Danino, basing his findings on study of ruins found along the dry bed of the Sarasvati River, discusses the Indus-Sarasvati civilization and refutes the notion of an Aryan invasion of the Indian subcontinent and the racializing of a division between Aryans and Dravidians.

10. A Taliban spokesman in Afghanistan in 2013 cited Macaulay's "Minute" in justification for the violent assault on a young woman who publicly advocated education for girls. https://www.facebook.com/pages/HBN-CHANNEL/159810344087950

11. One translator writes: "This duty I have accepted, as I said, in obedience to God's commands given in oracles and dreams . . ." (33b). "Socrates' Defense (Apology)," trans. Hugh Tredennick, in *The Collected Dialogues of Plato,* ed. Edith Hamilton and Huntington Cairns (Princeton, NJ: Princeton University Press, 1961), 19.

12. Paul Connerton, *How Societies Remember* (Cambridge: Cambridge University Press, 1989), 45.

13. David V. Barrett, ed., *Christian Encyclopedia: A Comparative Study of Churches and Religions in the Modern World A.D. 1900–2000* (Oxford: Oxford University Press, 1982).

14. Cited in Basil Williams, *The Whig Supremacy: 1714–1760,* rev. ed. (Oxford: The Clarendon Press, 1962), 75.

15. Roger Scruton, *Our Church: A Personal History of the Church of England* (London: Atlantic, 2013).

16. Mark C. Taylor, *After God* (Chicago: University of Chicago Press, 2007).

17. Taylor further argues that "The Infinite is not God but is always after the God who is after it" (345).

18. Mark C. Taylor, ed., *Critical Terms for Religious Studies* (Chicago: University of Chicago Press, 1998).

19. Rosemary Ruether, *Gaia and God: An Ecofeminist Theology of Earth Healing* (San Francisco: Harper, 1992).

20. Jonathan Z. Smith, "Religion, Religions, Religious," in *Critical Terms for Religious Studies*, 269-284

21. Guy Stroumsa, *A New Science: The Discovery of Religion in the Age of Reason* (Cambridge, MA: Harvard University Press, 2010).

22. For a detailed discussion of the developments in the notion of idolatry, see Stroumsa, *A New Science,* 88–90: "Discourse on idolatry not only reflected the discovery of nonmonotheistic religions, East and West but was also directly linked to Protestant apologetics against papism" (90).

23. Garry Wills, *Why Priests? A Failed Tradition* (New York: Viking Adult, 2013), location 4292.

24. C. P. Macpherson, *The Political Theory of Possessive Individualism: Hobbes to Locke* (Ontario, Canada: Oxford University Press, 2011 [1962]), 269.

25. René de Chateaubriand, *The Genius of Christianity, or the Spirit and Beauty of the Christian Religion,* trans. Charles I. White (Philadelphia: J. B. Lippincott, 1856 [1802]).

26. See P. duBois, *Slaves and Other Objects* (Chicago: University of Chicago Press, 2003) and *Slavery: Antiquity and Its Legacy* (London: I. B. Tauris, 2012).

27. G. W. F. Hegel, *Lectures on the Philosophy of Religion,* 1 vol. edition, *The Lectures of 1827,* ed. P. C. Hodgson, trans. R. F. Brown, P. C. Hodgson, and J. M. Stewart, with the assistance of H. S. Harris (Berkeley: University of California Press, 1988). The 1831 lecture on these religions adds: "While humanity is, of course, implicitly free, Africans and Asiatics are not, because they have not the consciousness of what constitutes the concept of humanity" (202, n. 3).

28. http://answers.yahoo.com/question/index?qid=20090219170408AAMmU65 (consulted 11/01/2013).

29. www.religiousforums.com/ . . . /148535-monotheism-superior-polytheism (consulted 11/01/2013).

30. Thucydides, vol. 1, *History of the Peloponnesian War Books I and II,* trans. C. F. Smith (Cambridge, MA: Harvard University Press, [Loeb], 1969).

31. Richard E. Nisbett, *The Geography of Thought: How Asians and Westerners Think Differently . . . and Why* (New York: Free Press, 2003), 3.

32. Macpherson, *The Political Theory of Possessive Individualism.*

33. Pascal Boyer, *Religion Explained: The Evolutionary Origins of Religious Thought* (New York: Basic Books, 2001).

34. Assmann, *The Price of Monotheism,* 43ff.

35. Marc Augé, *Génie du paganisme* (Paris: Gallimard, 1982, translations mine).

36. Michael York, *Pagan Theology: Paganism as a World Religion* (New York: NYU Press, 2003); York describes pagan behaviors and theology and categorizes paganism and gnosticism as "ideal types" (158–159). Gnosticism, not restricted to the historical phenomenon of the name, perceives "divine reality as purely transcendent and matter as evil, something from which to escape" (158). Any actual religion can be placed on a spectrum in relation to the ideal opposition between the two. "Gnostic by category, as distinct from historic or nominal manifestation, would be official Hinduism with its Vedantic or Brahmanic theologies" (159).

37. Gilles Deleuze and Félix Guattari, *Anti-Oedipus: Capitalism and Schizophrenia*, trans. M. Seem, R. Hurley, H. Lane (Minneapolis: University of Minnesota Press, 1985 [1977]), especially "Psychoanalysis and Familialism: The Holy Family," 51–137.

38. Gish Jen, *Tiger Writing: Art, Culture, and the Interdependent Self* (Cambridge, MA: Harvard University Press, 2013). The distinction between independent and interdependent relies on H. Markus and S. Kitayama, "Culture and the Self: Implications for Cognition, Emotion, and Motivation," *Psychological Review* 98 (1991), 224–253.

39. Nisbett, *The Geography of Thought*. A study conducted on "Hindu East Indians" and "Americans" found that there were cultural differences in causal attribution, with Hindu East Asians offering more contextual explanations of actions described, while Americans saw individual "dispositions" as responsible. "Miller [author of the study] also questioned Anglo-Indians whose culture is Westernized to a degree. The attributions, both for dispositions and for contexts, were midway between those of Hindu Indians and Americans" (115); see J. G. Miller, "Culture and the Development of Everyday Social Explanation," *Journal of Personality and Social Psychology* 46 (1984), 961–978.

40. Prema A. Kurien, *A Place at the Multicultural Table: The Development of an American Hinduism* (New Brunswick, NJ: Rutgers University Press, 2007).

41. See the work of Rajiv Malhotra, e.g., "Geopolitics and Sanskrit Phobia," Sulekha.com, July 5, 2005. Rand-rambler.blogspot.com/2005/ . . . /geopolitics-and-sanskrit-phobia-by (consulted 11/05/2013).

42. Gilles Deleuze and Félix Guattari, *A Thousand Plateaus: Capitalism and Schizophrenia*, trans. B. Massumi (Minneapolis: University of Minnesota Press, 1987), especially "Introduction: Rhizome," pages 3–26. "Any point of a rhizome can be connected to anything other, and must be. This is very different from a tree, or root, which plots a point, fixes an order" (7).

43. Eduardo Mendieta and Jonathan VanAntwerpen, eds., *The Power of Religion in the Public Sphere* (New York: Columbia University Press, 2011).

44. Judith Butler, "Is Judaism Zionism?" in Mendieta and VanAntwerpen, *The Power of Religion in the Public Sphere*, 70–91. See also Judith Butler, *Parting Ways: Jewishness and the Critique of Zionism* (New York: Columbia University Press, 2012).

Here and in *Is Critique Secular?* Butler proposes "that there are Jewish values of cohabitation with the non-Jew that are part of the very ethical substance of diasporic Jewishness" (*Parting Ways,* 1). See also Chapter 6, "Quandaries of the Plural: Cohabitation and Sovereignty in Arendt," 151–180.

2. GREEKS, ROMANS, AND THEIR MANY GODS

1. M. N. Tod, *Greek Historical Inscriptions,* ii, 204. Cited in J. O. Burtt, *Minor Attic Orators,* vol. 2 (Cambridge, MA: Harvard University Press [Loeb], 1954), 68–71. Passage cited from Lycurgus, "Against Leocrates," 77.

2. Sarah Kate Istra Winter, *Kharis: Hellenic Polytheism Explored,* 2nd ed. (Lexington, KY: Cafepress, 2008).

3. Jean Seznec, *The Survival of the Pagan Gods: The Mythological Tradition and Its Place in Renaissance Humanism and Art,* trans. Barbara F. Sessions (Princeton, NJ: Princeton University Press, 1953), 62; see also Edgar Wind, *Pagan Mysteries in the Renaissance,* rev. ed. (New York: Norton, 1969), and Leonard Barkan, *The Gods Made Flesh: Metamorphosis and the Pursuit of Paganism* (New Haven, CT: Yale University Press, 1990).

4. William Butler Yeats, 2nd rev. ed., ed. R. J. Finneran (New York: Scribner, 1996), 214.

5. G. W. F. Hegel, *The Phenomenology of Spirit,* trans. A. V. Miller (London: Oxford University Press, 1977), 266ff.; George Steiner, *Antigones* (New Haven, CT: Yale University Press, 1996 [1984]); Jacques Lacan, *The Seminar vol. 7: The Ethics of Psychoanalysis, 1959–1960,* trans. D. Porter (New York: Norton, 1992 [1986]); Judith Butler, *Antigone's Claim: Kinship Between Life and Death* (New York: Columbia University Press, 2000), Bonnie Honig, *Antigone, Interrupted* (Cambridge: Cambridge University Press, 2013).

6. Simon Goldhill, *Love, Sex, & Tragedy: How the Ancient World Shapes Our Lives* (Chicago: University of Chicago Press, 2005), 87.

7. Marie Phillips, *Gods Behaving Badly* (London: Jonathan Cape, 2007).

8. For an account of these debates, see H. S. Versnel, *Coping with the Gods: Wayward Readings in Greek Theology* (Boston: Brill, 2011), especially pages 23–149. Versnel contrasts the orderly pantheon of the Paris school of J.-P. Vernant with the more chaotic version of the Greek divinities explored by Walter Burkert, and concludes that Greek culture "displays an unmatched capacity to unashamedly juxtapose the two, tolerating glaring contradictions and flashing alternations" (149).

9. Robert Parker, *Polytheism and Society at Athens* (Oxford: Oxford University Press, 2005). On the conflict of views between kosmos and chaos, see H. S. Versnel, *Coping,* 26–37.

10. Marcel Detienne, "Experimenting in the Field of Polytheisms," *Arion* 3rd ser. 7 (1999), 127–199.

11. *The Poetry of Sappho,* trans. John Daley with P. duBois (San Francisco: Arion Press, 2011). All citations of Sappho's verse refer to this edition, n.p.

12. *The Love Songs of Sappho,* trans. Paul Roche (New York: Prometheus, 1998), 11.

13. *Greek Lyric: Sappho and Alcaeus,* trans. D. Campbell (Cambridge, MA: Harvard University Press [Loeb], 1982).

14. Giovanni Tarditi, "Dioniso kemelios (Alceo, fr. 129, 8 L.-P.)," *Quaderni Urbinati di Cultura Classica: Studi di poesia greca e Latina,* 4 (1967), 107–112.

15. For an analysis of fragment 16, see "Helen," in P. duBois, *Sappho Is Burning* (Chicago: University of Chicago Press, 1995), 98–126.

16. From a vast bibliography of work on Dionysos, I single out T. H. Carpenter and C. A. Faraone, eds., *Masks of Dionysus* (Ithaca, NY: Cornell University Press, 2003).

17. *The Homeric Hymns,* 2nd ed., trans. Apostolos Athanassakis (Baltimore, MD: Johns Hopkins University Press, 2004), no. 26, 58.

18. On Apollo, see Marcel Detienne, *Apollon, le couteau à la main* (Paris: Gallimard, 2009).

19. Euripides, *Bacchae,* trans. William Arrowsmith, in *The Complete Greek Tragedies,* ed. David Grene and W. Arrowsmith (Chicago: University of Chicago Press, 1959).

20. *Homeric Hymns,* 57.

21. *Homeric Hymns,* 57

22. See Froma Zeitlin, *Playing the Other: Gender and Society in Classical Greek Literature* (Chicago: University of Chicago Press, 1995), and *Nothing To Do with Dionysos? Athenian Drama in Its Social Context,* F. Zeitlin and J. J. Winkler, eds. (Princeton, NJ: Princeton University Press, 1992).

23. Aristophanes, *Frogs,* in *Aristophanes 4,* trans. J. Henderson (Cambridge, MA: Harvard University Press, 2002), lines 479–485, 89.

24. T. M. Mathews, *The Clash of Gods: A Reinterpretation of Early Christian Art,* rev. ed. (Princeton, NJ: Princeton University Press, 1999), 45.

25. Plato, *Collected Dialogues,* ed. Edith Hamilton and H. Cairns (Princeton, NJ: Princeton University Press, 1961), 576.

26. Ovid, *Heroides. Amores,* trans. G. P. Goold (Cambridge, MA: Harvard University Press [Loeb], 1914). Translation modified by John Daley.

27. Jörg Rüpke, *Religion of the Romans,* trans. and ed. R. Gordon (Cambridge: Polity, 2007 [2001]).

28. Clifford Ando, *The Matter of the Gods: Religion and the Roman Empire* (Berkeley: University of California Press, 2008).

29. *Juvenal and Persius,* trans. Susanna Morton Braund (Cambridge, MA: Harvard University Press [Loeb], 2004).

30. See Keith Hopkins, *A World Full of Gods: The Strange Triumph of Christianity* (New York: Plume, 2001), and Selina O'Grady, *And Man Created God: A History of the World at the Time of Jesus* (New York: St. Martin's Press, 2012).

31. *The Transformations of Lucius, Otherwise Known as The Golden Ass,* trans. Robert Graves (New York: Farrar, Straus and Giroux, 1951).

32. Jacques Lacan, *The Seminar, Book VII, The Ethics of Psychoanalysis 1959–1960,* ed. Jacques-Alain Miller, trans. D. Porter (New York: Norton, 1992 [1986]).

33. See Florence Dupont, *The Invention of Literature: From Greek Intoxication to the Latin Book,* trans. Janet Lloyd (Baltimore, MD: Johns Hopkins University Press, 1999 [1994]).

34. Jan Assmann, *The Price of Monotheism,* trans. Robert Savage (Stanford, CA: Stanford University Press, 2010 [2003]), 40.

35. Versnel addresses this question, taking issue with those who see Greek antiquity as "desperately alien," and also noting that all scholarship on antiquity is by necessity "etic," that is, performed from outside the culture being studied. *Coping,* 11–18, 73, 243.

36. G. S. Kirk and J. E. Raven, *The Presocratic Philosophers: A Critical History with a Selection of Texts* (Cambridge: Cambridge University Press, 1966). For a more recent view on Thales and Xenophanes, neither of whom is identified as a monotheist, see Robin Waterfield, *The First Philosophers: The Presocratics and Sophists* (Oxford: Oxford University Press, 2009), 3–24.

37. Kirk and Raven sum up: "Although these [his] ideas were strongly affected, directly or indirectly, by mythological precedents, Thales evidently abandoned mythic formulations . . ." (*Presocratic Philosophers,* 98).

38. Clémence Ramnoux, "Sur un monothéisme grec," *Revue philosophique de Louvain* 82 (1984), 175–198, passage quoted, 198, translations mine. Xenophanes, from Colophon, may have come into contact with an eastern monotheism, according to Ramnoux, linked by Darius to the destiny of his own imperial power (196). Ramnoux stresses that the wandering Xenophanes, who left his home in Asia, never became a citizen of a Greek colony, nor did he occupy any function in a panhellenic sanctuary, nor attempt to found an order, nor reform a city, as did Pythagoras. Yet Ramnoux designates Xenophanes's views as "une idéologie neuve" (197). But the fragments, lacunose and contradictory, do not, I would say, constitute monotheism.

39. *Texts of Early Greek Philosophy,* #35 (Fr. 23, from Clement *Miscellanies,* 5. 109), p. 111.

40. Versnel discusses Xenophanes as well (*Coping,* 244–268): "The *arche* devised by Xenophanes was the product of natural philosophy, not of theology. As *physical* 'all' it did encompass, but it encompassed everything that is, because it *was* everything that is: not only gods, but also men, and the whole material world. Just as men were both part of it *and* were independent beings, so were the (traditional) gods" (266). He sees coexistence, and complementarity, as inconsistency rather than a strict monotheism. See further Richard Bodéüs, *Aristotle and the Theology of the Living Immortals,* trans. Jan Garrett (Albany, NY: SUNY Press, 2000), for a similar argument concerning Aristotle's preservation of the polytheist pantheon as he developed and defended his teachings.

41. Richard Armstrong, *A Compulsion for Antiquity: Freud and the Ancient World* (Ithaca, NY: Cornell University Press, 2006), 96.

42. H. S. Versnel, *Inconsistencies in Greek and Roman Religion,* vol. 1, *Ter Unus: Isis, Dionysus, Hermes. Three Studies in Henotheism* (Leiden: Brill, 1990).

43. The issue is addressed again, in similar terms, in *Coping with the Gods,* 290ff.

44. Euripides, *Bacchae,* trans. W. Arrowsmith in *The Complete Greek Tragedies: Euripides 5,* ed. David Grene and Richmond Lattimore (Chicago: University of Chicago Press, 1968).

45. *Pagan Monotheism in Late Antiquity,* Polymnia Athanassiadi and M. Frede, eds. (Oxford: Clarendon, 1999), 1. John Dillon, in "Monotheism in the Gnostic Tradition" (69–79 in this volume), makes a distinction between "hard" and "soft" monotheisms: he finds "hard monotheism" in Jewish and Islamic traditions, "where nothing more formidable than an angel is allowed to compete with the supreme and only God." Soft monotheism is visible in "the intellectualized version of traditional Greek religion to which most educated Greeks seem to have adhered from the fifth century BC on . . ." Here we find Zeus as "supreme cosmic intellect," with "on a lower level of reality, as it were, the full Olympic pantheon of traditional deities, and a host of little local gods as well, who can all be, if necessary, viewed merely as aspects of the supreme divinity . . ." (69).

46. *One God: Pagan Monotheism in the Roman Empire,* Stephen Mitchell and Peter van Nuffelen, eds. (Cambridge: Cambridge University Press, 2010). This volume responds to the earlier *Pagan Monotheism in Late Antiquity* (note 44).

3. THE POLYTHEISM OF MONOTHEISM

1. Emily Schmall and Larry Rohter, "A Conservative with a Common Touch," *New York Times,* March 14, 2013, 1.

2. David Hume, "The Natural History of Religion," in *Essays Moral, Political and Literary* (London: Longman, Green, 1875), 334. Cited in Peter Brown, *The Cult of the Saints: Its Rise and Function in Latin Christianity* (Chicago: University of Chicago Press, 1981), 14.

3. From another vast bibliography, I cite Mark S. Smith, *The Early History of God: Yahweh and the Other Deities in Ancient Israel,* 2nd ed. (Grand Rapids, MI: Eerdmans, 2002).

4. *The New Oxford Annotated Bible, New Revised Standard Edition,* 3rd ed., Michael Coogan, ed. (Oxford: Oxford University Press, 2001). All subsequent Biblical citations refer to this text.

5. On the Pentateuch, see the article by David Noel Freedman in *Eerdmans Commentary on the Bible,* J. D. G. Dunn and J. W. Rogerson, eds. (Grand Rapids, MI: Eerdmans, 2003), 25–31, with bibliography on 30–31.

6. The commentator also here notes that the *New Revised Standard Version* has added "own" to the phrase "the LORD's own portion," "to identify Yahweh with

Elyon and avoid the impression that Yahweh is merely a member of the pantheon"
(302).

7. *New Oxford Annotated Bible,* commentary on *Jeremiah* 44.15–28, 1147.

8. See the commentaries on Exodus by William Propp, *Exodus 1–18* (New
Haven, CT: Yale University Press, 1999), and *Exodus 19–40* (New Haven, CT: Yale
University Press, 2006).

9. Tikva Frymer-Krensky, *In the Wake of the Goddesses: Women, Culture and the
Biblical Transformation of Pagan Myth* (New York: Fawcett Columbine, 1992).

10. These inscriptions are also discussed by Raphael Patai, who concludes: "the
worship of Asherah as the consort of Yahweh ('*his* Asherah'!) was an integral element
of religious life in ancient Israel prior to the reforms introduced by King Josiah in
621 BCE." *The Hebrew Goddess*, 3rd ed. (Detroit, MI: Wayne State University Press,
1990), 53. See also Ephraim Stern, "From Many Gods to the One God: The Archaeological Evidence," in *One God—One Cult—One Nation: Archaeological and Biblical
Perspectives,* R. G. Kratz and H. Spieckermann, with B. Corzilius and T. Pilger, eds.
(Berlin: De Gruyter [Beihefte zur zeitschrift fuer die alttestamentliche wissenschaft,
vol. 406], 2010), 395–403. Stern bases his understanding on archaeological evidence: "among all of them [the eight nations settled in Palestine in the 7th century
BCE] including the Philistines and even the Judaeans, the chief female deity was
Ashtoret (Ashtart) or Asherah" (395). He also discusses the great number of so-called
pillar figurines of females with breasts, noting that they must be Judaean; "a cult
existed between the foreign pagan practices and the pure monotheism of Jerusalem,
which may be called 'Yahwistic Paganism,' common to all other Judaean settlements"
(400). Evidence of such polytheism disappears from the archaeological record at the
beginning of the period of return of exiles in the Persian period, and Stern concludes
that it was then that "pagan cults ceased to exist among the Judaeans, who purified
their worship, and Jewish monotheism was at last consolidated." He attributes this
development to the Babylonian exiles and their return. But pagan customs persisted
in the Jewish communities of Egypt. "To sum up: the change from many gods to one
god in Judah was established by the Jews in Babylon, and from there it was brought
back to Judah" (402).

11. Discussion of the Cherubim can be found in Patai, *The Hebrew Goddess,*
67–95.

12. Jan Assmann, *The Price of Monotheism,* trans. Robert Savage (Stanford, CA:
Stanford University Press, 2010 [2003]). See also Regina Schwartz, who argues in
The Curse of Cain: The Violent Legacy of Monotheism (Chicago: University of Chicago
Press, 1998), that Judaic and Christian ideologies share with psychoanalysis a notion
of scarcity that defines them. She describes a "'Noah complex' in which love/hate for
the father with whom the son identifies issues in intolerable guilt for that incestuous
desire, a guilt projected onto an omnipotent monotheistic deity who punishes, maintaining his preserve at the price of his sons' dissension, turning the brother into the

reviled Other—is thoroughly predicated upon the supposition of scarcity. Scarcity imposes sibling rivalry: a shortage of parental blessings and love yields fatal competition for them. Scarcity imposes parental hostility; it presumes that in order to imitate the father successfully, he must be replaced, not joined. . . . Scarcity imposes patriarchy . . . Scarcity imposes monotheism: one god must maintain his singleness defensively, against the difference of other gods." (115)

Schwartz further argues that:

The "scarcity at the heart of the legacy of biblical monotheism is also part of Freud's biblical legacy of psychoanalysis. . . . Moreover, the competition / identification with the father that issues in excessive solicitude toward him presumes, like the biblical scheme, that the father must be replaced, not joined." (116)

Schwartz contrasts the Abrahamic view of scarcity, the violent legacy of monotheism, with a vision of plenitude, proliferation, enriching variety and multiplicity (173). She presents a Deleuzian "proliferation of nonidentical repetitions . . . that open up the Same into endless difference . . . Plenitude proliferates identities without violence . . . And when such plenitude is figured as a God, it is as a God who gives and goes on giving endlessly without being used up, and certainly without jealously guarding his domain" (117–118). God, or *gods* . . .

13. *Ancient Egyptian Literature: A Book of Readings,* vol. 2: *The New Kingdom,* trans. Miriam Lichtheim (Berkeley: University of California Press, 1976), 91.

14. See also Baruch Halperin, "Brisker Pipes than Poetry: The Development of Israelite Monotheism," in *Judaic Perspectives on Ancient Israel,* J. Neusner, B. A. Levine, and E. S. Frerichs, eds. (Philadelphia: Fortress, 1987), 77–115.

15. Commentary, *New Oxford Annotated Bible,* 908.

16. Midrash Ps. 16.2: H. L. Strack and P. Billerbeck, *Kommentar zum Neuen Testament aus Talmud und Midrasch* (Munich: C. M. Beck, 1926), 1: 892. Cited in Brown, *The Cult,* 3.

17. Within another vast bibliography, see Elaine Pagels, *The Gnostic Gospels* (New York: Vintage, 1989) and David Brakke, *The Gnostics: Myth, Ritual and Diversity in Early Christianity* (Cambridge, MA: Harvard University Press, 2012).

18. G. R. Hawting, *The Idea of Idolatry and the Emergence of Islam: From Polemic to History* (Cambridge: Cambridge University Press, 1999), 53.

19. William G. Dever, *Did God Have a Wife? Archaeology and Folk Religion in Ancient Israel* (Grand Rapids, MI: Eerdmans, 2005), 4.

20. See Elaine Pagels, *The Origin of Satan: How Christians Demonized Jews, Pagans, and Heretics* (New York: Vintage, 1996).

21. The commentator of the *New Oxford Annotated Bible* remarks here: "The scene is a meeting of the council of heavenly beings presided over by the LORD." (Jeremiah recounts his vision of the heavenly throne room, attended by seraphim, the "burning ones," who cover their faces and genitals with their wings; *Jeremiah* 6.1–2). "In the book of Job, Satan is not yet the personal name of the devil, as in

later Jewish and Christian literature. Rather, the Hebrew (with the definite article) simply means "the adversary" or "the accuser, a reference to one of the members of the divine council who served as a sort of independent prosecutor" (728).

22. See the work of Dayna Kalleres, *City of Demons: Violence, Ritual, and Christian Power in Late Antiquity* (Berkeley: University of California Press, forthcoming 2014).

23. *New Oxford Annotated Bible: Hebrew Bible,* 999.

24. See Lynn Huber, *"Like a Bride Adorned": Reading Metaphor in John's Apocalypse* (Atlanta, GA: Emory Studies in Early Christianity, 2007).

25. Marina Warner, *Alone of All Her Sex: The Myth and Cult of the Virgin Mary* (London: Quartet, 1976).

26. Peter Paul Vergerius the Younger (1498–1564), cited in Marina Miladinov, "Madonna of Loreto as a Target of Reformation Critique," in *Promoting the Saints: Cults and Their Contexts from Late Antiquity until the Early Modern Period,* O. Gecser, J. Laszlovszky, B. Nagy, M. Sebok, and K. Szende, eds. (New York: Central European University Press, 2011), 291–303.

27. David Brading, *Mexican Phoenix: Our Lady of Guadalupe: Image and Tradition across Five Centuries* (Cambridge: Cambridge University Press, 2001), 3.

28. T. H. Carpenter and C. Faraone, eds., *Masks of Dionysus* (Ithaca, NY: Cornell University Press, 1993).

29. Rennell Rodd, *The Customs and Lore of Modern Greece* (London: David Stott, 1892).

30. Rodd cites the story collected in Boeotia in 1846 by Christian Siegel.

31. Thomas F. Mathews, *The Clash of Gods: A Reinterpretation of Early Christian Art,* rev. ed. (Princeton, NJ: Princeton University Press, 1999).

32. Anne Marie Yasin, *Saints and Church Spaces in the Late Antique Mediterranean: Architecture, Cult, and Community* (Cambridge: Cambridge University Press, 2009), 288.

33. H. S. Versnel, *Coping with the Gods: Wayward Readings in Greek Theology* (Boston: Brill, 2011), 66.

34. "Academic Freedom and Tenure: Brigham Young University," *Academe, American Association of University Professors,* September–October 1997, 52–68; passage quoted, 59.

35. http://www.dailykos.com/story/2011/07/13/994153/-Michele-Bachmann-2004-Gays-are-Part-of-Satan# (consulted 11/05/2013).

36. See W. S. Poole, *Satan in America: The Devil We Know* (Lanham, MD: Rowman and Littlefield, 2009).

37. J. Budziszewski, *How to Stay Christian in College: An Interactive Guide to Keeping the Faith* (Colorado Springs, CO: Navpress, 1999), 125.

38. Hawting, *The Idea of Idolatry,* 14. Hawting suggests that the *Qur'an*'s polemic against idolators and polytheists may correspond to arguments with Jews and

Christians and their impure practices of monotheism, evolved not against polytheist Meccans in Muhammad's lifetime, but rather in the Middle East after the Arab conquest, where there was more contact with the other Abrahamic monotheisms. Hawting sees the traditional scholarship's emphasis on the Meccan idolators as a symptom of a desire to represent Islam as dependent entirely on divine revelation in the remote area of Arabia, rather than as influenced by earlier Hebrew, Judaic, and Christian ideas concerning their god.

39. Jamil M. Abu-Nasr, *Muslim communities of grace: the Sufi brotherhoods in Islamic religious life* (New York: Columbia University Press. (2007), 94. See also Fred M. Donner, *Muhammad and the Believers: At the Origins of Islam* (Cambridge, MA: Belknap Press of Harvard University Press, 2010).

40. Hawting, *The Idea of Idolatry,* defines *shirk* as "the association of other gods or beings with God, according them the honour and worship that are due to God alone" (3).

41. On the beginnings of Islam, see Donner, *Muhammad and the Believers.*

42. *The Qur'an,* 5th rev. ed., trans. N. J. Dawood (London: Penguin, 1999). All citations from the *Qur'an* refer to this translation.

43. Salman Rushdie's novel *The Satanic Verses* (New York: Viking, 1989) features two central characters, Gibreel Farishta ("Gabriel Angel"), and Saladin Chamcha, who becomes the embodiment of Shaitan, the devil. Gibreel falls in love with and then kills the Englishwoman Allie Cone and eventually commits suicide, while the devil survives.

44. Hawting, *Idea of Idolatry,* 141. On Athena and Allat, 141; Aphrodite, 85; Venus and other astral bodies and al-Uzza, as well as the other goddesses, 142, 147.

45. Henry Corbin, *Le Paradoxe du monothéisme* (Paris: L'Herne, 1981). Translations mine.

46. Corbin, influenced by Martin Heidegger, represents this distinction as that between Being and beings, *l'être* and *les étants.*

47. See Phiroze Vasunia, *Zarathustra and the Religion of Ancient Iran: The Greek and Latin Sources in Translation* (Mumbai: KRCOI, 2007).

48. Jenny Rose, *Zoroastrianism: An Introduction* (London: I. B. Tauris, 2011).

49. Vasunia, *Zarathustra,* 26, citing Xenophon's *Anabasis* 5.3.6; Strabo, *Geography* 14.1.23. See also Phiroze Vasunia, *The Classics and Colonial India* (New York: Oxford University Press, 2013).

50. M. Stausberg discusses what is called "memetic transmission," the movement of elements of Zoroastrian thinking across religious and cultural frontiers, in "Para-Zoroastrianisms: Memetic Transmission and Appropriations," in *Parsis in India and the Diaspora,* J. R. Hinnells and A. Williams eds. (London: Routledge, 2007), 236–254.

51. In Greek the word is used for medicines that are to be rubbed on as balms, or ointments, as opposed to those that are for drinking.

52. For a fascinating study of the beliefs of the imperial Persians, see Bruce Lincoln, *Religion, Empire, Torture: The Case of Achaemenian Persia, with a Postscript on Abu Ghraib* (Chicago: University of Chicago Press, 2007).

53. Saint Augustine, *Confessions*, trans. R. S. Pine-Coffin (London: Penguin, 1961).

4. THE POLITICS OF POLYTHEISM

1. Jacques Derrida, "Faith and Knowledge: The Two Sources of 'Religion' at the Limits of Religion Alone," in *Religion*, Jacques Derrida and Gianni Vattimo, eds. (Stanford, CA: Stanford University Press, 1998 [1996]), 25. "No Muslim is among us" [!] (5). Nor any Hindu, nor any woman. Are they so far to seek?

2. Wendy Doniger, *The Hindus: An Alternative History* (New York: Penguin, 2009), 43.

3. Thucydides, *The Peloponnesian War*, trans. Steven Lattimore (Indianapolis, IN: Hackett, 1998).

4. Andocides, "On the Mysteries," in *Antiphon and Andocides*, trans. M. Gagarin and D. M. MacDowell (Austin: University of Texas Press, 1998), 113–114.

5. Robert Parker, *Polytheism and Society at Athens* (Oxford: Oxford University Press, 2005).

6. Cyril Aldred, *The Egyptians*, rev. ed. (London: Thames and Hudson, 1987), 166. See also Jan Assmann, *The Search for God in Ancient Egypt*, trans. D. Lorton (Ithaca, NY: Cornell University Press, 2001 [1984]).

7. Jan Assmann, *The Price of Monotheism*, trans. R. Savage (Stanford, CA: Stanford University Press, 2010 [2003]), 48.

8. Arnaldo Momigliano, "The Disadvantages of Monotheism for a Universal State," in *On Pagans, Jews, and Christians* (Middletown, CT: Wesleyan University Press, 1987), 142–158.

9. The development of the concept of the trinity—three divine beings in one—a questionable feature of an avowed monotheism, created new difficulties for this affirmation of the correspondence between the kingdom of the one god and the Roman empire. "Augustine was less certain than Orosius that one god in heaven should be mirrored by one king on earth" (Momigliano, "Disadvantages," 153). Momigliano here makes reference to these arguments in the twentieth century, with the "theological Nazism" of Carl Schmitt (153).

10. Paul Veyne, *When Our World Became Christian, 312–394*, trans. Janet Lloyd (Cambridge: Polity Press, 2010 [2007]).

11. J. B. Bury, *A History of the Later Roman Empire*, 2nd. ed., vol. 1 (New York: Dover, 1958), 360.

12. *Julian*, trans. W. C. Wright (Cambridge, MA: Harvard University Press), 345.

13. Momigliano believed that Julian, "committed to pluralism both in heaven and on earth," "wanted the restoration of the Temple to be a proof that Jesus was no god" ("Disadvantages," 157).

14. James C. Scott, *The Art of Not Being Governed: An Anarchist History of Upland Southeast Asia* (New Haven, CT: Yale University Press, 2009), 155.

15. Stephen Mitchell and Peter Van Nuffelen, "Introduction: The Debate about Pagan Monotheism," in *One God: Pagan Monotheism in the Roman Empire,* S. Mitchell and P. Van Nuffelen, eds. (Cambridge: Cambridge University Press, 2010), 1–15; passage quoted, 1.

16. Scott also notes: "For the most part, hill peoples did not follow valley religions. Whereas the valley Burmans and Thais were Theravada Buddhists, hill peoples were, with some notable exceptions, animist and, in the twentieth century, Christians" (58).

17. *The Story of Guadalupe: Luis Laso de la Vega's Huei tlamahuiçoltica of 1649,* ed. and trans. Lisa Sousa, Stafford Poole, and James Lockhart (Stanford, CA: Stanford University Press [UCLA Latin American Studies vol. 84; Nahuatl Studies Series, no. 5], 1998); D. A. Brading, *Mexican Phoenix: Our Lady of Guadalupe: Image and Tradition across Five Centuries* (Cambridge: Cambridge University Press, 2003), 1–2.

18. *Mission archéologique et ethnologique française au Mexique:* Jacques Gailiner, Dominique Michelet, Anne-Marie Vié, "Mesoamerican Religion," in *American, African, and Old European Mythologies,* ed. Yves Bonnefoy, trans. under the direction of Wendy Doniger (Chicago: University of Chicago Press, 1993 [1981]), 46.

19. Rigoberta Menchu, *I Rigoberta Menchu: An Indian Woman in Guatemala,* ed. Elizabeth Burgos-Debray, trans. Ann Wright (London: Verso, 1987 [1984]). Nelson Reed's *The Caste War of Yucatan* (Stanford, CA: Stanford University Press, 1964) describes the synthesis of Christian and Mayan religious practices around "the speaking crosses" in the nineteenth century, at the heart of a short-lived but independent nation in the Yucatan, "a unique example of Spanish-Indian cultural synthesis" (209).

20. *Mission archéologique,* "Mesoamerican Creation Myths," in Bonnefoy, *American . . . Mythologies,* 56.

21. *Mission archéologique,* "Mesoamerican Religion," in Bonnefoy, *American . . . Mythologies,* 46.

22. *Mission archéologique,* "The Sky: Sun, Moon, Stars, and Meteorological Phenomena in Mesoamerican Religions," in Bonnefoy, *American . . . Mythologies,* 61.

23. Judy Rosenthal, *Possession, Ecstasy, and Law in Ewe Voodoo* (Charlottesville: University Press of Virginia, 1998).

24. George Brandon, *Santeria from Africa to the New World: The Dead Sell Memories* (Bloomington: Indiana University Press [Blacks in the Diaspora], 1993), 166.

25. See Joseph M. Murphy, *Santeria: African Spirits in American* (Boston: Beacon Press, 1993), Brandon, *Santeria,* and Leslie G. Desmangles, *The Faces of the Gods: Vodou and Roman Catholicism in Haiti* (Chapel Hill: University of North Carolina Press, 1992).

26. Jorge Amado, *Sea of Death,* trans. G. Rabassa (New York: Avon Books, 1984).

27. J. Lorand Matory, *Black Atlantic Religion: Tradition, Transnationalism, and Matriarchy in the Afro-Brazilian Candomblé* (Princeton, NJ: Princeton University Press, 2005), 246–248.

28. On the goddess, see Suzanne Cahill, *Transcendence and Divine Passion: The Queen Mother of the West in Medieval China* (Stanford, CA: Stanford University Press, 1993).

29. On Lewton's wartime films, see Alexander Nemerov, *Icons of Grief: Val Lewton's Home-Front Pictures* (Berkeley: University of California Press, 2005).

30. Richard Erdoes and Alfonso Ortiz, *American Indian Trickster Tales* (New York: Viking Penguin, 1998), 63. See also William Bright, *A Coyote Reader* (Berkeley: University of California Press, 1993).

31. Paul Axelrod and Michelle A. Fuerch, "Flight of the Deities: Hindu Resistance in Portuguese Goa," *Modern Asian Studies* 30:2 (1996), 387–421.

32. On psychoanalysis in India, see Ashis Nandy, *The Savage Freud and Other Essays on Possible and Retrievable Selves* (Princeton, NJ: Princeton University Press, 1995), especially "The Savage Freud: The First Non-Western Psychoanalyst and the Politics of Secret Selves in Colonial India," 81–144, on Girindrasekhar Bose (1886–1953). "[Bose] traces the hostility of Western scholars to things Indian . . . western scholars project into the Indian situation the enmity between Church and State existing in Europe. This makes them hostile to Hinduism and virulently anti-Brahminic. Under such circumstances, given that the organizing principle of Indian culture has always been religion, any serious consideration of India's past cultural achievements is bound to look like an exaggeration" (123). See also Ranjana Khanna, *Dark Continents: Psychoanalysis and Colonialism* (Durham: Duke University Press, 2003); Sudhir Kakar, *The Inner World: A Psychoanalytic Study of Childhood and Society in India* (Delhi: Oxford University Press, 1979), referring to the hegemonic core fantasy of the "split mother" in Indian culture; Alan Roland, *In Search of Self in India and Japan: Toward a Cross-Cultural Psychology* (Princeton, NJ: Princeton University Press, 1988); Ashis Nandy, *At the Edge of Psychology: Essays in Politics and Culture* (New Delhi: Oxford University Press, 1980).

33. This claim has been repeated even in children's books; see Subhadra Sen Gupta, *A Man Called Bapu* (Bangalore: Pratham Books, 2008), 5.

34. For a recent assessment of Gandhi's career, see Perry Anderson, "Gandhi Centre Stage," *London Review of Books* 34:13 (July 5, 2012), 3–11: "The composition of Gandhi's faith, Tidrick has shown, was born of a cross between a Jain-inflected Hindu orthodoxy and late Victorian psychomancy, the world of Madame Blavatsky, theosophy, the planchette and the Esoteric Christian Union. The two were not unconnected, as garbled ideas from the former—karma, reincarnation, ascetic self-perfection, fusion of the soul with the divine—found occult form in the latter. Little acquainted with the Hindu canon itself in his early years, Gandhi reshaped it through the medium of Western spiritualisms of the period. His one aim in life, he

decided, was to attain *moksha:* that state of perfection in which the cycle of rebirth comes to an end and the soul accedes to ultimate union with God. 'I am striving for the Kingdom of Heaven, which is *moksha,*' he wrote, 'in this very existence.' The path towards it was 'crucifixion of the flesh', without which it was impossible to 'see God face to face' and become one with him. But if such perfection could be attained, the divine would walk on earth, for 'there is no point in trying to know the difference between a perfect man and God.' Then there would be no limit to his command of his countrymen: 'When I am a perfect being, I have simply to say the word and the nation will listen'" (7).

35. Dipesh Chakrabarty, "Radical Histories and Question of Enlightenment Rationalism: Some Recent Critiques of Subaltern Studies," in Vinayak Chaturvedi, ed., *Mapping Subaltern Studies and the Postcolonial* (London: Verso, 2000), 256–280.

36. R. E. Frykenberg, "The Emergence of Modern 'Hinduism,'" in G. D. Sontheimer and H. Kulke, eds., *Hinduism Reconsidered* (Delhi: Manohar, 1991), 29–49.

37. *The Rig Veda: An Anthology, One Hundred and Eight Hymns,* selected, translated and annotated by Wendy Doniger O'Flaherty (London: Penguin Books, 1981).

38. *The Upanishads,* trans. Juan Mascaro (New York: Penguin, 1965), *Brihadaranyaka Upanishad,* 3.9.1.

39. For an accessible translation and abridgement of this immense epic, see Valmiki, *The Ramayana,* trans. Arshia Sattar (New Delhi: Penguin Books, 2000).

40. A. K. Ramanujan, cited by Wendy Doniger, from remarks made at a Harvard conference on Radha, in Doniger, *Hindus,* 390; and Wendy Doniger O'Flaherty, *Women, Androgynes, and Other Mythical Beasts* (Chicago: University of Chicago Press, 1980), 90–91. See also A. K. Ramanujan, "Is There an Indian Way of Thinking? An Informal Essay," in *India through Hindu Categories,* McKim Marriott, ed. (New Delhi: Sage Publications, 1990), 41–58. Ramanujan posits an opposition between "context-sensitive" thinking in India, and "context-free" thinking in the West, finding these not to be absolutes of difference, but "emphases," "biases."

41. Dipesh Chakrabarty, *Provincializing Europe: Postcolonial Thought and Historical Difference* (Princeton, NJ: Princeton University Press, 2000), quoting Edward Thompson, *Rabindranath Tagore: Poet and Dramatist* (Calcutta: Riddhi, 1979 [1926]), 24.

42. Alain Daniélou, *The Myths and Gods of India: The Classic Work on Hindu Polytheism* (Rochester, VT: Inner Traditions International, 1991 [1964]).

43. The Cyrus Cylinder, cited in Pierre Briant, *From Cyrus to Alexander: A History of the Persian Empire,* trans. P. T. Daniels (Winona Lake, IN: Eisenbrauns, 2002 [1996]). The Greeks, like the Israelites, saw Cyrus as a relatively benign conqueror (Xenophon, *Cyropaedia* 1.1.4).

44. Lindsay Allen, *The Persian Empire* (Chicago: University of Chicago Press, 2005), 131.

45. Beni Madhab Barua, *Asoka and His Inscriptions,* 3rd ed. (Calcutta: New Age Publishers, 1968), 271.

46. *The Edicts of Ashoka,* ed. and trans. N. A. Nikam and R. McKeon (Chicago: University of Chicago Press, 1959), 51.

47. Romila Thapar, *Asoka and the Decline of the Mauryas,* rev. ed. (Delhi: Oxford University Press, 1997), 159.

EPILOGUE

1. Neil Gaiman, *American Gods* (New York: William Morrow, 2003).

2. Anne Fadiman, *The Spirit Catches You and You Fall Down: A Hmong Child, Her American Doctors, and the Collision of Two Cultures* (New York: Farrar, Straus, Giroux: 1998).

Acknowledgments

I am fortunate to have been enlisted into teaching in a two-year sequence on "the making of the modern world," a.k.a. MMW, at Eleanor Roosevelt College, at the University of California at San Diego, by my dear friend William Fitzgerald. Compelled to achieve some degree of competence in teaching the ancient world, including not just my own field of expertise, ancient Greece, but also the "Near" East, Africa, India and China, Mesoamerica, and the rest of the world, I have been fascinated by the diversity of cultural traditions, their links with one another, but also their profound differences, which continue to have their impact on everyday life today. Confronted by undergraduates whose family histories look back to all these places, and who live in the modern world, I have learned more than I could ever have expected about differences, and ignorances, and prejudices, and racisms.

My thanks go to the undergraduates of MMW, as well as to the graduate students who have helped me teach this course for many years. And to the graduate students of my 2013 seminar at the University of California at San Diego on "The Question(s) of Religion"—Alex Chang, Jane Coulter, Sarah Hendy, Gibran Guido, Nadeen Kharputly, Kedar Kulkarni, Norell Martinez, Crystal Perez, Reema Rajbanshi, Laura Ha Reizman, Vineeta Singh, Josh Tremill, and Ting Ying Wu, who taught me so much about the varieties of religious experience in the present. And to friends and students Eunsong Angela Kim, Sarika Talve-Goodman, Anthony Kim, and Niall Twohig. And I am grateful in a multitude of ways to my colleague, Sara Johnson.

I thank many kind hosts, interlocutors, and audiences, in Chicago, Princeton, London and Paris, including Jonathan Hall, Shadi Bartsch, Bruce Lincoln, Claude Calame, Ellen O'Gorman and Vanda Zajko, Brooke Holmes and Joshua Katz, Michèle Lowrie, Mark Payne, Tim Whitmarsh, my colleague Dayna Kalleres, and David Frankfurter. I owe a special debt to Miriam Leonard and Simon Goldhill, who helped set me straight at the beginnings of this project.

I thank Dr. Tai-Nan Wang, for conversation and care.

I am, as ever, so grateful to Antonia Meltzoff, who changed my life, always for the better, and continues to do so.

Sharmila Sen makes writing books a joy, and I thank her.

My friends Lisa Lowe, Melvyn Freilicher and Joe Keenan, Sheldon Nodelman and Susan Smith, John Granger, Kate Harper and Harper Page Marshall, and Froma Zeitlin know, I hope, how much their loving support has meant to me over many years.

Most of all I thank John Daley, for happiness.

Index

Abraham(ic), 13, 20, 23, 28, 49, 84, 86, 117
Adam and Eve, 3, 122
Aeschylus, 17–18
Africa, 41, 76, 142–143, 178n27
Agamben, Giorgio, 9, 14
Ahura Mazda, 123, 125, 128
Akhenaten, 94, 134–135
Alexander, 66
Alkaios, 63
Amado, Jorge, 144–145
Amazons, 108–109, 124
Anahita, 96, 109, 124
angelology, 120–121. See *also* angels
angels, 118–121, 148
aniconism, 118
Antigone, 52, 79
Antiochus, 100
Aphrodite, 53, 56, 58–61, 63, 65, 72, 83, 85, 108, 118

Apollo, 22, 52, 56, 62, 64, 76, 83
Apuleius, 76–78
Arendt, Hannah, 12
Ares, 6, 50, 55–56, 83, 108, 137
Aristophanes, 69–70
Aristotle, 80–81, 182n40
Artemis, 55–57, 83, 109–110
asherah, 91–92, 93, 133, 184n10
Ashoka, 161–164
Assmann, Jan, 14, 16, 41, 80, 93, 96, 135
Astarte, 91–92
Aten, 94
Athena, 50, 54, 64, 108, 118, 137
atheists, 33, 172
Athens, 12, 33, 39, 50, 54–55, 64, 68, 76, 130–133
Atran, Scott, 7
Augé, Marc, 41–42
Augustine, 5, 84, 127–128, 188n9

Ba'al, 88, 92–93, 98, 100, 103–104, 133

Bacchus, 66, 73, 75, 76

barbarism, 23

Baron Samedi, 148–149

Bhagavad–Gita, 156

Black Power, 143

Boyer, Pascal, 40, 176n5

Brazil, 144–147

Brown, Peter, 14, 87, 111–112

Buddhism, 23, 28, 35, 128, 138, 147, 161, 163

Burkert, Walter, 51, 180n8

Butler, Judith, 11–12, 14, 48, 52

caesaro-papism, 135

Canaan, 90, 93, 104, 115

Candomblé, 144–147

Catholicism, 2, 8–9, 20–21, 26, 28, 30, 31, 110, 130

Chakrabarty, Dipesh, 14, 153, 158–159

Chateaubriand, René de, 32–34

Chaucer, Geoffrey, 5

China, 25–26, 31, 35, 45

Christianity, 2, 4, 19, 23, 41, 55, 78, 79, 150; defense of, 32–34; and monarchy, 136–138; and polytheism, 137, 98–115; privileging of, 9; resistance to, 136, 139–147, 148–152

Cicero, 4

cohabitation, 8, 11–13, 153, 161–166, 180n44

colonialism, 21, 28, 29–30, 31, 41, 129, 141, 153

comedy, 69–70

Confucianism, 30, 41

Connerton, Paul, 23

Constantine, 136–137

Corbin, Henry, 120–121

Coyote, 149–150

cultural psychology, 7, 44–46

Cyrus, 126, 162–163

Daniélou, Alain, 159–160

Dawn, 62–64, 154

deity, 5–7

Deleuze, Gilles and Félix Guattari, 44, 48, 179n42, 184n12

democracy, 15, 53, 85, 130; in ancient Athens, 39, 57, 70, 130–133; in India, 153

Derrida, Jacques, 129

Detienne, Marcel, 56

Deuteronomy, 89, 91, 95, 133

Devi, 156–158

devil(s), 55, 86, 121, 122–123, 187n43. See *also* satan/Satan

dharma, 36, 156–157, 163

Diana, 109–110. See *also* Artemis

diaspora, 12, 107, 116, 125, 142–143, 146–147, 160

Dickens, Charles, 138

Dillon, John, 183n45

Dionysus, 53, 58, 61, 63, 64–71, 82–83, 111

Doniger, Wendy, 14, 130, 156, 159–160

Egypt, 1, 17–18, 52, 75–78, 90–91, 93, 96, 134–135, 162

emperor, 75, 130, 136–137, 161–164

empire, 75, 78, 84, 136–138, 161–164

Enlightenment, 31–2

Ephesus, 108–110, 124

Ethiopians, 19, 77

Euripides, 66, 82–83

euro, 19

Europa, 19, 64

European Union, 9–10, 19

evil, 3–4, 127–128

evolution, 38, 84

Francis, Pope, 86, 115

Freud, Sigmund, 10, 44, 82, 94, 97

Frymer–Krensky, Tikva, 91, 95

Gabriel, 119

Gaiman, Neil, 149, 167

Gandhi, 152–153 190n34

Genesis, 2–3, 25

Gnosticism, 84, 98–99, 179n36
God, 5–6, 11, 22, 27, 31, 32, 37, 43
god, 5–6, 16, 27, 31
gods, 3–7, 15, 16, 21, 43, 53–59, 88–97, 107–116, 117–128
Gods Behaving Badly, 52
Goldhill, Simon, 52
Greek(s), ancient, 6, 12, 14–15, 17–19, 25, 29, 35, 41, 48, 50–72, 130–133
Guadalupe, Virgin of, 7–8, 139–140
Guanyin, 147–148

Habermas, Jürgen, 48
Haiti, 34
Hajj, 122–123
Halbertal, Moshe and Avishai Margalit, 10, 21, 43–44
heathen, 5, 20, 22, 26, 28, 49, 88
heavenly mother, 114
Hebrew Bible, 1, 2–4, 10, 18, 24, 29, 33, 43, 88–98
Hegel, G.W.F., 34–36
Hellenismos, 51
henotheism, 60–61, 82, 156
Henry VIII, 138
Hera, 61–65, 83, 108
Heraclitus, 31
Hermes, 137, 148
herms, 131
Herodotus, 18
Hindus, Hinduism, 2, 21, 23, 26, 35–36, 46–47, 150–164, 179n36
Homeric Hymn(s), 64, 67
How to Stay Christian in College, 115
Hume, David, 87

I Walked with a Zombie, 148
idol(s), 6, 46, 93, 100, 152, 158. See *also* idolatry
idolatry, 10, 17, 20, 26, 28, 29, 31, 38, 43, 49, 55, 87, 95, 97–98, 110, 116–117, 136, 139, 152, 161, 178n22. See *also* idol(s)
Iemanja, 144–145

India, 35, 47, 65, 86, 87, 150–164
Indo-European, 6
Is Critique Secular?, 9, 11
Isis, 75, 77–78
Islam, 2, 11, 19, 23, 49, 116–123, 148, 186n38

Jahweh, 24, 89, 91, 128, 183n6
Jen, Gish, 44–45, 179n38
Jeremiah, 1, 90–91
Jerusalem, 1, 12, 137
Jesus, 24, 31, 44, 71, 99, 112–113, 119, 128
Jezebel, 91
jinn, 121
Job, 90, 102–103
Judaism, 19, 23, 24, 78, 84
Judas, 104
Julian, 137, 188 n13
Julius Caesar, 74
Justin Martyr, 30–31
Juvenal, 75

Kant, Immanuel, 32
King, Richard, 4
Krishna, 156, 161
Kurien, Prema A., 46–47

Lacan, Jacques, 44, 52, 79
Lactantius, 4
Legba, 148
Lenin, 137
Lesbos, 61–63
Lilith, 96
Lincoln, Bruce, 14
Livy, 75
Locke, John, 31–32
London, 160–161
Lucretius, 73

Macaulay, Thomas, 21
Maccabees, 99–101
Macpherson, C.P., 31–32, 39–40
magic, 49, 76, 80, 153

Mahmood, Saba, 9, 11, 14
Mami Wata, 142
Manicheanism, 99, 126–128
Marcion of Sinope, 24
Mars, 73, 76
Mary, Virgin, 10, 108–110, 124, 142, 144
Mater Magna, 74
Mathews, Thomas, 112–113
Matory, J.L., 14, 47, 146–147
Maya, 3–4, 7, 189n19
Menchu, Rigoberta, 141, 189n19
messiah, 119, 126, 162
Mexico, 139–141
missionary, 7, 20–21, 33–34, 42, 139–141, 147, 151–152
Momigliano, Arnaldo, 136, 188n9
monarchy, 92, 94–95, 134–135, 138, 162
monism, 84, 155
monotheism, 20; and Christianity, 22; ethical, 25; as inevitable, 12; and monarchy, 133–138; premature, 12, 78–85
Montaigne, Michel de, 110
Mormonism, 2, 114

Nandy, Ashis, 14, 190n32
Native American, 49
Nazi, 43–44
neopagans, 42–43
Nietzsche, Friedrich, 43
Nisbett, Richard, 39, 45, 179n39

Osiris, 135
otters, 124
Ovid, 73

Pagans/paganism, 12, 20–22, 26, 28, 30, 42–43, 50, 84, 88, 99, 106–107, 136, 179n36, 180n3, 184n10; genius of, 41–42
Pagels, Elaine, 106–107
Pan, 19, 56, 83
pantheism, 156
Paper, Jordan, 20, 42

paradeisos, 126
Parker, Robert, 14, 54, 132–133
Patai, Raphael, 92, 96, 184n10
Paul, 55, 105–106
Pausanias, 19, 54
Persia, 57, 76, 99, 123–128, 162–163
Pitt, William the elder, 26
Plato, 22, 54, 71, 79
pluralism, 2, 8–9, 10, 13, 164, 175n1
Plutarch, 19
polytheism, 7, 19; in Christianity, 98–115; and democracy, 130–133; in Hebrew Bible, 88–98; as norm, 7, 20; prejudice against, 8, 12, 16–49; as resistance, 138–153; survival and persistence of, 2, 8, 10, 12, 16, 129–166
polytheos, 18
Popul Vuh, 3
popular culture, 10, 36–38, 52–53, 72, 84–85, 111–112, 113–114, 115, 121, 145, 167
possessive individualism, 12, 31–32, 39–40
prisons, 150
Protestant, 1–2, 9, 13, 20, 25–26, 28, 30, 33, 35, 38, 40, 45, 48, 110, 130, 138
psychoanalysis, 10, 44, 79, 82,190n32
public sphere, 48–49
Purchas, Samuel, 20, 151

Queen of heaven, 1, 90–91, 92
Qur'an, 11, 116–123

racism, 12, 129
Ramakrishna, 168
Ramanujan, A.K., 191n40
religion, 4–5, 9, 23, 28, 48–49
rhizome, 179n42
Rig Veda, 154
Rodd, Rennell, 111
Rome, 30, 34–5, 72–78
Rosenthal, Judy, 142–143
Ruether, Rosemary, 27
Rüpke, J., 74

saints, 87, 108–115, 122

Santeria, 7, 51, 143–144

Sappho, 53, 59–64, 85

satan/Satan, 7, 101–107, 115, 127; in *Hebrew Bible*, 90, 102–103, 185n21; in *New Testament*, 104–107; in *Qur'an*, 119

Scott, James C., 138, 139, 189n16

Schwartz, Regina, 184n12

secularism, 8–9, 10, 176n13

separation of "church" and state, 8–9, 13

Seznec, Jean, 51

Shiva, 155, 156, 158, 161

slavery/slaves, 33–34, 65, 67, 69–70, 71, 72, 74, 76, 82, 83, 106, 113, 114, 115, 122, 134, 143–144, 146, 148, 150, 153, 163

Smith, Jonathan Z., 28–29

Socrates, 22, 71

Solomon, 92, 95

Soma, 155

Sophia, 95, 98

Sophocles, 52, 54, 72, 79, 82

Stroumsa, Guy, 29–30, 178n22

Sumerian Reconstruction, 50

Tagore, Rabindranath, 158–159

Taoism, 168

Taylor, Charles, 48

Taylor, Mark C., 26–27

Tertullian, 30–31, 107

Thales, 80–81, 182n37

theological Nazism, 188 n9

Tonantzin, 140

tragedy, 66–67, 69, 82–84

translation of names, 18

trinity, 9, 107–108, 188n9

True Blood, 145

U.S. Army manual for chaplains, 165

Varro, 74

Vasunia, Phiroze, 14, 124

Venus, 73, 76

Vernant, J.-P., 180n8

Versnel, Henk, 14, 82, 114, 180n8, 182n35, 182n40

Veyne, Paul, 137

violence, 2, 21, 99–101, 163

Virgil, 73

Vishnu, 155–158

war, 6, 45, 55–57

Warner, Marina, 108–110

West, Cornel, 48–49

whoredom, 43, 77

Wills, Garry, 30

Xenophanes, 19, 81–82, 182n38, 180n40

Yajnavalkya, 155

Yasin, Anne Marie, 113

Yeats, William Butler, 51–52

York, Michael, 42–43

Zeitlin, Froma, 181n22

Zeus, 17–19, 50, 51–53, 56–57, 61, 79, 82, 108

zodiac, 19, 51

Zoroastrianism, 86, 99, 123–128, 187n50